## The Meditator's Handbook

**Dr David Fontana** is Reader in Educational Psychology at the University of Wales, Cardiff. He is the author of a number of highly acclaimed books in psychology and has spent many years in both personal and professional study of the psychological and spiritual benefits of meditation, learning from both Eastern and Western teachers.

Selected titles by the same author

*Dreamlife*
*The Elements of Meditation*
*Managing Stress*
*Space in Mind (Edited with John Crook)*

# *The Meditator's Handbook*

A COMPREHENSIVE GUIDE
TO EASTERN AND WESTERN
MEDITATION TECHNIQUES

## DAVID FONTANA

Foreword by
Michael West

ELEMENT
Shaftesbury, Dorset ● Rockport, Massachusetts
Brisbane, Queensland

© David Fontana 1992

Published in Great Britain in 1992 by
Element Books Limited
Longmead, Shaftesbury, Dorset

Published in the USA in 1992 by
Element, Inc.
42 Broadway, Rockport, MA 01966

Published in Australia in 1993 by
Element Books Limited for
Jacaranda Wiley Limited
33 Park Road, Milton, Brisbane 4064

Reprinted May 1993

Cover design by Max Fairbrother
Designed by Roger Lightfoot
Typeset by Footnote Graphics, Warminster, Wiltshire
Printed and bound in Great Britain by
Redwood Books, Trowbridge, Wiltshire

British Library Cataloguing in Publication
data available

Library of Congress Cataloging in Publication
data available

ISBN 1–85230–320–4

To the memory of Carl Jung,
psychologist, meditator, mystic
and explorer extraordinary of
the human spirit.

# CONTENTS

# FOREWORD

There is enormous turbulence on the surface of the earth. Yet at the same time most of us experience in our day-to-day relationships the closeness, warmth, trust, honesty and generosity, which is characteristic of individuals in their behaviour towards each other. It often seems as though collectively we are unable to manage the way we live, but at an individual level it is clear that there are good intentions and that there is great morality in human behaviour. One solution that people have adopted over the ages, in trying to manage the demands and challenges of living, is to turn to the world religions. But even here cynicism has grown about the extent to which they too have been responsible for increasing destruction, terror and war, rather than solving the problems which face us.

Meditation is a practice which, across traditions, is intended to still the turbulence of our outer and inner lives, and to create harmony between the individual and his or her social, spiritual and even metaphysical world. It is a practice, not necessarily based on belief, which ultimately may produce still completeness within us and on the surface of our lives. It is a practice which spans religions and secular traditions. It offers stillness, understanding, freedom and tranquillity.

David Fontana's book, simply titled *The Meditator's Handbook*, is no small undertaking and its title perhaps belies its important aims. The book aims to provide an introductory guide to the place of meditation in all of the great and many of the lesser traditions of human society, through history, across nations and across philosophical traditions. It is, in that sense, a guide to the many alternative meditation practices which exist for attempting to cope with the turbulence which we have created in our individual lives and in our world.

But what is meditation? This simple question is very difficult to answer, simply because meditation spans so many traditions. Over the years I have read accounts of the meditative traditions in Hinduism, Buddhism, Sufism, Judaism, Christianity and in Shamanism. My experience has been that, after a little time of reading or study, my eyes glaze over as I find myself slipping beneath the waves of obfuscation that advanced scholars, either advertently or inadvertently, create for the swimmer in their rarely charted waters. Much of the writing about meditation in different traditions is so obscure for the naive reader that it becomes almost impossible to understand the nature of the practice, the purpose of meditation and how it relates to the broader spiritual context within which it is taught. Consequently, confusion rather than understanding, and turmoil rather than stillness, are created. One has a sense, sometimes of scholars so enamoured of their own understanding of a particular tradition that they mystify this understanding to maintain their ascendency over the naive reader or aspiring scholar. None of these accusations can be levelled against David Fontana in this enlightening book.

The book is a guide which takes the reader gently by the hand and walks him or her through vast traditions of complex knowledge. It provides clear and simple directions for routes ahead, and is written in a language which is immediately accessible without being either condescending or simplistic. It is a tribute to David Fontana's writing that I, who have practised and studied meditation from a psychological orientation for more than twenty years, felt that I had learned far more by reading this one book about meditation, than I had from most of the others put together. The complexities of different spiritual traditions are clearly outlined, and the place of meditation simply explained. Repeatedly throughout the book, straightforward instructions for the practice of different kinds of meditation techniques within those different traditions are presented.

But the book is not merely an academic and dispassionate guide to meditation. It is written with sensitivity and, at the end of the book, there emerges a sense of what is common to meditation practice across the traditions, and coupled with this, a sense of David Fontana's own rich experience of meditation. He communicates the products of meditation as being stillness, beauty, fullness, understanding, engagement with, rather than separation from, truth, honesty and sincerity. At the end of the book I tried to summarize for myself what meditation is. I began by thinking that meditation is the experience of oneself. Then it becomes the experience of one's being. And then, more spiritually, a celebration of one's being. As a consequence of this there is a celebration of others' being, and then a celebration of all beings. Finally, there is a celebration simply of Being. Indeed, I concluded that Meditation is Being. This is what, for me, is the conclusion of this vast, yet easy, journey across traditions – an understanding based on my own experience and David Fontana's guidebook. Meditation is a way of learning to be, without attachment, greeds, desires, antipathies, aggressions or guilts. Consequently it is truly a practice to still the turbulence of the inner and outer world. It does seem to me that, along with a collective intent to heal ourselves and our planet, meditation represents a straightforward path to stillness and understanding which can help us learn to be in our world and live with each other, rather than live off our world and be separate from one another.

Dr Fontana's sincerity, enormous depth of both scholarship and practice of meditation all combine to make this book a beautiful companion for meditators at any stage of their own spiritual journeys.

Michael West
Author of *The Psychology of Meditation*

# INTRODUCTION

In writing about meditation, one is also writing about religion, since it is within the context of religion – or, more properly, of spirituality – that all the great meditative traditions have grown and flourished. But I hope that the reader who takes no particular interest in religion won't be put off by this. The book isn't an attempt to convert anyone to a spiritual way of thinking, for it is up to each of us to find our own way through life, and our own sense of its meaning or lack of it. Nor is the book written from the standpoint of any one particular religion. If there are more references to some religions than to others, this is simply because they are the ones that have placed most emphasis upon the meditative tradition.

For my own part, my interest has always been to look for the one truth that lies behind all religions. The teachings, both practical and theoretical, I have been privileged to receive in many of the major Eastern and Western traditions, together with the sense of the sacred I have experienced in temples, churches, mosques, chapels and meditation halls, have shown me that it is human fallibility and not truth itself that is responsible for setting people against each other.

At the same time, as a psychologist, my interest has also been to study the mysteries of the human mind, the richness of which we can live and die without even suspecting if we fail to explore them. Meditation is one way, perhaps the only way, to conduct this exploration and enter into the heart of this richness.

# 1

## *Who am I? The Exploration of the Inner World*

Each of us lives in two worlds. One world is obvious enough. Look around you and you see it. Notice how familiar it is, how well known. Notice how you can put a name to each of the things you see, how you can say what each thing is for, where it comes from, what it costs, who owns it, how attractive or unappealing it is, how long it will last and what will happen to it at the end of its days. Observe how you can put a name to the faces you see, how you can divide people into men and women, children and adults, old and young, friends and strangers, loved ones and acquaintances, fair-haired and dark-haired, fellow countrymen and foreigners. Notice how easily things fall into categories, assume labels, become understandable and predictable. The world that meets our senses is for most of the time and for most of our lives a clear and comprehensible one, full of sights and sounds, tastes and sensations that define for us what it means to be alive.

But there is another world, equally vivid at times, but much less easily described and understood. An inner world of thoughts and emotions, a world of imagination and dreams, a world that contains a shadowy 'I', a mysterious person whom we never actually see but who appears to be able to watch and observe both the outer and the inner worlds. A person whose existence we may forget about from time to time, as for example when we are totally absorbed in a task or lost in a Beethoven symphony or fast asleep, but who always re-emerges the moment we start thinking our own thoughts once more, or when we wake up in the morning and come to ourselves again.

## WHO IS THIS 'I'?

It is strange how seldom we stop and reflect upon the existence of this elusive 'I'. Who actually *is* this person who lives inside us and is in touch with both outer and inner worlds? Where did this person come from and where is he or she going? Undoubtedly he or she is experiencing life, but what actually *is* life, this strange, magical, frustrating, infuriating thing which expresses itself through us, and for so much of the time balances us uneasily between sadness and joy? What is it for? Does it have a purpose and if so, what is it? Can we know it, and if we can know it, can we understand it?

The more we ponder these questions, the more we become aware that to answer the first of them is to answer all the rest as well. Because to know who we are is also to know where we came from and where we are going, and to know what life is and what, if anything, it is for. Each of these questions is in fact only a version of the one eternal enquiry, 'Who am I?'. 'Who am I?' The fundamental existential question from which all other existential questions arise, and on which they depend for their meaning and importance.

For thousands of years, probably since the dawn of consciousness in the mists of pre-history, men and women have been pondering this fundamental question, and listening to those strange individuals who from time to time have appeared among us and seemed to know the answer, an answer they couch in strange, symbolic language which doesn't sound like an answer at all. And when we seek clarification of this answer, what they then give us is an enigmatic set of techniques through which, they imply, we can find this clarification for ourselves. We are thus being told, it seems, that the answer to the question 'Who am I?' is not a formula handed to us by someone else but a direct personal *experience*. And when we come to think about it, what else could the answer possibly be, since it is *we ourselves* who are what we are?

## KNOWING OUR OWN MINDS

One shorthand term for this 'I', this 'self' whose nature we want to know, is 'mind'. 'Mind' is a useful, general term that covers everything that goes on in our inner world, both at conscious and unconscious levels. Our 'mind' is our thoughts, our feelings, our memories. It is the pictures and images we visualize, the music we sing to ourselves, the sense we make of the outer world, the consciousness we have of our own existence, the hopes and dreams we have for the future, the morals and values we carry with us and by which we live, the expectations and demands we make of ourselves and of others. And at the same time it is those deeper, hidden reaches which lie below the level of immediate awareness, but which nevertheless, in ways I shall discuss as we go along, profoundly influence our thoughts, our actions and our emotions. The 'mind' is in fact the inner magic theatre where we enact the drama of our lives, and like any theatre it includes both the action on-stage and the action off-stage, the actors and the playwrights, the conscious mind that thinks and knows that it thinks, and the unconscious mind that moves in quite different, hidden ways.

So to know ourselves, to know who we are, is to know our own minds, both at conscious and unconscious levels. Which is a quite different form of knowing from the kind we imply when we say of decisive people that they 'know their own minds'. It is a form of knowing which takes in, directly, what our minds actually are. A form of knowing which involves the – at first sight impossible – task of being at the same time both the mind that is known and the mind that knows. A form of knowing that at first seems as out of the question as being asked to gaze into our own eyes.


## THOSE WHO KNEW

Let's pause before going any further and consider the men and women who appeared to know the answer to the question 'Who am I?' By identifying these people more clearly, we put ourselves in a position to learn and use the practices they taught, the practices which may or may not (wait and see) lead us to find in our own turn the answer to this oddly baffling question.

The first thing to say about these men and women is that they have appeared in many different centuries and cultures. And the second is that although the language they use to talk about this answer and about the practices that help us look into it may be different, as may be the symbols they use to express the truth that underlies the answer, nevertheless the essence of what they are saying does not seem to change. Whether they come from the East or from the West, from highly complex or from apparently simple cultures, from centuries back or from modern times, the teachings they give us remain consistent in essentials. The science and technology of the outer world are changing rapidly, exponentially, even as I write these words, but the inner world of which these men and women talk would appear to be timeless, and the maps they have left to help us find our way within it would not appear to change.

The third thing to say about these men and women is that they recognize no boundaries within the inner world. The maps they left us contain no dotted lines for frontiers, no border posts, no customs sheds, no changes in tariffs, currency or laws. For them, there were no divisions between the three great studies of the mind that we moderns label as religion, philosophy and psychology. For them, there was only the mind. There was no division even between conscious and unconscious, or even between sleeping and waking, between thoughts and dreams. For them, there was just an all-embracing *knowing* or, since the term 'knowing' is often now debased into mere factual knowledge, an all-embracing wisdom.

We shall meet some of these men and women as we go through the book but, because our modern mind insists on placing people in categories, we recognize them best under the title of religious or spiritual teachers. In the East, they include the Buddha and many others practising in the Buddhist tradition, and Patanjali and many others in the Hindu (and particularly Vedanta) traditions. In the Middle East, they include Rumi and others in the Sufi tradition, and the anonymous writers of the *Sepher Yetzirah* and the other Kabbalistic texts. And in the overlap between the Middle East and the West, they include Christ and many others working in the Christian (and particularly in the gnostic) traditions, and the mythical Hermes Trismegistus and others working in the mystery religions and the Hermetic tradition.

In less obvious ways, we can also add Pythagorus and other figures working in the Greek mystery tradition, and those practising in the shamanic and American Indian traditions, and even then the list is by no means complete. The unifying principle behind the work of all these men and women is that they taught practices designed to help the individual look into him or herself, and find within the inner world the reality from which all existence flows, the reality which is at one and the same time our own true nature and the creative force that brings into being and sustains the outer world.

## THE VIEW FROM MODERN PSYCHOLOGY

Let me at this point say something about why modern Western psychology should take note of the teachings of these men and women. The very fact that I have to spend time on such an exercise illustrates not only the artificial distinction we in the West make between psychology, religion and philosophy, but also the narrowness with which much modern Western psychology goes about its business.

It is this narrowness that leads people (mostly fellow psychologists) to ask why I, raised as I am within the Western psychological tradition, should concern myself with what is sometimes described as the 'unscientific mystical nonsense' which these teachings represent. In the West, we have the habit of regarding ourselves as at the pinnacle of human achievement. We tend to see history as the process of humankind's steady climb from superstition and primitive notions about the world and ourselves to a sophisticated body of knowledge which represents a true and objective picture of how things really are. In defence of this way of seeing things, we point to the achievements of modern science and technology, to the space rockets, the electronic wizardry, the breakthroughs in biology and medicine, and to the extraordinary discoveries which have fuelled the progress we are making in learning to manipulate and control virtually every aspect of our physical world.

But there are two inter-related fallacies here. The first is that 'progress' of itself means that earlier ideas, earlier ways of looking at the world, were necessarily wrong. Much depends upon the concerns that lay behind these ideas. If your concern is to demonstrate that the world is simply a vast machine, produced by a combination of blind chance and natural selection, then you are going to interpret the evidence turned up by your science in the terms dictated by this concern. On the other hand, if your concern is to demonstrate that the world has other dimensions, and that it is these dimensions that give meaning and purpose to life, then you are going to interpret the evidence in a very different way.

A helpful analogy is to think of a car and its driver. If you are only interested in the mechanics of the car, you spend your time with your head under the bonnet and are not concerned with the man or woman who sits inside it. If you should chance to think about them at all, you dismiss them as non-existent because they are not made of the steel and plastic which is all your equipment is designed to detect. On the other hand, if you are interested in those who drive the car, you open the door and look inside, and begin to see very different things.

It would be wrong to dismiss the importance of looking under the bonnet. Looking under the bonnet is appropriate when it comes to tinkering with the car's mechanics. But similarly it would be wrong to dismiss the importance of looking inside the car. Looking inside the car is appropriate when it comes to knowing the driver. Neither set of actions is 'wrong' in any absolute sense. They both have their uses, depending upon the kind of questions we are asking. But although the person looking under the bonnet has the easier task (machines are more predictable and more easily dealt with than the people who drive them), it is the person looking inside who is asking the more fundamental question, and who will find the answer that explains not only the driver but also the car itself, since it is the human mind that ultimately is responsible for both.

The second fallacy is that apparent progress in *some* areas of our knowledge is progress in *all* areas. Modern science and technology have made great strides in studying the material composition of inanimate things, as has modern biology in studying the material composition of living things. But comparable strides have not taken place in studying human psychology. We know, in fact, very little more (and in some areas a great deal less) about the human mind than men and women did in the time of the Buddha 2500 years ago, and in the time of the anonymous authors of the Hindu *Vedas* centuries earlier even than that. In fact, the detailed mapping of the human mind and of the states of human consciousness carried out by Eastern sages in those remote times is unequalled in complexity and precision by anything that our modern Western psychology has attempted.

For those who recoil at the mention of things such as Buddhism and the Hindu *Vedas* that smack to them of magic and superstition, I can point instead to the great literature of the Western world. Although we fail to find here anything comparable to the mapping of mental states carried out in the East, it is right to say that for observation of human thinking and behaviour, it is hard to surpass the insights of a Shakespeare or a Goethe or even a Molière. The literature produced by these writers has survived over the centuries not just because of the beauty of its language but because of the insights it gives us into the human condition, and because we find in it a series of mirrors which reflect for us the realities of our own experience.

Literature of this magnitude, together with that produced in the millennia before Christ by Greek writers such as Sophocles and Euripides, shows that men and women were asking and trying to answer the same questions about human psychology and the origin and destiny of human life as we are asking and trying to answer today.

No, it would be wrong to think that just because we moderns have successfully looked inside the atom and penetrated outer space we have also successfully looked inside the human mind and penetrated the mysteries of inner space.

## MIND AND BRAIN

In fact, in a sense modern science hasn't tried to look into the mind at all. It has preferred to see mind as synonymous with brain; in other words, to see mental activity as nothing more than the electrochemical processes that go on in the brain and which can be measured by the right kind of instruments. The fact that, no matter what the electrochemical activity of the brain happens to be, we experience thoughts *as thoughts*, as mental, non-physical events rather than as electrochemical processes, is regarded as irrelevant.

The motivation behind this approach has been to present men and women as biophysiological machines, susceptible to study just as mechanical machines can be studied. The trouble is, of course, that human beings do not experience themselves as machines and persist (very inconveniently for scientists) in acting unpredictably, untidily, unconventionally, and occasionally gloriously.

They persist in imagining, in dreaming, in creating, in innovating. They persist in showing initiative, in breaking rules, in producing great works of art and literature, in surviving against all the odds, and in adapting mentally and biologically even to the weightlessness of outer space – a real scientific poser since humans have never previously experienced weightlessness in their evolutionary history, and thus in theory should be unable to adapt to it. And they persist in inventing and discovering, and even in taking over the course of genetic evolution itself – another poser for science, since genetic evolution must now be seen as subject to mind and not due solely to random mutations and the law of natural selection.

And they persist in having this troublesome thing called consciousness, self-awareness, for which even the most die-hard Darwinian can find no evolutionary explanation and no evolutionary purpose.

## THE INNER WORLD

Thus, to return to the position of modern Western pyschology, it has long been clear to me that if one wishes to be a psychologist, then one must study people as they are, and not as one would have them be. We must take psychology on its own terms, as a subject with its own rules and procedures. Which means listening to people and taking into account the things they say about themselves. It means making use of introspection and allowing people to reflect on and report their own experience. And it means showing a respect for this introspection and this reflection, instead of telling people that the experiences they have within their own minds are only the electrochemical workings of a biological machine located inside the skull.

Ultimately it means taking seriously this inner world in which we each live and from which we look out upon the outer world; this inner world within which we interpret and make sense of life, and grapple with the fundamental 'Who am I?' question.

Recognition of the need for such an approach to human psychology set me off on a search for methods and techniques for exploring this inner world, and ultimately brought me to the subject of meditation. I first became seriously interested in meditation as a postgraduate student nearly twenty-five years ago, when in the course of pursuing a lifelong interest in yoga I came upon a reference in Desmond Dunne's book *Yoga Made Easy* (still a good introduction to hatha yoga, and much less basic than the title would have you believe) to the effect that through its practice one learns 'to be truly and fully conscious of himself as a unit ... not merely in the highly personal, individualistic Western sense, which all too often leads to egocentricity and uneasy self-absorption, but in a serene, detached way that makes him immune to superficial influences'.

A practice that could do this, I reasoned, deserved a psychologist's attention. Anything that could help the individual to become serene and detached and 'immune to superficial influences' seemed to me to bear comparison with even the best that our modern psychological techniques and therapies have to offer. The more one works within the field of human psychology, the more one realizes the extent and magnitude of human psychological suffering. Whether we have reached the stage of wanting to look more closely into our inner world or are still firmly located in outer concerns, most of us are greatly in need of a serenity which can make us less vulnerable to the many problems that life puts in our path.

## MEDITATION AND CONCENTRATION

In those days nearly twenty-five years ago, there was far less material available on meditation than there is now, and far fewer meditation teachers. But I began to read all I could about the subject, and was especially fortunate to come across Ernest

Wood's excellent – if a little dry and academic – *Yoga*. On the strength of what he and other writers such as Dunne had to say, I realized that whatever else meditation was about, it was certainly about concentration. In fact, concentration seemed to be the essential first step. And concentration of a special kind. Not concentration upon an ever-changing stimulus, as when we concentrate upon a book or a chess problem or a symphony, but concentration upon a single stimulus, either an unchanging one or one with a simple repetitive rhythm.

Thus I learnt, for example, that the meditator can concentrate upon a geometrical shape or a blank wall or a rhythmical chant or a physical movement or the rise and fall of the breath. And that, it seemed, was all there was to it. Armed with this knowledge, I decided to put things to the test, so one evening when I was alone in the house, I placed a cushion on the floor and, somewhat self-consciously (and rather uncomfortably), sat cross-legged, closed my eyes and tried to concentrate upon my breathing. At that stage, I had no idea what to do about the thoughts that crowded into my head and persisted in affecting my concentration, but whether by happy chance or by some gift of grace I did succeed for some ten minutes or so in staying fairly well focused upon the rise and fall of my own abdomen.

And when, disturbed by the sound of someone returning to the house, I opened my eyes, I was surprised (and rather proud) to find myself in a calm and very pleasant state of mind. The room around me had taken on a strange new quality in which the colours and the shapes of everyday objects possessed a special soft beauty under the electric light, and I seemed, without knowing why, to be in touch with something of the same quality inside myself.

'This', I thought to myself, 'is it', and I saw before me a lifetime of regular meditation in which I grew apace in Desmond Dunne's serenity and detachment and went through my days spreading peace and joy. It was clear that meditation was easy. I had only to sit down in a quiet place, close my eyes, concentrate upon my breathing, and that was that.

Needless to say, the next evening when I sat again on my cushion and confidently expected to re-enter the same state, I met with dismal failure. The moment I closed my eyes and tried to focus on my breathing, my mind said in effect, 'I know

**BOX 1**
**CONCENTRATION**

What exactly *is* concentration? In view of its great importance in meditation, we need to know more about it.

Psychologists define concentration as a special form of disciplined, sustained attention, an attention which involves a narrowing down so that extraneous stimuli which normally distract us are not allowed to intrude. The whole of our consciousness becomes directed towards one thing, becomes in effect 'one-pointed'.

The benefits of concentration in daily life are obvious. If we concentrate upon what we are doing, we are able to do it more effectively, and better able to remember the details associated with it. Most of our lapses of memory are caused by the fact that we were not paying proper attention in the first place.

But why is concentration so vital in meditation? The answer is that only when the mind is concentrated are we able to clear the way for it to experience itself. Normally we are mentally and emotionally so pushed and pulled by a constant bombardment of things clamouring for our attention that we never really know what this 'attention' actually is. We are so busy gazing out of the window that not only have we never explored our own house, we are unaware of its very existence. Through concentration, we train the mind to be much clearer and sharper whatever we are doing and give it the space in which to turn inwards and see what's there.

But how can the mind come to know itself? Isn't that rather like the eye seeing itself? An impossibility, surely. Certainly it is, if you take the view that in order for us to 'know' there must always be two things, a mind that knows and a thing to be known. In other words, that the mind must always be concentrating upon something that *is not itself*, that mind and the contents of mind are two separate things. Through concentration, the mind reaches a point where it is empty of contents. What then? Has mind ceased to exist? Your own direct experience will provide the answer.

The concentration can be trained, and just as concentration is essential for meditation, so meditation is the best way of training concentration. But there are two helpful preliminary exercises.

*Exercise 1*  Take any common word such as 'tree' or 'water'. Write it down on a piece of paper. Now write down the first word that comes to mind in association with it, and *immediately go back to your original word*. Now another word will come to mind. Write it down and again go back at once to your starting point. Do this for as long as word associations come to mind. When they cease just stay with your original word. Hold it in your mind. Concentrate upon it, without any thoughts about it. Continue for as long as feels comfortable.

**BOX 1**
CONCENTRATION

*Exercise 2*  Do this on the day following Exercise 1. Start with the same original word. Hold it in your mind. As soon as the mind leaps to one or other of the words that came up in Exercise 1 (or to a new word), bring it back at once to your starting point. Repeat this exercise at least five minutes a day for a month.

At the end of the month, note your improvement in concentration.

exactly what you want. Leave it to me. I can get us there with no problem.' But although my mind certainly got me into mental chatter, physical discomfort, boredom, and pretty soon extreme irritation, it certainly did not get me *there*. The whole session was a complete failure. Or a complete failure in one way, and a great success in another. Because, as I came to see in due course, it began the process of teaching me that meditation certainly isn't something one enters through force of will, through an ego that says, 'Leave it to me, it's dead simple. All I have to do is consciously re-create the state we want'.

It took a while for the lesson to sink in, because all my education up to that point had left me believing that if you want to achieve something you must consciously work hard. It wasn't easy for me to recognize that I was now embarking upon something much more subtle that obeys (if 'obeys' is the word) quite different laws. And the first of these laws is that, although you may sit down with the *intention* of meditating, as soon as the process begins you must drop any idea of intention, any sense of a mind fixed on achieving some pre-determined goal. Instead, you must concentrate upon the object of concentration, whatever it happens to be, as if you are doing it for the very first time. Without expectation, without hope or the absence of hope, you sit and concentrate, you sit and do the practice of meditation, and then you watch (but remain detached from) what comes.

## THE EXPANDING VIEW OF A PSYCHOLOGIST

In spite of the apparent failure of my second attempt (and of many subsequent attempts) at meditation, my interest in the subject continued to grow. At times I had glimpses of a stillness inside myself that was paradoxically – and the meditator soon learns to live with paradox – both calming and exciting. And at times I found in my daily life something of the serenity and detachment of which Desmond Dunne spoke; a serenity and detachment which, although they didn't render me 'immune to superficial influences', at least gave hints that there is a way of living life in which one is not pulled this way and that by external influences, and put always under threat by the myriad frustrations and difficulties that life puts in the way of living.

And when, in the fullness of time, I came to write my first book, I found that a few minutes meditation before I started a writing session helped clear my mind and open it to the flow of ideas that comes from that mysterious place within the inner world where creativity has its birth. Although in those days I had still not met my first meditation teacher, I found one or two people who shared my interest in the subject, and together we swapped bits of information gleaned from books and from attending the occasional lecture given by someone from that community of Tibetan lamas who, after the Chinese invasion, found their way to the West. And my reading began increasingly to uncover gems, such as the statement by Edward Conze, one of the leading Western translators and interpreters of Buddhist texts, that:

> Enlightenment, or the state of Nirvana, is, of course, the ultimate aim of Buddhist meditations. On the way to Nirvana they serve to promote spiritual development, to minimise the impact of suffering, to calm the mind, and to reveal the true facts of existence. Increased gentleness and sympathy are among their by-products, together with an opening up to life's message, and a feeling that death has lost its sting.
>
> *Buddhist Meditation*, p. 11

This was even better than Desmond Dunne's serenity and detachment, but along with Dunne it emphasized firstly that meditation reveals 'the true facts of existence' (and therefore must answer the question 'Who am I?'), and secondly that it minimizes 'the impact of suffering'. A way of self-discovery on the one hand, and a way of psychotherapy on the other. Two ways, separate at first but, as I came to learn later, very much part and parcel of the same thing. (The extract I've quoted from Conze goes further and makes reference to concepts of 'Nirvana' and 'enlightenment', but these weighty matters were beyond my scope at the time.)

I went on from these early discoveries to find one major Western psychologist, Carl Jung, who had taken meditation seriously, and also the whole range of psychological insights provided not only by Eastern traditions but by those of the Western Hermetic, gnostic and alchemical systems to boot. Jung regarded these insights as providing a guide to inner space, and the more I studied his compelling writings the more I became convinced that, far from being the mixture of ignorance and superstition that Western science takes them to be, both the insights and the traditions from which they sprang provide us with the deepest store of psychological and spiritual wisdom known to humankind.

In the course of time, I was able to commence practical study under a number of meditation teachers from these different traditions, and much of what I learned forms the substance of this book. But I hope that this brief diversion into personal reminiscences will explain why, for all my affection and respect for Western psychology, I found it inadequate when it comes to the inner world and to the states of mind that represent for each of us what it really means to be ourselves. And I hope that before the book is over, I will have indicated why meditation is the supreme practice for exploring this inner world and these states of mind, and for uncovering the truths which only this exploration can reveal.

I hope I will also have shown why meditation can, in the course of such exploration, bring with it psychological benefits that, in Conze's words, 'minimise the impact of suffering'. In spite of all the effort and attention paid by Western psychology to the alleviation of human psychological misery, we are still in our infancy when it comes to helping people feel at peace with themselves. Psychological suffering is every bit as real as physical suffering, and those caught up in it look desperately for something, anything, which will help them find a way out of their self-imprisonment. If meditation can provide them with that something, then this is another good reason why the Western psychologist should enter and probe its mysteries.

# 2

## Why Meditation?

In view of the way Western psychology ignores the inner world of the mind, and meditation as a method for exploring it, it is hardly surprising that Western research has produced little conclusive research evidence on whether or not meditation lives up to the claims made for it by writers like Dunne and Conze. In a recent book, *The Psychology of Meditation*, Michael West has brought together this evidence, and although the book is excellent, much of the research it describes shows the difficulties of research into meditation.

How do you research the benefits of meditation? How do you assess whether people have become more 'serene' or 'detached' or resistant to the 'impact of suffering'? The simplest way is to ask them, but Western psychology regrettably does not much like direct enquiry of this kind, since it involves introspection and thus relies on the accuracy and integrity of what people say about themselves. For this reason, much of the psychological research into meditation has involved physiological measurements. Psychologists generally feel safer (equally regrettably) with physiological factors, since they record objective facts; for instance, what is actually going on in the physiological system in terms of blood pressure, electrical activity in the brain, and chemicals such as adrenalin and noradrenalin in the bloodstream.

Thus, if meditation is claimed to enhance serenity, the psychologist will ask whether it produces the physiological changes that usually accompany physical relaxation, such as reduced blood pressure and heart rate, a change in electrical brain rhythm from the customary beta to the slower alpha, and a reduction in the level of stress-related hormones such as adrenalin and noradrenalin. This is all very well as far as it goes, but it doesn't go far enough since it doesn't tell us how the meditator's inner experience actually *feels* to him or her. Two people may apparently be equally relaxed physiologically and show equal changes in blood pressure and brain rhythms, but their relaxed states may have very different causes and be experienced in very different ways. One may be having a rambling daydream while the other may be focused clearly and steadily upon his or her breathing. The physiological effects will look similar, but the nature and quality of the inner experiences which give rise to them will be quite different.

In view of the relative crudity of physiological measurements, it is not surprising that research shows that meditation is little better at putting the individual into a calm physiological state than are the simple relaxation techniques taught by psychologists themselves. The result is that there appears to be nothing about meditation to commend it to psychologists above these much less 'mystical' procedures.

A second method used by psychologists to research into meditation is the questionnaire. Psychologists are happier with questionnaires than with introspection because the questions which they contain can be highly specific and they can include trick questions designed to catch respondents out if they give inaccurate or falsified information. Further, the questions can be designed to reveal objective facts such as whether the individual experiences nervous sweating or butterflies rather than asking subjective questions such as how does he or she feel.

Once again, research of this kind is all right as far as it goes, but it still doesn't tell us how the individual actually experiences his or her inner life. For example, two people may both answer 'yes' to test questions that ask them whether they sweat or have butterflies in their stomachs before an interview or before public speaking, but these answers tell us nothing of how the individuals concerned relate to their condition. One person may identify with it and become overwhelmed, while the other may observe it objectively, and get on effectively with the job in hand. In other words, although both people may be experiencing anxiety, their respective coping behaviours may be quite different, and this fact will be of enormous importance in the lives of the individuals concerned.

In view of the shortcomings of questionnaire tests, it is predictable that the research carried out with them once again tells us little about the value of meditation. Certainly, results show that, while people who take up meditation tend to be more anxious as a group than the majority of their fellow men and women, meditation does appear to lower their anxiety levels somewhat, but again the results are no better than those obtained from relaxation training. A further finding, that people who score *very* high on anxiety in the questionnaire tests are more likely to withdraw from meditation training than are those with lower scores, is of interest since it indicates that such people should be given extra support, but the inability of the tests to tell us what goes on in the inner world of such people to prompt their withdrawal limits its practical value.

In the general field of personality, questionnaire research shows that introverts (those more orientated towards inner states of mind) are more likely to take up meditation than extroverts (those more outgoing and socially orientated), which is hardly surprising. More interestingly, it suggests that introverts become *less* introverted as a result of meditation, which is reassuring for those who fear that meditation increases tendencies towards solitariness, although this may be due more to the social benefits of belonging to a meditation group (meditators tend to be pleasant people) than to meditation itself. The evidence also suggests that experienced meditators score more highly than non-meditators on self-esteem (the value we place on ourselves), but since research also shows that low self-esteem individuals are particularly prone to drop out of meditation, this may simply suggest that high self-esteem is a cause of perseverance in meditation rather than an effect.

Which doesn't necessarily mean meditators are a conceited bunch of people, by the way! Conceit is frequently a defence against *low* self-esteem, an absurd attempt to convince everyone how marvellous you are because at base you don't believe it yourself. The ability to value ourselves has far more to do with self-acceptance, with an awareness that, whatever our good and bad points, we all deserve self-respect and self-cherishing by virtue of the possession of a precious human life.

## MEDITATION AS PSYCHOTHERAPY

None of the research summarized above was carried out with highly advanced meditators. Most researchers were – and are – more interested, rightly or wrongly, in assessing the effects of meditation upon ordinary mortals than upon a few rare and highly advanced individuals. There are reports from India of experienced yogis who, under carefully monitored laboratory conditions, can control bodily metabolism to such an extent in meditation that they are able to survive for long periods of time in oxygen-free conditions that would kill the rest of us. There are also accounts of advanced meditators who can continue to produce relaxed alpha brain rhythms even when engaged in complex arithmetical problems (an activity normally guaranteed to flip the brain into a beta rhythm, no matter how calm one is able to remain). One of my own meditation teachers, the Venerable Ngakpa Chögyam, has demonstrated this effect under strict test conditions in a hospital neurology department, and an account of the proceedings is given in the Introduction to his book *Rainbow of Liberated Energy.*

Another limitation of the above research is that much of it has involved meditators who are using the transcendental meditation (TM) technique. This is a *mantra* technique (Chapter 10) which has attracted a large number of enthusiastic followers. But some of the research carried out with transcendental meditators has failed to meet the strict standards that ensure reported results are accurate, or that results which are attributed to one particular cause may not be due to something else. For example, beneficial physiological results attributed to the effects of meditation could be due simply to physical relaxation since, as we have seen, physical relaxation often parallels the physiological results produced by meditation. Or they could be due simply to the belief that the meditation works (the so-called 'placebo effect') – in which case playing a tin whistle might be equally beneficial provided you regarded it with the same level of belief.

However, although the picture produced by research is rather unsatisfactory, this isn't the end of the story. Psychologists who use meditation with patients in actual *clinical* work have produced case studies to show that, when used with suitable individuals, meditation is helpful in reducing tension, anxiety, stress-related abnormalities (such as insomnia, stuttering, high blood pressure, and abnormal heart rhythms), and self-blame. They have also found it valuable in reducing drug dependence, increasing a sense of personal identity, improving mood, facilitating emotional expression, and increasing creativity, energy and general productivity levels.

Since evidence of this kind isn't produced under strict research conditions, we don't know whether relaxation training would have produced comparable results. But certainly these clinical studies go deeper into the lives and the subsequent progress of the individuals concerned than the other studies mentioned, in that they take into account introspection and thus respect what individuals say about their responses to meditation practice. These clinical studies still don't tell us all we would like to know, but within their limitations they support Dunne's claims that meditation leads to increased serenity and detachment, and Conze's claims that it produces a calmer mind and a decrease in the impact of suffering.

However, clinical studies also suggest that meditation isn't suitable for everyone. In order to use meditation successfully, they indicate that the meditator should have a degree of self-discipline (though this need be no more than that required for relaxation training), and should not have an excessive need for self-control. The latter need may result in the meditator feeling insecure, even frightened, by the loss of the sense of 'being in command' that meditation brings, and this may lead him or her not only to give up meditation but to feel actively harmed by it.

A further (not surprising) suggestion is that simpler forms of meditation such as concentrating upon the breath or a mantra bring more immediate results than more complex forms of meditation such as visualization. Clinical results also suggest that there can be certain dangers in meditation, and these are worth listing. None of them is particularly serious, and none is a reason for not taking up meditation. They are simply things against which you should be on your guard.

1. Meditation can lead to feelings of personal power and superiority which are not only unhelpful in themselves but which can conflict with the meditator's more 'objective' feeling that he or she really isn't that successful in daily life. Alternatively they may cloak this latter feeling, and prevent the meditator from confronting it and dealing with it realistically.

2. The optimism and well-being reported by many meditators may produce an unrealistic euphoria that actually impedes attempts to identify and reduce psychological problems.

3. Meditation can lead to an easing of the pace with which one handles things, and this easing may be inappropriate for the life the individual actually has to lead. As a result he or she may become *less* effective in a career or in domestic life than hitherto.

4. For some people, the sense of ease and well-being that can come with meditation may result in the conviction that one has become self-indulgent and lazy, or that one is wasting time instead of getting on with the real business of living.

5. Entry into meditation with unrealistically high expectations may lead to disillusionment, and even to a dislike for any activity that looks into the inner world.

Experienced meditators reading through this list will say, 'Ah yes, but these things only happen if you are going about meditation in the wrong way. You shouldn't have high initial expectations, for example, and if you're meditating properly you shouldn't develop feelings of personal power or unrealistic optimism.' And they may add that if slowing the pace of life means you are less effective in your career, this suggests you are in the wrong career in the first place. And of course, they are right. If you are working with a meditation teacher, he or she will point these things out to you, and will counsel you accordingly. Even if you are working alone, a proper initial understanding of meditation will allow you to steer clear of these pitfalls, or to cope with them should they appear.

But these dangers do emphasize the need to know something of the theory involved in meditation, as well as the practice. This theory isn't particularly demanding, and for anyone interested in the inner world explored in meditation, it carries enormous fascination in itself. Indeed, in meditation, theory and practice are two sides of the same coin. The one is incomplete without the other, as I hope to make clear as we go along.

## MEDITATORS ON MEDITATION

As psychological research tells us so little about the actual experiences of the meditator, the sensible thing is to go to meditators themselves and ask them to tell us in their own words the effect that meditation has upon them. Let's choose two examples from Westerners who have studied meditation under Eastern meditation teachers.

The first is by Jane Hamilton-Merritt, an American writer who spent some time in intensive meditation practice in Thai monasteries.

> Meditation . . . is among many things a learning to still the mind, to control it, to centre the mind's potential energy . . . the mind expands and is capable of producing more acute realizations . . . the body and mind seem to come together in a harmony or centring because separateness, or duality, of the body and mind is diminished and at times even absent . . . it is this separateness of body and mind which prevents humans from knowing their true self and is consequently the source of much struggle, of much unhappiness, of much suffering. The process of meditation seems to involve a shedding of desires, of the need for unnecessary possessions, of a demanding ego . . . when these fall away . . . it becomes possible to know something of the true self. In this new state minus all these hindering distracting trappings, the mind can be centred and achieve personal equanimity.
> *A Meditator's Diary*, p. 142

On the subject of this personal equanimity, Hamilton-Merritt confirms that 'there is a calmness, an understanding, a harmony in my life which has developed as a result of meditation'.

The second example is by Timothy Ward, another American who studied in a Thai monastery, and gives us a taste of the experience of *samadhi*, a deep level of meditation.

> My breath came through clearly, easily. It sustained itself with a perfect concentration never before achieved. Thoughts arose from time to time but they could not intrude. I was aware only of balance,

of ease . . . It was a surprisingly active state of mind, neither automatic nor trancelike. Only moment by moment concentration could sustain it. It required energy but produced no stress . . . I felt I could sustain the state indefinitely . . . What I cherished was the feeling of ease.

*What the Buddha Never Taught*, p. 150

Both these examples describe something over and above what emerges from techniques like relaxation training, no matter how similar the physiological effects may be. The literature produced by relaxation training contains no accounts of the knowledge of the 'true self' gained by Jane Hamilton-Merritt, no accounts of the samadhi experienced by Timothy Ward. Even the literature produced by those who have undergone the various psychotherapies developed in the West contains nothing directly comparable.

The literature produced by meditators is full of similar examples. The more one delves into this literature and talks to and observes practising meditators, the more one becomes aware that here is a technique like no other technique, a practice like no other practice. A practice that can transform, that brings with it a richness of understanding and imparts a wisdom hard to put into words but which transports those who sample it into a deeper dimension of experience.

For in the way that my first tentative attempt at meditation twenty-five years ago subtly transformed the shapes and the colours of the room around me, so meditation alters not only the perspective one has of oneself – the way one thinks and feels about and experiences oneself – but also the perspective one has of the outer world. There is a shift not only in one's mental and emotional condition but also, as it were, in one's sense perception. One becomes more open to the environment, more aware of the beauties and colours of nature, of the joys and sorrows of others. One *feels* the texture of life, in the way that a parent feels the smooth warm skin of a baby, or the potter the clay on the wheel, or the gardener the petals of an opening flower.

## SO WHAT IS MEDITATION?

So far, I have discussed meditation without offering any clear definition of what it actually is. I have discussed it as a way of looking into the inner world, and finding an answer to the question 'Who am I?', an answer which also changes the way we experience and understand the outer world. This looking inwards to help understand what lies outwards should not surprise us. Because everything in the outer world only exists for us when we become aware of it through our senses and register it in our own minds. So it follows that only through understanding the mind can we understand the external phenomena that play out their existence for us within its magic theatre.

I have also said that the starting point of this process of looking inwards, of meditation, is concentration upon one particular stimulus to the exclusion of all others.

But this still doesn't define what meditation actually *is*. And here we run up against a difficulty which has to be faced before we go any further. Namely that definitions are a particularly Western way of making 'sense' of the world. We all of us love definitions. 'What is it?', we ask, and immediately we come up with the answer, 'Well it is . . .' this or that or the other. And having offered this definition, we feel that we have answered the question and encapsulated the *essence* of whatever it is we're talking about.

But have we? Our definition is simply a set of words. And the words are no more the thing we are talking about than the word 'horse' is the animal itself. We have cleverly deceived ourselves into believing that our definition and whatever it is we are defining are one and the same thing. We go further, and believe that our definition is also an *explanation* and that by defining something, we have said all there is to say about it.

Take the definition of a common substance like water. 'What is water?', we ask, and tell ourselves that it is a colourless liquid essential to life. We go further and say that it is a chemical substance made up of hydrogen and oxygen, with two parts of the former to one of the latter. All very clever, and very useful if you are a chemist. But is this what water really *is*? Go and look at it. Splash it on your face. Drink it; take a bath in it. *That* is what water is, that experience of sight, touch, taste and wetness.

But there is even more to water than this. Your body is largely made of water. *You* are largely water. You are a mobile column of water. *You* are what water is. Feel water from the inside, not just from the outside. Water is your blood and your tissues, your brain and your skin, your heart and your lungs. Water is not just something in the outer world, water is in the inner world. If it were not, there would be no one to write these words and no one to read them.

Once we begin to think in this way, we can see how meaningless is the definition of water as a colourless liquid, or as two parts hydrogen and one part oxygen. And we can go on and demolish the definition of other things in the same way. Stay for a moment with what the ancients in their wisdom called the four elements – water, air, fire and earth. We've looked at water, so what about the other three? Air is a gas, says the chemical definition, made of oxygen mixed with a few other gases. Is it? Move your hand backwards and forwards in space and feel the sensation against your skin. Fill your lungs and focus on the sensation in your nostrils and in your chest. Look out of the window and see the trees moving in the wind. *That* is what air is.

But again, it is more even than that? Your blood is full of oxygen, pulsing along each artery in your body and feeding each tissue. That is air. You are air. A balloon filled with air. So what of a definition that says air is simply a gas made up of bits and pieces of other gases?

What about fire? Gas in combustion? Feel the warmth in your body. Put your hand on your arm and feel this strange, mysterious thing called heat. Feel it glowing inside every fibre of your being. That is fire. You are fire. A furnace of gently burning fire.

And earth, the last of the four elements? You are earth, too. Iron, copper, phosphorus, zinc, magnesium, manganese, and several others, are all present in your body and without them you would die. Each of these minerals is identical to the minerals in the earth. There is no real difference between the iron in your body and the iron in an iron nail, or between the copper in your body and the copper in a copper pipe. We are these minerals, and these minerals are us. (You will notice I have resisted the temptation to say that you are a clod of earth, but this is only because that might give the wrong impression!)

And the more we ponder this, the more we realize that when the ancients identified the four elements, they meant something much more profound than we give them credit for.

We can pursue the matter even further. The four elements

came, literally, from the stars. We are star dust, star people, star children. We are the stars and the stars are us, not in some absurd science fiction sense, but in the cold hard sense of modern science. The stars are not simply things that twinkle in the heavens on a clear night; they are the stuff of our flesh and bones, the stuff of our brains and hearts. The stars are inside us as well as outside, and any definition that ignores the fact is at best a dangerous half-truth.

'Definitions', therefore, are simply ways of giving snippets of information, useful for their own narrow purposes but useless if we take them to be what things actually *are*. And this is why symbols, whose place in meditation I will be returning to again and again, can be much more powerful ways of understanding than the words in a dictionary. And humankind has always realized this. A national flag conveys the idea of their country to people much more strongly than does a geographical description. The symbol of the cross can say far more to Christians than can attempts to list the dry bones of beliefs. Symbols can convey the essence of something, and arouse an inner response to that essence in a way that definitions on their own can never do.

Modern psychology is only now trying to tease out why this should be – and risking in the attempt the very error from which symbols allow us to escape; namely, trying to explain one thing in terms of another instead of allowing it to speak through direct experience. By trying to define symbols in any 'scientific' sense, the essence of what they are slips through the fingers. Only Jung of modern psychologists seems fully to realize this. He writes that:

> ... a word or an image is symbolic when it implies something more than its obvious and immediate meaning. It has a wider 'unconscious' aspect that is never precisely defined or fully explained. Nor can one hope to define or explain it. As the mind explores the symbol, it is led to ideas that lie beyond the grasp of reason ... Because there are innumerable things beyond the range of human understanding, we constantly use symbolic concepts that we cannot define or fully comprehend. This is one reason why all religions employ symbolic language or images. But this conscious use of symbols is only one aspect of a psychological fact of great importance: Man also produces symbols unconsciously and spontaneously, in the form of dreams.
>
> *Man and His Symbols*, p. 4

Jung's reference to the unconscious is vitally important here, and takes us one step further into the apparent mysteries of meditation. For the unconscious, that vast reservoir of the mind in which is stored so much that is inaccessible to consciousness, is part of the inner world that meditation allows us to enter. No one can grasp the importance of meditation to our psychological lives and to our psychological well-being without realizing this. Our conscious mind is only a small part of our mental life, the tip of an iceberg that stretches down into unfathomable depths, and that at the same time reaches up into the heavens and what lies beyond (I've mentioned already that the meditator soon learns to live with paradox).

This paradox of reaching downwards and upwards at the same time is easier to accept if we remember that the term 'unconscious' is itself simply a definition. We use it (and we psychologists are more guilty than anyone) as if it explains the vast hidden areas of the mind. And of course it does no such thing. We simply do not, in any scientific sense, know what the unconscious actually is. Ideas, memories, dreams come into the mind from some unknown sources, and we simply say, 'Ah yes, that's the unconscious at work', as if the unconscious is a tangible object like a bowl or a bucket. By using the term in this way, as if it explains everything, we put a full stop to our enquiry, and risk trivializing the larger part of our mental life.

And there is worse to come, because for some psychologists the unconscious is simply our animal nature, the source of the instinctive drives from which we had much better emancipate ourselves as quickly as possible. But in meditation we realize that this earthy, animalistic aspect of the unconscious, far from being merely brutish and instinctive, carries a wisdom of its own. More, we find that there is another aspect to the unconscious, an aspect in communion with a deeper wisdom which some call spiritual and some call our higher self. We stand, as it were, astride a stream with one foot in the rich and fruitful world of nature and the other in the rarified world of the spirit, and in meditation we may even see that for all their apparent differences, these two worlds are ultimately part of one another.

**BOX 2**
**CONSCIOUS AND UNCONSCIOUS**

Western psychology doesn't possess an accurate map of the mind, but one of the most useful was put forward by Sigmund Freud, the founder of psychoanalysis. This model has three levels.

*Level 1    The Conscious Mind* consists of whatever is occupying your awareness at any one moment, whether this be thoughts, sensations, feelings or emotions. The conscious mind – consciousness – is essentially the part of the mind in which we feel ourselves to live.

*Level 2    The Preconscious Mind* is the term used for all that information we have in our heads and which, although it is not occupying our conscious attention at the moment, we can recall more or less at will. Think about your home, for example. The chances are this wasn't in your thoughts before I mentioned it, but the moment I did so all sorts of ideas and visual impressions associated with it come readily into consciousness. These emerge from your preconscious.

*Level 3    The Unconscious* consists of those mysterious depths which I talk about in the text, and which are generally inaccessible to the conscious mind without the use of appropriate techniques (hypnosis, dreaming and, above all, meditation). Jung divided the unconscious into the *personal unconscious*, which consists of all those elements which have to do with your own personal history, and *the collective unconscious*, which is (put at its simplest) the inherited predispositions which we all share, the ways of thinking and feeling which are common to the human race. The collective unconscious seems to be the home of our common aspirations such as our emotional and spiritual longings, and also of the patterns, the *archetypes* as Jung called them, on which we model powerful universal concepts such as 'mother', 'father', 'hero', 'wise old man/woman', 'god' and so on. In other words, the primordial symbols that have been meaningful for all time and for all races, as witnessed by their appearance over and over again in the fairy tales, myths, legends and art forms of all cultures; the symbols which help define the way in which we conceptualize and relate to the world.

In meditation, the mind opens itself firstly to the preconscious – the rush of thoughts and memories that immediately crowd into the mind when we try and turn inwards. Then, as the ability to meditate deepens, the mind opens to the unconscious. Long-forgotten memories from the personal unconscious may be the first things to arise, and only later come universal symbols and archetypes from the collective unconscious.

**BOX 2**
CONSCIOUS AND UNCONSCIOUS

The collective unconscious is the level at which our minds expand, as it were, and join with the unifying psychological and spiritual forces that underlie the human race. It is possible that extrasensory powers, some of which the meditator may find he or she develops, stem from our ability to make direct contact with the thoughts and feelings of other men and women through the collective unconscious.

## THE POWER OF SYMBOLS

Which brings me back to symbols and metaphors. In its attempt to understand symbols, Western psychology suggests they gain their power through association. A cross means nothing of itself, but acquires meaning as it becomes linked in our minds with Christianity. The one stands for the other, in the same way that a logo or trade mark stands for a particular commercial product. But this denies the fact that the symbols that have the power to stir the imagination and to carry levels of inner meaning emerge, as Jung tells us, from the unconscious mind rather than from the conscious.

In making this point Jung is referring not just to those rare individuals who first wove the great patterns of thought and practice of the world's religions, but ordinary men and women living ordinary lives. For example, Jung found that in his clinical work his clients, on their inner journeys towards wholeness and mental health, frequently reached a stage where spontaneously they began to dream *mandalas* (the symbolic shapes and pictures used in many forms of meditation – see Chapter 7), and that by working with these mandalas – painting them, drawing them, meditating upon them – they opened themselves to otherwise inaccessible inner truths.

Further evidence of the fact that certain symbols have a universal, archetypal power is that in both the East and West, the same ones occur time and time again (the cross, for example, was in use as a religious symbol many centuries before the coming of Christianity). No matter how remote and isolated they may have been from each other, different communities and different cultures have produced and revered the same symbols. The cross, the circle, the triangle and the square, for instance, occur time and again as representations of inner meaning. And – here lies their particular relevance for the meditator – just as these symbols emerge *from* the unconscious, so they act as keys *into* the unconscious. By meditating upon these universal symbols, in ways to which I return in Chapter 7, the meditator is able to open doors and set out on pathways that otherwise would be difficult to find.

We also detect the power of symbols in the creative arts, in painting, in music and in poetry (certain sounds and words carry symbolic meaning just as do certain shapes). This is one reason why the creative arts have such a power to stimulate the imagination, and to stir us in ways that simple representational material cannot do. Symbols allow the creative artist access to our inner being, allowing him or her to communicate directly to us in an inner shorthand that brings a profound sense of 'knowing', even when we do not know exactly what it is we know.

There is a wealth of difference between the words of poets and writers and the words of the scientists. In poetry and in the great stories of mankind, words carry their impact through metaphor, through myth. And as we respond to this metaphor and myth, we understand that ultimate truth – or as much of it as we can encompass – is poetic and not scientific. Science, for all its power and usefulness, has the limited range of convenience imposed by the rules of its own language. Within that range of convenience it is relevant and appropriate. Outside that range, it gives you a razor blade when you have asked for a flower.

Meditation takes us deep into this poetic world of metaphor and symbol. We pass from the land of the razor blade into that of the flower. We move from the rational, linear, logical world into the world of intuition, where truth presents itself in flashes of insight and causes profound changes in the way we respond to experience. A world of being instead of reasoning, a world where to be human is what it is instead of what we are told it is, and where life is lived instead of talked about.

So, to take up once more the question 'What is meditation?', it makes sense to avoid scientific definition and say that meditation is a lotus flower emerging from still waters. Or a monk or nun sitting in the silence of towering mountain peaks. Or the line of trees on the skyline. Or a man or woman sitting in peace in the midst of a busy city. Or a traveller walking a pathway through the trees of a great forest. Or the still music of a flute on a summer's evening.

A wise person once said that the tragedy of the Westerner is that 'he cannot sit quietly in his own room'. Meditation is this sitting quietly in one's own room, whether it be the physical room of the outer world or the mental room of the inner world. Meditation is the experience of your own being, the experience of what lies behind the thousand and one thoughts and emotions that usually clutter up life. Think of your *own* symbol for it. Find a symbol that embodies meditation for you, however tentatively. If one doesn't immediately emerge, put the exercise to one side and let the symbol arise from the unconscious in its own good time, perhaps during actual meditation. Remember that symbols are the language of the unconscious, and that meditation allows us to listen to that language.

Finally, remember that meditation is already there inside you. Although for convenience we often refer to it as a technique, in reality it is not something waiting to be learned. It is not something additional to who you are now, an extra waiting to be studied in the way that we study the language of the computer or how to say hello in Chinese. Meditation is the experience of who you already are, and have always been and will always be. If you want a final metaphor, it is how the world looks when you stand still and see it for what it is instead of distorted into a blur by your own perpetual motion.

**BOX 3**
**THE LANGUAGE OF SYMBOLS**

Take a piece of paper and draw on it a circle. Now contemplate the circle for a moment, and then write down all the associations it suggests for you. These are the 'language' of the circle, the things which it symbolizes for you.

If a number of people carry out the same exercise, they invariably come up with much the same 'language'. The circle is one of the most powerful universal symbols, used not only as a design but also as a lived experience – as, for example, in the round table of King Arthur and his Knights, and the circle dances that are a feature not only of folk customs but also of shamanic and sacred rituals.

**BOX 3**
**THE LANGUAGE OF SYMBOLS**

The circle represents wholeness, completeness, fulfilment, unity, the absolute. It is as near perfection as we can achieve, since it has no beginning and no end, and each point is equidistant from the centre. The circle makes its appearance in all religions, from the Celtic cross to the Buddhist wheel to the yin-yang symbol of the Taoists to the domed cupola of the Islamic mosque. There is no other symbol that unlocks such a rich outpouring from the unconscious, or that can lead more easily to the sense of tranquillity and peace in meditation.

Now try the same exercise in turn with the cross, the square and the triangle. These are more arousing, challenging symbols than the circle, but again they carry important levels of meaning that have been put to use in all the great religions.

The cross symbolizes, amongst other things, the meeting point between heaven and earth, the tree of life (note how Christ is often referred to symbolically as crucified on a 'tree'), infinite expansion in all directions, the four elements with the fifth (ether) in the centre. The square symbolizes strength, integrity, steadfastness, and the triangle the trinity (which occurs in various forms in nearly all religions), male energy when pointing upwards, female energy when pointing downwards, and the union of male and female when upward and downward triangles are put together to form a star.

Now try combining two or more of these four symbols to make further symbols. Experiment until you find something that carries special meaning for you. This, in a sense, is your own symbol.

When meditating on symbols, put all the above associations out of your mind, however. Ultimately, they are only words. Allow the symbol to speak directly to you, to produce its effect at the level of feeling, of being. It is one thing to talk about 'harmony', for example, or 'peace', and quite another to feel *in* harmony or *in* peace. When meditating on a symbol, pay no more attention to the verbal associations that arise in response to it than you would to any other thoughts. They can be remembered and recorded afterwards, but during the meditation, let the symbol speak for itself.

# 3

---

## Concentration, Tranquillity, Insight

### THE BASICS OF MEDITATION

It is useful at this point to pause and summarize the basics of meditation practice (fuller details are given in my book *The Elements of Meditation*). If you're just taking up meditation, this will help you know where to begin, and if you're already experienced, it will allow you to recap on your practice in the way we all need to do from time to time. It is too easy to allow the practice to become mechanical. We sit in meditation out of habit, but quickly let ourselves become lost in thought. A pleasant enough pastime, assuming the thoughts are happy ones; but the result is that as the weeks and months go by we don't make any real progress. For whatever else meditation is, it most certainly isn't getting lost in thought.

As I mentioned in Chapter 1, the essential first step in any meditation practice, no matter what form the practice takes, is concentration. The mind must have something upon which to concentrate, and must stay with it. Whenever the attention drifts away, through intruding thoughts, tiredness or boredom, it must be brought gently but firmly back to the point of focus. This point of focus can be virtually anything, but especially in the early stages of meditation it should be something simple and/or rhythmical. This is why, since the time of the Buddha 500 years before Christ – and probably from time immemorial before that – the breath has been used.

The breath is both simple and rhythmical, a steady coming and going, rising and falling, inflowing and outflowing. And as the breath is always with us, in good times and in bad, it tends not to carry any specific personal associations. It is the unacknowledged background to our lives, vital to our very existence yet taken so completely for granted that mostly we are unaware it is happening. If you have asthma or bronchitis or other breathing problems you will be more conscious than the rest of us just how precious each breath is, but you will still usually give little particular attention to it.

## WORKING WITH THE BREATH

The breath, therefore, is a good point of focus. But the meditator doesn't follow the breath from the nose down into the abdomen, but instead chooses one or other of these places and stays there. Either the nostrils where the air is cool as we breathe in and warm as we breathe out, or the position in the abdomen where we feel the rise and fall of the diaphragm. Shifting from one point of focus to the other by following the passage of the breath is too distracting. Our concentration needs to be, in the Buddhist term for it, *one-pointed*.

So having first sat down in a quiet place, either in the lotus position or one of its variants, or upright in a chair with the back straight and hands flat on the thighs and feet flat on the floor, you place your attention at the nostrils or the abdomen and keep it there, refusing to be distracted by thoughts or outside events. In theory, nothing could be simpler. You feel the air drawn in, then observe the slight pause between the in-breath and the out-breath, then you feel the air expelled and once again observe a slight pause, this time between out-breath and in-breath. At least at first, you don't strive for any special pattern to your breathing, such as longer out-breaths than in-breaths; you just allow your breath to come and go naturally, allowing it to settle down and become softer and softer as your mind and body relax into your meditation.

To help your concentration you can count your breaths, counting from one to ten on each out-breath, and then returning to one and beginning again. Should you lose track of your counting, go back to the count of one each time.

**BOX 4**
PRANAYAMA

Concentration upon the breath in meditation often leads people to ask whether they should breathe in any special way. The best advice is to breathe naturally, and become aware as the meditation deepens of how the breath becomes gentler and more subtle until finally it is almost imperceptible.

There are, however, a number of special breathing techniques, known as *pranayama*, taught in yoga and these are said to be methods by which the meditator can gain increasing control over the vital forces in the body, and use them not only in the promotion of physical health but also in the transformation of physical into spiritual energy (Chapter 4). It is inadvisable to use the more advanced of these techniques without a teacher, since they can prove dangerous (for example, by affecting the rhythm of the heart) but there are several introductory ones which help mind and body enter more rapidly into meditation, and I give examples below. Practise them if you wish for a few minutes each time you take your place on your cushion or chair, and then allow the breath to settle back into its natural pattern.

● The simplest form of pranayama is to breathe in through the mouth with the lips pursed as in whistling until the lungs are full, then to swallow, close the mouth and breathe out equally slowly through the nose. This exercise is said to bring sweetness of disposition, friendliness and cheerfulness of personality, beauty of form, and a long life.

● One of the most relaxing forms of pranayama is to allow the out-breath to take longer than the in-breath. Ideally, the former should occupy a silent count of eight and the latter a count of four. But to begin with, it is enough merely to ensure that the one is longer than the other.

● A more advanced form of this practice is to retain each in-breath for twice the time taken by the out-breath. Thus the rhythm is 4-16-8, which can be increased to 6-24-12 with practice. No strain should ever be involved, and there should be no appreciable pause between the out-breath and the in-breath. To gain maximum benefit, close your right nostril with your right thumb, breathe in through the left, close both nostrils while the breath is held, then close the left nostril with the left thumb and breathe out through the right. For the next breath, reverse the procedure, breathing in through the right and out through the left, and continue by reversing nostrils on each breath. (Incidentally, this north-south breathing, as it is called, is the best method I know for warding off a cold or for clearing the sinuses.)

BOX 4
PRANAYAMA

Remember that there should never be any tension in these breathing exercises. And if they produce adverse effects (light-headedness, palpitations, feelings of breathlessness) stop at once. You have been trying too hard. Go easier next time.

If you're just beginning to learn meditation, you sit for five or ten minutes each session; try to sit each day at the same time, morning or evening, whichever suits you best. You allow the daily five to ten minutes to expand to fifteen or twenty minutes as the weeks go by, but you never try and force the pace. Meditation isn't about gritting the teeth in determination. It's about sitting quietly with yourself, and although it requires its own kind of discipline this has less to do with toughness than with yielding and letting go.

When the inevitable thoughts or emotions arise, you allow them to pass into and out of awareness like clouds reflected in water. You don't try and push them away, but leave them to move of their own accord. No matter how 'important' the thoughts seem to be or how pressing or disturbing the emotions, you don't hang on to them or allow one thought or emotion to set off another and another until you are off on a wool-gathering trail that takes you further and further from the simple matter of the in-breath and the out-breath. If, nevertheless, you do get carried away, gently but firmly return to your breathing the moment you realize this has happened. Avoid being impatient with yourself or convincing yourself you'll never learn to meditate. Your wandering mind is simply demonstrating to you just how much you need to meditate. It is helping you, prompting you, showing you how little control you have over your own thinking. The right response is gratitude, gratitude towards that part of your mind that has become aware you are wool-gathering and that has reminded you to return to your point of focus.

I cannot overstress how important this attitude of gratitude is. If you curse yourself each time you become aware you are lost in thought, you will not only be arousing the unwelcome emotion of self-disgust, you will be conditioning your mind *not* to

## BOX 5
## DEALING WITH DISTRACTIONS

Once we begin to meditate, we become aware of just how many distractions there are each moment of our lives, pulling our attention away from whatever we happen to be doing. Distractions such as physical discomfort (a pain in the leg, an itch on the nose), extraneous noises (the television next door, children's voices), the rumblings of hunger, the emergence of thoughts and emotions.

What should one do about them? These distractions are always there, but in meditation they become more obvious, sometimes till we're ready to scream. A minor itch grows into a raging irritation, the murmur of voices becomes the bellowing of savages, the memory of a popular tune a blaring military band, a quiver of anger a blast of fury.

The standard advice – the only advice – is that we simply note these things, and get on with our meditation. But this is easier said than done. How can you 'simply note' something that is clamouring for your attention? The answer lies in the attitude of mind with which you do the noting. Fierce, grim determination *not* to be distracted by what you regard as unwarranted intrusions only makes things worse. The right attitude is that these distractions are a perfectly natural part of living. Normal life isn't going to pack up and go home just because you want to meditate. True meditation is the ability to remain centred in the midst of life, not to run away from it. So these distractions are part of what *is*, part of the activity that is going on all the time in both outer and inner worlds.

Once matters are viewed in this light, you can see that paradoxically all these distractions are there to help you by testing the depth of your concentration.

Never try and shut out external distractions. Allow them to pass in and out of awareness like all the other things registered by the mind. Similarly with minor discomforts in the body. Don't resent them, and don't rush to put them right. As soon as you get into the habit of shifting or scratching, you'll have to do it more and more often. Sit with physical discomforts, and most of them will pass out of your awareness just like everything else. If they become really troublesome deal with them, but the stillness of the body helps the stillness of the mind, and sitting with a little discomfort trains you not to feel you must be constantly trying to alter your surroundings just to suit yourself.

All this becomes easier if – as with thoughts and emotions – you don't *identify* with distractions. Observe them, but keep the mind separate from them. They are the temporary contents of the mind, not the mind itself. The less you identify with them, the more you will become conscious of this, and the less hold they will have on your awareness.

remind you when it is wandering in the future. You are in effect punishing it each time for reminding you, and naturally it doesn't like being punished. So it will remind you less and less often, and you will find concentration becomes harder and harder. In response to the frustration that this brings, your mind will then start whispering persuasively to you that meditation is a total waste of effort, and that you would be well advised to find something better to do with your time.

## MEDITATION ISN'T ANTI-INTELLECTUAL

None of what I have said so far means that meditation is anti-intellectual, and suitable only for those with undemanding minds. On the contrary, meditation engages the whole of what you are, including your intellect. You don't have to leave your intellect at the door each time you enter the meditation room. The intellect is a very powerful tool, and it is given to us to use. But the intellect isn't engaged during the actual meditation practice in the sense that it is given an intellectual problem to solve and expected to work on it with rational, logical, analytical thinking. The intellect is certainly there in meditation. Where else could it be? If you doubt this, notice the subtle changes that come over it as a result of meditation, the way it becomes more open to new ideas, more fertile, more creative, more balanced, less rigid in its outlook.

And you can certainly use the intellect to ponder over the nature and meaning of meditation in your non-meditative moments. But in meditation itself, the task given to the mind is to practise one-pointed concentration, and not to become distracted by the thoughts, whether trivial or profound, that happen to arise. We each have to learn this and to learn that we are all equal when we sit down to meditate. Our academic qualifications, the size of our bank balance, our status in our jobs and in society at large, count for nothing. We are each of us back where we started from, and beginning all over again.

## CONCENTRATION PLUS TRANQUILLITY

Let us return now to the summary of the basic practice involved in meditation. One-pointed focusing upon your breath, without irritation at your wandering mind, and without expectations or elevated goals, develops your concentration. Gradually, over a period of time, this concentration becomes clearer and the mind wanders less. Progress isn't in a straight line. Some days you feel you're well on your way, other days you're convinced you're going backwards. Some days your mind stays aware and centred, other days it chatters away like a cartload of monkeys. But even the very worst meditation session can be a strengthening experience if you treat it as a reminder of how much you need to practise, and if you are willing afterwards to review the session and identify why and in what way your concentration was so wayward. If this review is successful, then a 'bad' session can sometimes be more helpful than a 'good' one. And of course the very struggle to stay concentrated during such 'bad' sessions can contribute more towards the development of your abilities than a session in which the mind obediently follows the breath throughout. Viewed thus, 'bad' sessions can be amongst your most valuable teachers.

When you are able to maintain concentration even for a few minutes, spontaneously, as if through an act of grace, calmness begins to emerge. Your mind and body enter a state of still, quiet peace. Your breathing, your heart rate, your metabolism itself settle down. The rhythm of your being slows as you sit and becomes softer, gentler, more subtle. This is the second stage of meditation, the stage of *tranquillity*. But a special kind of tranquillity. I said in Chapter 1 that, according to some psychological research, meditation carries with it no greater physiological benefits than does relaxation training. Maybe not. But once you enter meditative tranquillity, you become aware of the gulf that exists between it and simple relaxation.

In the former, the mind is aware of letting go of the distractions which come between it and its peace; of finding itself instead of being lost in the confusions of its own thinking; of becoming clearer, sharper, like sunlight dispersing clouds. In simple relaxation, by contrast, the mind typically freewheels through any mental experience, imaginary or remembered, that brings with it pleasant, peaceful feelings. The mind is put into a dreamy, trancelike state, quite different from the alert, watchful serenity of meditation. In most relaxation training, the mind is allowed to drift, to switch off, whereas in meditation there is a switching on, an awareness of a new and much more subtle awareness than that experienced in even the most alert moments of normal life.

Of course, this tranquillity comes only rarely during the early stages of meditation training, just as deep relaxation only comes briefly to the novice in relaxation training. Meditative tranquillity does not stabilize itself without long practice, and it is often unclear why it arises easily in some meditation sessions once concentration is there, while in others it appears only fleetingly even when the concentration seems deep and sustained. There are also different levels of tranquillity, including those deep states of bliss of which experienced practitioners speak. But tranquillity at first is the absence of emotions rather than the arousing of deeper levels of existential joy. These levels may one day come or they may not. Through the experience of meditation itself, the meditator becomes conscious that the practice of meditation is an end in itself rather than a means towards an end. It may indeed lead one day to an unimaginable, unknowable goal, but for the moment it is the practice itself that matters. And to think about such a goal once the practice starts is to put it ever further beyond reach.

## CONCENTRATION PLUS TRANQUILLITY PLUS INSIGHT

For some people, the tranquillity achieved in meditation – at whatever level – is an end in itself, and there is no doubt that such tranquillity brings great benefits in terms of a serener, more productive, more balanced approach to living. But there is a third stage to meditation, and it is this stage that takes the meditator into the heart of the meditative experience. This is the stage of *insight*, the stage in which one begins to make the discoveries that answer the question, 'Who am I?'. At times this stage is entered spontaneously in meditation, again as if through grace, but usually it requires a clear commitment, a commitment that some find demanding and into which they are reluctant to enter.

This commitment is to see exactly what is going on in your own mind, whatever that happens to be. And it requires a form of *activity*, as opposed to the more passive state experienced in tranquillity. Yet it is a form of activity that can only be entered into once tranquillity has been achieved (we are up against paradox again). To try to enter it prematurely only agitates the mind, like stirring up the mud on the bottom of a pond. Once tranquillity arises, this activity does not disturb the mind, and uses no more mental energy than that employed when simply watching the breath. Far from stirring up the mud on the bottom of the pond, this activity is more like moving your hand in bright water and watching the crystal ripples spread out endlessly in all directions.

You can in fact practise the activity of insight by staying with the breathing, in ways defined by the Buddha in the *Satipattha-nasutta* (*Sutra on the Application of Mindfulness*). This involves examining minutely the in- and out-breaths to see if they are long or short, fast or slow, coarse or subtle, and examining minutely the sensations caused by them (ultimately studying what these sensations *are*). Strange as it may seem, this apparently simple exercise ultimately opens up the mystery of both the perceiver and the perceived, and reveals reality itself.

Another way of practising the activity of insight is to turn attention from the breath to thoughts themselves. Previously thoughts have remained in the background during meditation, with breathing placed at the centre of awareness. Now your thoughts themselves become this centre, but you still refuse to become caught up in them either mentally or emotionally, or to let them take you on their daydreaming journeys. You simply observe them, with the same alert detachment with which you watched the breath. Again, they are allowed to pass like the reflection of clouds across water, but now you are focused on the point from which they arise and into which they disappear, and on the space between them when the mind becomes empty and is simply its own self in its bare essence.

There is nothing that can be said of this state, this experience of insight, which approaches in value actually entering it for yourself. But it is at this stage of insight that the various meditation practices begin to diverge from each other – in technique though not in direction – for there are many other things upon which one can focus instead of the breath or the thoughts. I will look at some of these things and the techniques connected with them in the next section, and a more extended discussion of them forms a large part of subsequent chapters. But before leaving this summary of meditation practice, let me re-emphasize the three stages that form the centre of all of them, namely:

> **Concentration**
>
> **Tranquillity**
>
> **Insight**

Or to put them another way:

> **Focus your mind**
>
> **Allow it to be still**
>
> **See what's there**

## TYPES OF MEDITATION

It would be wrong to over-emphasize the divergences between the various meditation techniques at the insight stage, but some attempt to classify them is necessary to obtain an overall picture of this vast and incredibly rich subject. Claudio Naranjo, a Chilean psychiatrist who has made a special study of meditation, suggests in his book *How to Be* that one practical method of classification is to talk of two bi-polar dimensions (two dimensions each of which has two poles or extremes). One of these he calls the *stop–go* dimension, and the other the *mindfulness–God-mindfulness* dimension. Let's look at these dimensions in turn.

*The stop–go dimension*   This involves, at the 'stop' end, what Patanjali in his *Yoga Sutras* (see Chapter 4) refers to as 'the extinction of the movement of the mind'. The mind remains focused upon the initial stimulus and is held there steadily while insight develops of its own accord. At the 'go' end of the dimension, the meditator watches thoughts as they arise and then allows him or herself to follow the insights and revelations provided by the inner voices, feelings or intuitions which may arise; in the way, for example, that the Christian or the Mohammedan listens to the voice of God or the shaman listens to spirit voices.

*The mindfulness–God-mindfulness dimension* The 'mindfulness' end of this dimension refers to the insight gained through awareness of immediate experience such as the sensations in one's body, the emotions one is feeling, or the thoughts that arise and pass away. At the 'God–mindfulness' end, the meditator gains insight by focusing upon an external symbol such as a *mandala* or a *mantra* or the attributes of God or the flame of a candle, and allows the symbol to act as a key to a part of the inner world which is beyond this immediate experience. With the help of this key, the meditator moves into new dimensions and follows hitherto untrodden pathways. (Naranjo's use of the term 'God' doesn't imply one must have theistic beliefs in order to operate in this mode; 'God' is taken to imply something seen initially as 'other' to, as outside oneself.)

Naranjo's two dimensions fit with my own preferred way of mapping meditational systems, although the terms I favour for the dimensions are *stilling–flowing* and *subjective–objective* respectively. These two bi-polar dimensions are not mutually exclusive. One can start meditation at the 'stilling' end of the *stilling–flowing* dimension, for example, and pass from it into the 'objective' mode of the *subjective–objective* dimension. Or one can start at the 'subjective' end of the *subjective–objective* dimension and pass from it into the 'flowing' mode of the *stilling–flowing*. One can even combine the dimensions, in that one can be in both the 'objective' mode and the 'flowing' mode at the same time (in the sense that one could be meditating upon a symbol of God and then hear God's voice, as happens to devout Hindus). But one cannot – at least until one reaches the point of ultimate truth itself, when all opposites are said to disappear! – effectively be simultaneously at the opposite ends of the *same* dimension (that is, in both 'stilling' and 'flowing', or in both 'subjective' and 'objective' modes), since to be so would fragment the one-pointed concentration without which progress is impossible.

In spite of the fact that in meditation we can move from one dimension to another, we shouldn't do this intentionally. In all meditation practice, it is vital to be aware before the start of a session both of the particular mode one is going to use and of one's intention to stay within it. Many people keep to one particular mode throughout their life. Others stay with one mode until they become familiar with another that seems more suitable. However, no experienced meditator will decide to switch *during* a session from one mode to another, although for a beginner the temptation to do so may be strong. Finding progress to be slow, the novice may commence a session already half-discouraged, and with the feeling that other techniques must be 'better' than the one in use. In this frame of mind, it's hardly surprising that a few minutes into the session, the feeling of discouragement gets the better of the mind and the meditator switches attention to another point of focus – from the breathing to the thoughts perhaps, or from the thoughts to a *mantra*, or from a *mantra* to a *mandala*.

The result is that even less progress is made, and in the end the meditator becomes completely disillusioned and gives up in disgust. For there is no short cut in meditation. Certainly, when you have developed concentration and tranquillity and are entering the insight stage, one form of meditation may be more acceptable to you than another because it fits better with your belief system or your temperament or your interests, but all meditations are built upon the same foundations, concentration and tranquillity, and these qualities only develop through the self-discipline that comes by working over time with the same focus of awareness.

Let's emphasize this by looking at what Conze has to say about concentration:

> ... concentration is a narrowing of the field of attention in a manner, and for a time determined by the will. The mind is made one-pointed, does not waver, does not scatter itself, and it becomes steady like the flame of a lamp in the absence of wind ... It is concentration which provides some stability in the perpetual flux [of the mind] by enabling the mind to stand in, or on, the same object, without distraction ...
>
> *Buddhist Meditation*, p. 19

It is this standing in or on the same object of awareness without distraction that is essential, whichever form of meditation you are using and no matter which end of the *stilling–flowing* or the *subjective–objective* dimensions you choose.

## A GROUPING OF THE MEDITATIVE PATHWAYS

Let me now group under the two dimensions some examples of major meditational traditions.

| *Stilling* | ← ——————————— → | *Flowing* |
|---|---|---|
| Vipassana | | Ecstatic prayer |
| Hatha yoga | | Quaker quietism |
| Tai chi | | Shamanism |
| | | Christian mysticism |

| *Subjective* | ← ——————————— → | *Objective* |
|---|---|---|
| Zazen | | Mystery religions |
| Koan meditation | | The Kabbalah |
| Shikantaza | | Bhakti yoga |
| | | Jnana yoga |

Three things must be stressed about these groupings:

1. They should not be taken too literally. With the exception that *within* a technique the meditator can't effectively be at both ends of a dimension simultaneously, there are no hard and fast lines to be drawn *between* techniques or on which technique belongs to which dimension. The techniques overlap and merge into each other at a number of points, and sensible arguments could be put forward for various groupings other than the one I've adopted. My grouping is merely a way of clarifying our thinking. The more we attempt such clarification, the more we see that a pattern underlies all techniques, and that the way in which it unites them is far more important than the way in which it divides.

I shall return several times to this matter of unity, to the underlying theme which binds the various traditions together, both at the level of practice and at the level of theory. And it is indeed a recognition of this unity which makes a study of the different traditions so vital. This whole book is in fact an attempt to answer the question as to why any meditator should want to study traditions other than his or her own. And I hope this answer will show that just as foreign travel broadens our understanding not only of other cultures but also of our own, so studying other meditation traditions helps us understand better the one closest to our heart.

2.   None of the practices grouped under the two dimensions are necessarily less 'effective' or less 'advanced' than any of the others. It is the way in which we study and practise them that determines effectiveness and advancement. This is again why, if you wish to make full use of meditation, you should study theory as well as practice. The Buddha listed among the eight requirements for spiritual/psychological progress (the so-called Noble Eightfold Path) both *right view* and *right meditation*. The one is handicapped without the other. It is of limited value to go into meditation with the wrong view, whether it be simple misunderstanding or a desire to gain power over others through the development of the *siddhis* (see Chapter 9). Similarly it is of limited value to have the right view if one does not develop the direct experience of right meditation to support it.

'Right view' is essentially right understanding, a philosophy of life which strives to see things for what they are instead of from behind a veil of self-deception. One can learn this right view from whichever of the great spiritual teachings (in its pure form) fits best with one's temperament and cultural background. Its defining characteristics are two in number and suggest that all these profound teachings stem from the same source – namely that one must neither exalt the self above others, nor see the self as a separate individual ego distinct from the rest of creation.

But however firmly one holds to the right view, it operates only at the theoretical level, no matter how strongly buttressed it is by sound argument or faith or good works, until one has had direct experience of its reality, the direct experience provided by meditation, the direct pointing at reality that addresses the conundrum 'Who am I?'.

3.   Like any system which tries to draw a line between one level of inner experience and another, the groupings I've given reflect a dualistic form of thinking. This is such an important point that

I discuss it more fully at the start of Chapter 8. But let me stress here that even the dimensions themselves propose a fundamental distinction between what is 'me' and what is 'not me' (whether 'not me' is God or the rest of the world). This is largely because we grow up in a world that constantly proposes this distinction for us, and conditions us into accepting that it is the fundamental distinction upon which all other distinctions rest. But as Buddhism, Christian and Hindu mysticism make clear, there is a level of inner experience at which this distinction disappears. The Christian mystic Meister Eckhart, in Evans' translation, tells us

> God must be very I, I very God, so consummately one that this he and this I are one 'is', in this is-ness working one work eternally ... God's being is my life, but if it is so, then what is God's must be mine, and what is mine God's. God's is-ness is my is-ness, and neither more nor less. The just live eternally with God, on a par with God, neither deeper nor higher. All their work is done by God and God's by them.
>
> *The Works of Meister Eckhart*, p. 247

We may or may not feel that we know what Eckhart means. He is trying to convey to us the mystic's direct experience of the oneness of all things. But whether we know what Eckhart means or not, we may find it hard to get away from the idea that if we are using an objective form of meditation such as the person of Buddha or Christ or Krishna, then this objective focus upon which we are meditating is 'not me', is 'out there' rather than 'in here', is a distinct and personalized object with a separate self and a separate existence from ourselves.

Even if we do manage to get away from this idea, we may become caught in the opposite notion that Buddha or Christ or Krishna is 'in here' rather than 'out there'; in other words, that they are a creation of our own minds rather than possessed of any objective reality. We become trapped in the 'either/or' distinction of our Western way of thinking; the object of meditation is *either* out there *or* in here, it can't be both. Whereas the real implication of what Eckhart and other advanced teachers are saying is that our thinking should be in terms of 'both and'. The object of meditation is both this *and* that, both 'in here' *and* 'out there', and 'in here' and 'out there' in a way that dissolves the distinction between the two conditions.

I remember once, in my early studies in Tibetan Buddhism, the lama from whom we were receiving teachings was asked whether the Buddhas and bodhisattva (enlightened masters) used as the focus of meditation were in the mind or were real. At once he assured us, 'Yes yes, in mind'. Then a moment later, realizing Westerners do not understand the world in the way that Tibetans understand it, and not wanting us to be misled, he added with a twinkle, 'and real, and real'.

If it helps, think of the inner world as a shared world. It is not just your world, and neither is the inner world of the next man or woman their own inner world. Jung calls this concept the collective unconscious (see Box 2), and explains it in biological and psychological terms as a common inner inheritance, the aspect of the mind that we acquire along with our genes from the ancestors of our race and that lays down the pattern, the blueprint of our thinking. This aspect of the mind gives us the fundamental ideas by which the human race has shaped its destiny; our ideas of courage, for example, of honesty, self-sacrifice, true love and chivalry. And at a deeper level, it gives us the archetypal images, the gods, the heroes and heroines, the wise men and women, with which we have peopled our pantheons and our literature.

Joseph Campbell sums this up when he says that:

> You become the carrier of something that is given to you from what have been called the Muses – or, in biblical language, 'God'. This is not fancy, it is a fact. Since the inspiration comes from the unconscious, and since the unconscious minds of the people of any single small society have much in common, what the shaman or seer brings forth is something that is waiting to be brought forth in everyone. So when one hears the seer's story, one responds, 'Aha! This is my story. This is something that I had always wanted to say but wasn't able to say'.
>
> *The Power of Myth*, p. 71

I would part company with Campbell in that it is humankind itself, and not just the members of single small societies, who share this common inner heritage. Although there are aspects of the collective unconscious that may differ from culture to culture, the very consistency with which we find the same themes assures us that at a deeper level the contents of the collective unconscious are common to us all.

Thus, when I talk about the dualism present in groupings such as the one I have given, I mean that there is a sense in which whether we are using 'stilling' or 'flowing', 'subjective' or 'objective' meditation, we are in fact concentrating upon effectively the same thing. The mind and the content of the mind are one and same. Which is not to say that the content – the object or the symbol or the Buddha upon which we are concentrating – is subservient to the mind, or a figment of the imaginative play of the mind. Nor is it to say that the mind is subservient to the content. It is to say that they partake of the one reality.

When working with students, I find they have extreme difficulty with this concept. This is not surprising. I have extreme difficulty with it myself sometimes, since we are all of us so caught up in the idea of boundaries, of 'me' and 'not me'. I try to make things clearer by offering my students an analogy. I ask them where 'they' end and the 'rest of the world' begins. At each moment we are taking part of the 'rest of the world' inside us as we breathe. We do so each time we eat. And at each moment we are giving ourselves to the rest of the world as we perspire moisture, shed skin cells, breathe out, excrete body waste. Once they acknowledge this I go further and remind them of the points I made in Chapter 2 about our bodies being 'made' of the elements, or that there is no difference between the water, air, earth elements and fire in our bodies and the water, air, earth and fire elements in the outside world. I then go further still and remind them that we are taking in the 'rest of the world' every time we use our eyes or our ears, and giving ourselves to the rest of the world every time we recreate or reshape our environment.

Once we think along these lines, we begin to attain the right view and the boundary between 'me' and 'the rest of the world' grows shadowy. There are then meditations, such as those I describe in Chapter 10, which take the process even further, until we reach the point where we begin to experience – as well as just to acknowledge mentally – that the world is not made in the way which we had assumed it to be.

Thus although, because of our limited powers of concentration, we cannot be at both ends of one of the meditation dimensions at the same time, in a sense we are at both ends all the time. Another of the paradoxes with which the meditator learns to live and into which ultimately he or she sees to the heart.

With the above limitation firmly in mind, I shall use the groupings of meditation systems given above as I look at the individual meditation traditions in some detail.

# 4

## Stillness Meditation: Stopping the Mind

A Ch'an (the Chinese form of Zen) meditation teacher once said to me, when we worked together on the 'Tell me who you are' exercise described in Chapter 8, 'I want everything to just stop'. As he spoke he appeared to be in a deep inner state, his eyes cast downwards and half-closed. The words came very slowly and with great deliberation, as if they were spoken through him, not by him. We sat together side by side on the floor in the still, quiet meditation room, with the light from the single window enfolding the golden image of the crowned Buddha who sat with us. Behind the Buddha, framed in the window, were the rolling hills, crowned in their turn by blue-grey clouds.

We sat on and the silence lengthened and deepened, emphasizing the stillness and timelessness of the moment. I remember feeling an upwelling of great love for my teacher, as if he and I were one and I could not be sure whether the sadness which was also part of that moment came from him or from myself. A sadness born of our own vulnerability, as mortals on this changing, turning planet in the endless eternity of space. 'I want everything to just ... stop'. To just stop.

And what, my mind questioned, was this 'stopping' of which he spoke? Annihilation? Oblivion? The ending of everything, or of one's own experience of everything (which came to the same thing)? Time, space, the life we know but do not understand, the hills in the distance, the crowned Buddha with his inscrutable face and secret smile? What would happen if everything stopped? What could happen, since there would be nothing left to happen, and no one to whom it could happen? Was this wise, gentle Ch'an teacher wishing an end to his own existence, to the travelling and seeking of his long years from boyhood to manhood and now into middle age? What inner suffering or inner tranquillity could make him wish for that?

Then I saw how limited my view of stopping was, how easily I had fallen into the trap of seeing my teacher's 'stopping' as having anything to do with existing or not existing, with life or with the annihilation of life. His Buddhist path names 'holding to extremes' as the second of the five types of afflicted views, the afflicted view that believes either in permanence (that what we call the self is not changing moment by moment) or in annihilation (that what we call the self does not connect to a future lifetime).

No, what my teacher meant was that he wanted to achieve stillness, not just for himself but for all beings, for the whole of measureless existence. A stillness transcending either permanence or annihilation, being and non-being, becoming and not-becoming, arising and passing away. A stillness that had as little to do with stagnation as with activity, as little to do with boredom as with excitement, with coming as with going, with life as with death. A stillness that lies beyond definitions and the absence of definitions, and beyond both paradox and orthodox.

Is such a state possible? Certainly it is hard even to imagine it, let alone describe what it might actually be (one reason why the Hindus have always talked about such a condition as 'netti, netti – not this, not this', delineating it in terms of what it is not rather than what it is). In Buddhism, this state is called Nirvana, and it is stressed that Nirvana is 'something' about which 'nothing' can be said, just as the Hindus claim nothing can be said about Brahman, the ultimate ground of our being, the Christian mystics claim nothing can be said about the Godhead ('Everything in the Godhead is one', wrote Eckhart, 'and of that there is nothing to be said'), the Taoists claim nothing can be said about the Tao ('The Tao that can be told of is not an unvarying Tao', says the *Tao Te Ching*, 'The names that can be named are not unvarying names'), and the Jewish mystics of the

Kabbalah speak of Ain Soph as 'no-thing ... beyond compre-
hension, beyond classification ... it exists in its non-existence,
and in its non-existence it exists' (Poncé, *Kabbalah*, p. 95).

Men and women from the beginnings of recorded history
have been telling us of this ineffable state, the realization of
which we call enlightenment, and they speak as travellers who
know it well, who abide in it in this life rather than look forward
to it in what lies beyond. And as one progresses in meditation
there comes the sudden response to their teachings, 'Ah yes, of
*course*'. Without our knowing how it happens, meditation
brings the awareness that what they are saying is true; as if,
without quite remembering, we have actually seen the territory
of which they speak, or at least have experienced hints and
whispers of it as we walk the mystic pathways of our dreams.

So when my teacher spoke of wanting everything to 'just
stop', it was this territory of which he was speaking. A territory
towards which all meditation practices lead, a territory which is
both the centre of who we are and the centre of creation itself.


## STILLNESS

What does the word 'stillness' suggest to you? For the word is a
powerful symbol for the inner state, the state beyond all states,
to which I am trying to refer. It may suggest *tranquillity*, but
remember that tranquillity is a state achieved in meditation on
the way towards insight. So stillness is something more than
tranquillity; it is insight itself. But – and here again we move
into paradox – stillness is also part of the practice that takes us
into insight, part of the concentration and tranquillity that are
our first two stages. Because ultimately there is no gap between
the practice and the state to which the practice leads. How could
there be, if that state embraces all things, if it is indeed the unity
containing all unities of which the mystics of every great religion
have spoken?

The absence of a gap between the practice of meditation and
the state to which that practice leads is one of the most profound
teachings contained in Ch'an and Zen (from now on I shall use
the word 'Zen' to cover both terms). Special emphasis was
placed upon it by the thirteenth century Japanese master Dōgen,

the founder of the Soto sect within Zen. In his translations and commentary upon Dögen's major works (*Zen Master Dögen*), Yuhu Yokoi sums this up when he says that, in Dögen's teaching:

> ... there is no gap between practice and enlightenment, and there-fore ... neither precedes or follows the other. That is to say, enlight-enment is not something that is attained as the *result* of practice; it is embodied in practice from the very beginning.
>
> *Zen Master Dögen*, p. 58

Lest this leads to complacency, Yokoi adds the warning that, 'It is only through the single-minded practice of the Way, however, that this truth can be fully understood'.

By this, Yokoi means a single-minded dedication to the moment-by-moment of meditation. If we have in mind the idea of a 'goal' when we enter meditation, then we have an idea *about* stillness, *about* the enlightenment which we hope to attain. And inevitably this idea, since it is simply another mental construc-tion, gets in the way of this attainment. Our preconceived ideas of a 'goal' are the creation of our own thinking, and the essence of meditation is the dropping of preconceptions, and in their place the untarnished experiencing of what lies beyond these preconceptions and the thoughts of which they are composed.

Dögen himself, in his *Gakudo Yojin-shy* ('Points to Watch in Buddhist Training'), puts it that, 'To study the Way is to try to become one with it – to forget even a trace of enlightenment' (p. 57 in Yokoi's *Zen Master Dögen*). In other words, we do not meditate in order to become enlightened, we meditate because that is what enlightened people do. Meditation is both the path and the fruit of the path. 'The Way is completely present where you are, and if you forget this', Dögen warns us in his *Fukan Sasen-gi* ('A Universal Recommendation for Zazen'), and allow 'the slightest difference in the beginning between you and the Way, the result will be a greater separation than between heaven and earth' (p. 47 in Yokoi's translation).

## VIPASSANA

Although stillness is such a feature of much Zen training, it is in the *vipassana* practice of the Theravadin Buddhists that many people find stillness most strongly emphasized. For vipassana meditation stresses pure (or mere) attention. When first practising vipassana, it is helpful to express the stillness symbolically as the watchful, unmoving awareness that observes the coming and going of the in-breath and the out-breath. Without labelling, without the value-loaded discriminations of 'good' and 'bad', the mind observes the breathing and those turning moments in between in-breaths and out-breaths. So important are these turning moments between breaths, and so likely are we to lose our concentration in these moments, that some teachers speak of them as the moments in which truth reveals itself.

This again is symbolic, since truth reveals itself in all moments if we drop the ignorance (symbolized in meditation by mental chatter) that obscures it. But the symbolism is helpful, both because it reminds us that if we can stay concentrated in those moments our concentration will become deeper, and because in those moments there is a physical stillness, a stillness of body in which a stillness of mind can more easily develop. It is, to use a simile, like the moment when the wind in the trees drops, and the leaves, the branches, the surrounding landscape, stand revealed in a moment so empty of movement that it seems to show us emptiness itself. In just this way does the between-breaths stillness of the body allow the stillness of the mind to reveal itself, open and clear as the space that both contains and composes the motionless trees.

Thus through the outer stillness of the body and of the mind, the inner stillness of insight (in-sight, seeing *into* the real nature of things) is allowed to emerge. In vipassana, the process can be further assisted by what, for want of a better term, we can call gross insight. In this practice, the meditator removes the awareness from the nostrils and the breathing, and focuses it in turn, gently, softly, slowly on all parts of the body. In ordinary life, we are aware yet unaware of our bodies. We know they are there, but unless some discomfort or pleasurable sensation draws our attention to it, the body is left to get on with its own business unnoticed by the mind.

There is nothing wrong about this. The mind has other things with which to occupy itself. But the body is in fact sending out subtle signals to us all the time. By ignoring these, we blunt our awareness to them, and thus our awareness of who, physically,

**BOX 6**
**VIPASSANA MEDITATION**

*Vipassana* (insight) meditation is the method the Buddha himself taught, involving concentration upon the breath. As the Buddha said of the meditator, 'Mindfully he breathes in, mindfully he breathes out'. In these simple words lies the kernel of the practice. One is 'mindful' of the breath to such an extent that not a whisper of it passes in or out unnoticed. The meditator watches the breath with the total awareness with which a good sentry watches the comings and goings at the main gates into the city.

Normally, this watching is done at the tip of the nostrils, where one is most sensitive to the feeling of the cold air entering and the warm air exiting. But an alternative is to be aware of the gentle rise and fall of the abdomen. Both places are equally acceptable. The former is more subtle, the latter in closer touch with the body. Choose which you prefer, but don't keep switching between them. And if you decide on the nostrils, be careful not to follow the breath down into the lungs. The sentry does not leave his or her post without permission.

Once this mindfulness of the coming and going of the breath has been fully established, the meditator develops insight into the breathing. As the Buddha put it, 'Breathing out a long breath [he] knows "I breathe out a long breath", breathing in a long breath he knows "I breathe in a long breath".' And ditto for a short breath. What the Buddha was emphasizing was an awareness of the *quality* of the breathing, and once the concentration has deepened to this point the meditator can at last allow the sentry to leave the gates of the city and, using a technique called *sweeping*, allow awareness to travel minutely down the face, down the arms, down the body and legs, and back up again to the nostrils, travelling with infinite slowness and becoming conscious of each subtle sensation as it goes.

Gaining insight in this way immeasurably strengthens the powers of concentration and perception, and allows the meditator in due course to turn the attention upon the mind and examine what goes on there in the same minute, objective detail.

we are. In vipassana, this awareness can be rekindled by minutely, inch by inch, focusing attention first upon the face and head, then down each arm, then down the body and the legs and into the feet before returning back upwards to the nostrils and the breathing. At each point, the meditator becomes aware of the sensation there, the warmth or the cold, the tingling of the skin, the feeling of the clothes. And through this dawning insight into his or her physical being, the meditator is taken from gross to subtle insight into the stillness, the emptiness, from which each physical sensation, and ultimately the body and the play of thoughts within the mind, arise and into which they disappear.

## VIPASSANA AND TAI CHI

So vipassana is a practice of stillness. But since one remains in stillness while the awareness is sweeping the body, it is also a practice of stillness in movement. Stillness in movement. Yet another paradox. A paradox that resolved itself for me not just through vipassana but also through tai chi, that set of slow, concentrated, deliberate movements which some describe as a form of moving yoga. Once, in the early years of my tai chi training, my teacher asked me to video him as he went through the whole sequence of tai chi movements. We were alone in a bare still room, and in my anxiety to make a success of the video I concentrated totally upon every aspect of his movement, every smallest nuance. With a particular absorbed intensity, I watched as his black-clad form moved against the light colour of the walls, as his soft slippers stepped and turned soundlessly across the tiled floor, as his arms and his hands extended outwards and then drew back, as he filled space and then withdrew into space, making patterns in the stillness until I was not sure whether the patterns were the stillness or the stillness was the patterns.

And in that moment of not being sure, the movement and the stillness became one, part of the one unity. The distinction between them dropped away, like a pebble falling into water, and there were no longer any boundaries, any one and other, only a sense of single presence, of things in their place. Or, if you prefer, of absence and of no things and of no place in which they could be.

There is nothing unique or impossibly mystical about an experience like this. It can come to us, readily enough, when we focus our concentration steadily and unwaveringly upon a particular stimulus for any length of time. Some people find it comes when they listen intently to music, others when they gaze for a long time at a work of art. The characteristic of this state is the loss of boundaries, at first between the music and the silence in which it is taking place, or between the work of art and the space within which it is composed, and then ultimately between the self that is attending and the object which is attended to.

What happens is that one becomes aware (one *knows*) that the music or the work of art is not 'out there', located in separate space, but is existing within the mind that is registering it. Its reality is not foreign to the mind but shared with it, and there is no other way in which things could possibly be.

In vipassana – and when performing the movements of tai chi practice – the boundaries that dissolve are those between the mind and one's own breathing, or between the mind and the movements of one's own body. This is the point at which the dualism between the mind and the contents of the mind disappear. First the mind watches the breathing or feels the movement of the body, and then the mind and the breathing, and the mind and the movements of the body, become one. To return to my metaphor of a moment ago, it is a realization of the truth that everything we experience, the outside world, our bodily sensations, come into being for us only when we register them in the inner world of the mind. And this is why there can be no distinction in direct experience between the objects registered by the mind and the mind that registers them.

An analogy is the absence of distinction between a mirror and the images it reflects. If a distinction exists, then the images have an existence independent of the mirror, and the mirror has an existence independent of the images. If so, where are these two independent existences? Can I show you the image without also showing you the mirror? Can I show you the mirror without also showing you the image? As long as the mirror is reflecting the image, then they are not two separate realities but part and parcel of the one reality, and no boundaries exist between them.

In meditation, knowledge of the absence of distinctions between the mind and the objects it registers is experienced directly, from within. It thus becomes a truth of our own experience rather than a belief we have taken over from someone else. And once we reach this point of truth, we see that it is many-faceted, like a diamond, and that its implications reach into each corner of what we understand as reality.

## TAI CHI AS STILLNESS MEDITATION

Tai chi (or tai chi chuan to give it its full title) contains a sequence of connected movements or postures which, depending upon the actual version being practised, take between ten and twenty minutes to complete. Usually they are done very slowly, almost like a slow-motion ballet, with the practitioner covering a floor area of no more than 10 square feet. An onlooker may be captured by the deliberate, mesmeric beauty of the performance but may wonder what on earth it is for. Is tai chi an exercise, a dance routine, a slowed-down martial art? Or is the tai chi practitioner merely someone who has lost his or her senses?

There is an element of truth in all these possibilities. Tai chi is a form of exercise, and a kind of dance, and a version of the martial arts, and a way of losing one's senses. But it is a very special form of exercise, dance and martial art, and an even more special way of losing one's senses, because what one loses are the blunted, tired, everyday senses. For tai chi is at bottom a moving meditation, a meditation in which the mind takes as its point of focus the movement of the body (synchronized with the breathing) and/or the energy centre of the body, the so-called *tan t'ien* situated sóme 3 inches below the navel, around which this movement circles, from which it flows and to which it returns.

Tai chi chuan is said to have originated with Chang San-feng, a Chinese Taoist priest living in the thirteenth century Yuan dynasty, but some legends claim it to be older still, and to date back to the T'ang dynasty in the seventh century. Whether or not either of these stories is correct, tai chi as we know it surfaced in the eighteenth century Ch'ing dynasty. Originally taught as a martial art – called 'long boxing' because the opponent was never allowed to make body contact – it nevertheless differed from other such arts in that it was 'soft' rather than 'hard'. That is, it relied upon the development and use of 'internal' energy, rather than upon the external energy of rock-hard muscles and sinews.

This 'internal' energy, known as *ch'i* in Chinese, is said to be the basic life-force itself, a non-material substance that fills the universe and animates all living forms. Analogous to what the yogis call *prana*, it is said to circulate through the body in non-physical meridians, and to be the energy whose flow is re-directed and rebalanced by acupuncture. The tai chi movements, it is claimed, are a form of internal acupuncture, a series of postures which follow the flow of ch'i itself. Not only do they balance this flow but they also bring it under the conscious control of the practitioner, so that he or she can direct its power to any part of the body, allowing an opponent to be toppled with what appears to the onlooker as a gentle though lightening-fast touch, or rendering parts of the body resistant to blades, spears or physical pressure.

These are extravagant claims. But I have personally seen the most extraordinary feats performed by Chinese tai chi masters, many of which it would be well-nigh impossible to duplicate by normal means, even with the most elaborate trickery. For ex-ample, I have witnessed such a master balance a needle-sharp spear on his throat, while a chair complete with seated young lady was then balanced upon the spear. This feat was not trickery to encourage the gullible to throw coins, but a serious demon-stration of a technique known in translation as 'thrusting throat with spear', and possible only for a very advanced practitioner.

The control of ch'i for the purposes of strength and health still forms the basis of Chinese traditional medicine, and is referred to in China's oldest existing medical manual, the *Book of Inter-nal Medicine*, which goes back to 300 BC. Reference to the value of this control in the martial arts goes back equally far. The control itself is known as *yingqigong*, while the actual conscious direction of the ch'i to the required part of the body is called *qigong*, and depends equally upon the power of the will and the control of the breath, both developed through the tai chi move-ments supplemented by some more static exercises.

Tai chi chuan must be learned from a teacher, as the move-ments cannot be fully mastered from written descriptions or from photographs. The same is true of the static exercises. But the meditative philosophy from which tai chi flows is the Taoist teaching that life itself is movement. All living things move, in one way or another, whether that movement is expressed through mobility or through breathing or through the processes of physical growth. If we are therefore to experience true still-ness, we must be able to experience it not just in immobility but in the midst of movement itself. In seated meditation, however, the body remains motionless save for the merest whisper of breathing. Thus although it allows us to realize concentration, tranquillity and insight, what happens when we get up and start to move around? We are in danger of losing this realization as the mind becomes distracted by physical activity.

Tai chi chuan is therefore a way of practising physical action while staying centred in the meditative state. It helps us remain conscious of stillness even in the midst of the confusions of daily life. And, since it teaches us to concentrate upon action, it helps us to remain *mindful* in daily life, that is, to remain focused on what we are actually doing, instead of allowing ourselves to become distracted by the myriad outer and inner stimuli with which we are bombarded. At the insight level, it thus allows us to remain aware both of the stillness from which all movement arises, and of the way in which this movement is expressed in our dealings with the outer world.

It also helps us to be aware of the subtle flows of internal energy associated with this movement, and which so readily become blocked by physical tensions. Watch an experienced tai chi chuan practitioner walk across a room, or sit or stand. Notice their posture, the economy of effort with which they move, and the calm alertness with which they attend to life. Then turn and watch the average man or woman and note the difference. The practice of tai chi chuan leads to a poise, to a relaxed unhurried approach to existence, yet at the same time to a highly efficient use of the self and of the space-time within which that self has its being. As the tai chi chuan *Classics*, a slim volume handed down from the early tai chi chuan masters, puts it, in every action of the tai chi practitioner, 'the entire body should be light and agile and all of its parts connected like pearls on a thread ... the feet, legs and waist must act as one' (see Cheng and Smith, *Tai Chi*).

It is the movement of the body as a single unit rather than as a series of separate physical events held together only by flesh and bone that conveys to the onlooker the sense of stillness, of meditative awareness, which is such a feature of the advanced tai chi practitioner. No part of the body is uncoordinated, no part is at war with any other. Instead, there is a unity. When practising the postures there are no boundaries, no divisions between one posture and another. As a great modern tai chi master, the late Cheng Man-ch'ing, tells us, 'The postures flow evenly from start to finish. The ch'i is blocked when the flow is impeded ... Do the exercises as though "pulling silk from a cocoon" ...' (Cheng and Smith, *Tai Chi*).

But there is a deeper level still to tai chi, a level in which the practitioner gains even greater insight into stillness. For at the centre of tai chi there is a dropping of the personal ego, of the sense of being separate from the rest of existence. Tai chi is a meditation that gives direct insight into the artificiality of this ego, into the pretentiousness and pride with which it dominates our lives and demands we protect and feed it with a sense of its own importance. One interpretation has it that the postures themselves, which are said to follow the movement with which the life force flows into the world and into our own bodies, gradually strip away the falseness with which we construct this ego and come to believe it represents who we really are. The postures follow the blueprint upon which our being is actually constructed, and as we perform them this blueprint is revealed under the false scribbles we have imposed upon it, re-educating us first at an unconscious and later at a conscious level.

An alternative (perhaps complementary) explanation is that as we practise tai chi we become aware of the tensions in our bodies, of the artificiality of much of our physical movement. We also discover the crabbed and restricted thinking which has impressed itself upon our bodies and led to this artificiality, in the inexorable way in which the psychological life leaves its mark upon the physical. As tai chi re-educates us into more natural movement, so the process is reversed and our bodies start to re-educate our minds, changing the ways in which we think about ourselves, our relationships and our being. By learning natural physical movement we thus also begin to learn to function more naturally at the mental level, rather in the way that some brain-damaged children can gradually regain cerebral functioning if their limbs are consistently put through certain patterns of physical movement by adult helpers.

You may also like the explanation that, as we witness our own initial clumsiness when doing the postures (especially when in front of others!) or as we practise the exercise known as 'push-hands' in which you work with a partner and each tries to find the point at which the other loses balance, so we are brought face to face with the spoilt child inside us. The spoilt child who wants to do everything better than anyone else, who doesn't want to be made to look 'silly' or inadequate. The spoilt child that we carry with us into adult life and who forms a major part of our egos. We may also encounter the frightened, vulnerable child that we also carry with us, or the angry, irritated and rebellious one.

For example, in the push-hands exercise it is almost inevitable that your teacher, with his or her greater experience, will probe your physical balance and find the exact point at which this balance is lost. In the exercise, you stand face to face with your teacher and make contact only through the hands. Your teacher holds his or her hand, palm inwards, a few inches away from the chest, while you push gently against this hand until you reach the point where – since the feet must not be moved during this exercise – your teacher either has to allow the body to yield and turn in response, or else to lose balance and fall backwards.

Having completed your push (which ends at the point at which, reaching forward, you are in danger of losing your own balance), you then reverse the position of your hand and now it is your teacher's turn to push towards your chest. And it is now that he or she probes your weakness, because however much you try to turn the body in the way that he or she has just done, your teacher gently but unerringly finds the point in your chest which is unable to soften, relax and yield, the point which feels trapped or angry, and which represents at a physical level what you are experiencing inside your mind.

Only when you learn to relax this point, to lose all thought of self and instead focus with all your meditator's concentration upon the pressure of your teacher's hand, do you find that your body will yield easily and will turn and move in response to it so that you can no longer be easily toppled. Only then have you learned to let go of the ego and what it represents, and in its place become fully present in the moment and in what is taking place within it.

And it is in this sense of total presence in the moment during the push-hands that you find stillness. The collection of Zen *koans* known as the *Mumonkan* ('The Gateless Gate' – more about koans in Chapter 8) contains an account of two monks watching a flag blowing in the wind. The first monk argues that it is the flag that is moving, but the second claims it is the wind. Eno, the sixth Zen patriarch, happens to be passing at the time and hearing the argument, says, 'Not the flag, not the wind, mind is moving'. Of all Zen koans, this is one of the most accessible. It is indeed the mind that moves, and it is only when the mind is still that true insight can arise. The Buddha taught:

> Do good,
> Refrain from evil,
> Pacify the mind.
> That is the way of the Buddhas.

## STILLNESS IN YOGA

Let me now turn from tai chi to a similar meditative discipline based upon the body, hatha yoga. I quoted in Chapter 3 Patanjali's reference to the stilling of the mind as 'the extinction of the movement of the mind', and in fact Patanjali's Yoga Sutras, written down somewhere between 400 BC and AD 400 (scholarly opinion differs widely), provide us with one of the best short manuals on meditation ever written. The term 'yoga' (which comes from the same Sanskrit root as our word 'yoke', and implies union with the divine) refers not just to hatha yoga but to several inter-related spiritual pathways. Starting with hatha yoga itself, the best known of these are:

*Hatha yoga*, the yoga of the body, in which one practises the familiar yoga asanas in order both to gain control over the vital energy flows in the body and to provide a focus upon which the mind can concentrate;

*Karma yoga*, the yoga of good works, in which one devotes oneself without thought of reward to the service of others;

*Bhakti yoga*, the yoga of devotion, in which one devotes oneself equally single-mindedly to the worship of God;

*Jnana yoga*, the yoga of knowledge, in which one works initially upon learning and understanding the deeper spiritual truths, and subsequently upon arousing one's own corresponding intuitive wisdom.

Each of these yogas, practised diligently, leads to the same goal, namely a loss of the personal ego and the realization of oneself as part of that unity which embraces all creation. And each of these yogas carries within it *rajah yoga*, the yoga of meditation. Whether one is working on the body, on service to others, on devotion to God, or on intuitive wisdom, one is concentrating and focusing the mind upon one over-riding and all-consuming stimulus and thus stilling the incessant preoccupation with one's own ego.

Yogacarya Krpälvanand in his *Science of Meditation* insists that hatha yoga and karma yoga, by controlling the physical sense organs, act as a necessary preliminary to the development of the higher level of jnana yoga. What Krpälvanand means is that until one has mastered the physical self, one cannot develop the mental or spiritual self. This is because the physical self – the senses and the sensual desires that go with them – will inevitably distract the seeker, and consume the vital energy which should be applied to the quest for spiritual development.

In Western psychological language, we would say that the craving for sensual satisfaction diverts our powers of motivation and attention away from the mental and spiritual side of life, but whichever language we use, the message is clear. The practice of karma and/or hatha yoga develops the concentration, the tranquillity and the insight which allow for spiritual progress and for the wisdom which accompanies it. Whether we subdue our sensual desires in the service of others (as in karma yoga), or whether we work directly on transforming sensual energy into spiritual energy (as in hatha yoga), we must acknowledge that we are in and of the physical world, and must strive properly to order our existence within it if we are to prepare ourselves for progress to the higher levels of mental and spiritual truth.

There is a direct parallel between this teaching and the Buddhist guidance I quoted at the end of the last section. In this guidance, 'Do good' and 'Refrain from evil' are listed before 'Pacify your mind'. Work on and purify the physical self in order to put yourself in a position to purify the mental self. Failure to do this will not only impede progress, but may lead to the wrong kind of progress. Many well-intentioned spiritual pilgrims have plummeted from grace because they gained certain of the powers that come with spiritual practices (see Chapter 9), but without ensuring that they had made sufficient progress in morality to know how to use them properly.

The Buddhist guidance is particularly helpful because it places 'Do good' as the first step. Even if you cannot yet refrain from evil (thoughtless, self-centred behaviour), you can at least do good alongside it. Gradually the good actions will re-educate the mind into an awareness of the ignorance and futility that lie behind the evil actions, and these actions will begin to lose their hold over you. But Vedantic Hindus such as Krpälvanand are giving us very much the same lesson, the only difference being that in hatha yoga we are provided, as in tai chi, with a set of physical postures designed to hasten the process of transformation.


## HATHA YOGA

I said in Chapter 1 that it was Desmond Dunne's book on hatha yoga, *Yoga Made Easy*, that first sparked off my active interest in meditation. Through the odd way in which these things happen in life, it was a tai chi teacher rather than a yoga teacher whom I eventually found to initiate me into the stillness meditation that comes through physical movement. But nevertheless I have for many years had strong links with hatha yoga and with hatha yoga teachers and practitioners, and have been made aware that although the language and symbolism of tai chi and hatha yoga differ from each other, there are great similarities between the things they each achieve. (There is even a sequence of moving hatha yoga postures, 'Homage to the Sun', that parallels tai chi in some of its more subtle aspects.)

Hatha yoga does, however, lay particular emphasis upon presenting us with a picture of how the vital energy force – the ch'i or the prana – actually behaves within the body. The picture is of seven non-physical energy centres, known as *chakras* (Sanskrit for 'wheels'), which are situated respectively at the base of the spine, over the spleen, over the solar plexus, over the heart, at the front of the throat, in the space between the eyebrows, and at the top of the head. These centres are not only the focal points of *prana*, they are also said to be the points of connection between the physical body and the more subtle etheric body, which in yoga philosophy is claimed to permeate the physical body and to be the vehicle through which the life force actually flows. (The etheric body is further said to form the bridge between the physical body and the spiritual body, and its existence has been recognized by cultures since time immemorial – the ancient Egyptians called it the *ka*, and symbolized it as a bird with a human head.)

Of even greater importance from the point of view of meditation, a large part of the life force is said to enter the body at the *muladhara* chakra, the chakra at the base of the spine that controls our 'grosser' physical and sexual energies. In order to sustain the physical body, it then flows from there to the other chakras by means of two channels running up through the centre of the body known as *ida* and *pingala*. Provided the energy flow is balanced between these two channels, the body will remain in good physical health, and the yoga asanas are designed in part as ways of maintaining this balance. But there is a dormant third channel, the *sushumna*, that rises up between ida and pingala, and around which they intertwine much as the snakes intertwine around the staff in the caduceus (the symbol carried by the God Mercury and adopted as the medical logo in the Western world).

The life force that enters the body at the muladhara chakra carries more energy than the body actually needs, and this energy is stored at the base of the spine, where the yogis symbolize it as a coiled, sleeping serpent. Through the intensive use of asanas coupled with control of the breath (*pranayama*) and certain visualization practices (more on such practices in Chapter 7), this dormant reserve of energy, referred to as *kundalini*, can be awakened and allowed to ascend through the sushumna, illuminating in turn each of the chakras until finally it explodes in the crown chakra in a many-petalled burst of enlightenment.

These terms are of course symbolic. In Western language, we would say that energy which is normally only put to physical use is transformed into spiritual energy, allowing the individual to ascend from the animal side of his or her nature into the spiritual side.

But yoga tells us there are dangers in this transformation. If this stored energy arises not through sushumna but through either ida or pingala, neither of which is strong enough to accommodate it, then madness and even death can result. In itself this is a curious aspect of yoga teaching, but it is based upon literally thousands of years of observation of the human condition. We may reject it if we please, but at the very least it is a useful symbolic way of reminding us once again that we must effectively prepare our lower physical natures before we are ready to ascend to higher spiritual levels. We must do good and refrain from evil, we must practise hatha and karma yoga, in whatever form we interpret these two yogas of physical activity, before the body becomes a fit receptacle for the full force of spiritual power.

## KUNDALINI MEDITATION

In view of the reported dangers of abrupt and incorrect arousal of kundalini energy, any intensive work should be carried out under the guidance of an experienced teacher. But there is a gentle kundalini practice which is without risk, and this is given below. To use it, the powers of visualization must already be well developed (see Chapter 7).

Sit in your usual meditation position, and use the second of the pranayama exercises given in Box 4 (pp. 35–6). When you are concentrated and centred, continue the pranayama and visualize a luminous channel (the sushumna) running from the base of your spine – visualized as a point deep inside the abdomen some four fingerbreadths below the navel – via a pathway just in front of the spine up to the crown of your head. Now add to it a w-shaped junction at the base of the spine, with ida and pingala comprising the two outer columns and sushumna the centre one. Ida and pingala run from the left and right nostrils respectively up to the top of the head and down to this union with the sushumna (see Figure 1). Feel energy flowing with each of your breaths through these two outer channels, unblocking the point where they meet sushumna and awakening the kundalini lying dormant there into a red hot ember the size of a seed.

When these visualizations are fully established, gently contract and keep contracted the muscles of the anus and the floor of the abdomen. Now, immediately on completion of the next in-breath, swallow and push gently down with the muscles of

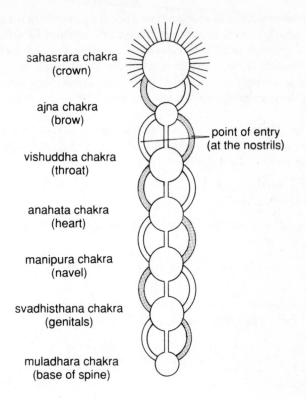

sahasrara chakra
(crown)

ajna chakra
(brow)

point of entry
(at the nostrils)

vishuddha chakra
(throat)

anahata chakra
(heart)

manipura chakra
(navel)

svadhisthana chakra
(genitals)

muladhara chakra
(base of spine)

Figure 1. *Sushumna, ida and pingala, together with the seven chakras. (For visualization purposes, the two outer channels can be thought of as rising on either side of the spine rather than twined around it.)*

the diaphragm, retaining the inhalation for as long as is comfortable. Visualize the kundalini flame increasing in heat as a result of this compressed inhaled energy.

On the next exhalation, relax all the muscles and, although the focal point of your concentration remains the hot ember at the base of the spine, see the heated air energy rising through the sushumna all the way up to your crown, clearing obstructions as it goes. Repeat the same process on the next six inhalations and exhalations, with the glowing ember at the base of the spine growing hotter each time.

On the seventh exhalation, visualize the ember bursting into a flame which travels slowly up through the sushumna and passes in turn through each of the chakras, visualized as drooping lotus flowers with closed petals. As the kundalini reaches each one, the lotus straightens up and opens out in the following order (note: the colours listed differ somewhat in the various systems):

The *muladhara* chakra, a fraction above the base of the spine, where the lotus flower opens to show a central disc surrounded by four petals, all a brilliant red;

The *svadhisthana* chakra at the genitals, where the lotus flower is six-petalled and vermilion;

The *manipura* chakra at the navel, with its ten-petalled scarlet and green lotus;

The *anahata* chakra at the heart, a twelve-petalled brilliant gold, awakening your spiritual powers;

The *vishuddha* chakra at the throat, sixteen-petalled silvery-blue, and awakening your mystical powers;

The *ajna* chakra just above and between the eyes, a two-petalled lotus of a brilliant white which radiates light in an aura around the head and which awakens your divine understanding;

The *sahasrara* at the crown of the head, where the sushumna ends and the kundalini explodes into the 1000-petalled lotus, seen as an ocean of light, in which the meditator discards the small self and becomes one with universal truth.

This last experience, when successfully achieved, may last only for seconds or for the remainder of the meditation. But when it fades, the silvery light descends once again through the sushumna until it meets the glowing ember in the abdomen, where there is a second explosion of bliss, which grounds and energizes the meditator and renders him or her ready to return to normal life.

This practice normally has to be repeated regularly over many months before the meditator feels as if energy is really ascending in the way described. Don't anticipate the process. Concentrate at first on increasing the sense of a glowing ember in the abdomen, and on the sense of heat rising and unblocking the sushumna.

Only when this visualization (with attendant feelings of physical heat) is well established should you proceed to the actual raising of the energy itself.

It is interesting to note how frequently this idea of raising physical energy until it unites with spiritual energy and produces a burst of enlightenment occurs right across many of the major traditions. Further examples are given in Chapter 9 when the Western traditions of alchemy and the Kabbalah are discussed, and other instances are given in Box 7 below. In all cases, however, the practice will only be fully successful if the meditator first purifies mind and body by developing concentration and tranquillity, and by following the Buddha's advice to do good and refrain from evil.

---

**BOX 7**
**RAISING PSYCHIC HEAT**

The Tibetan practice of *tumo*, 'raising psychic heat', has clear similarities to kundalini meditation and is in fact referred to as the 'Goddess Kundalini', the dormant divine female power in the body uniting with the male *devata* principle located in the 1000-petalled lotus. Success in the practice transmutes the gross physical body into *the rainbow body*, a state in which the consciousness is said to be able to leave the body at will, especially at the moment of death (recall the Biblical prophet Elijah, who was taken up into heaven in a 'chariot of fire', the symbol of the radiant glory of the transmuted form).

Objective proof of the *physical* effectiveness of the tumo practice is that, after completing their training, monks were 'tested' by sitting overnight on the ice of a frozen river while up to nine sheets, dipped into the freezing water, were dried on their naked bodies. Full details of the very complex tumo practice (which necessitates the presence of an appropriate teacher) are given in W. Evans-Wentz' monumental work *Tibetan Yoga and Secret Doctrines*. These details are far too lengthy to give here, but again they describe how energy is made to rise from the base of the spine through each of the chakras until it explodes into the 1000-petalled lotus at the crown of the head.

A similar practice is described in the Taoist text *The Secret of the Golden Flower* (translated by Richard Wilhelm). The language used is particularly poetic; for example:

... the blazing fire causes the water of the Abysmal to vaporize, the steam is heated, and when it has passed the boiling point it mounts upward like flying snow ... The way

**BOX 7**
**RAISING PSYCHIC HEAT**

leads from the sacrum upward . . . to the summit of the
Creative . . . then it sinks . . . in a direct downward-flowing way
into the solar plexus . . . Therefore it is said: 'Wandering in
heaven, one eats the spirit-energy of the Receptive' . . . how
otherwise should one be able to enter upon this far journey?
. . . Therefore it is said: 'And the still deeper secret of the
secret: the land that is nowhere, that is the true home'.

(pp. 60–61)

Carl Jung, in his foreword to *The Secret of the Golden Flower*,
writes that before Wilhelm made the book available to Western
readers he could find 'no possible comparison' with his own
theory of the collective unconscious (see Chapter 2), except in a
few scattered references in the literature on gnosticism.
However, Wilhelm's text 'contained exactly those pieces I had
sought for in vain'. For Jung, the secret of the golden flower, and
of the symbolic truth underlying kundalini yoga, is the union of
the individual conscious mind with the collective unconscious. It
is the breaking down of the barrier that keeps men and women
from their spiritual birthright, the barrier that maintains the illusion
of separateness one from another.
    Jung made a similar point in connection with the Tibetan texts
made available in the West a few years later by Evans-Wentz.
There can be no more ringing endorsement from Western
psychology for the need to take seriously these profound Eastern
meditative practices.

## OTHER FORMS OF PHYSICAL YOGA

There are many other ways of practising the physical postures
that reflect the spiritual philosophy of hatha yoga. Besides tai
chi, other martial arts such as aikido serve the same purpose
(see, for example, Peter Payne's *Martial Arts: The Spiritual
Dimension*). Tibetan Buddhism also teaches appropriate
postures, as described by Ngakpa Chögyam in *Journey Into
Vastness* and by Peter Kelder in *Tibetan Secrets of Youth and
Vitality* (though Kelder's claims for the extraordinary physical
benefits of the postures he describes need to be taken with a
large pinch of salt).
    Another example is the whirling, spinning movement of the

Dervishes, a school within the Sufi branch of Islam. Those who have seen this spinning movement speak not only of its mesmeric quality but also once again of the impression of stillness in movement that it conveys. My own response to it is an awareness of the still centre at the heart of the whirling activity of creation, the unchanging axis around which the impermanent world of change, growth and decay eternally circles, the one that gives rise to the many, the source from which movement constantly radiates and to which it constantly returns.

Reshad Feild, one of the few Westerners who has trained at first-hand in the Dervish tradition, gives an account of how the Dervish spins.

> He began to turn, slowly at first, his arms folded across his chest. Little by little the spin grew faster; as the young man unfolded his arms the rhythm increased and the drumming became more and more intense ... (he) was completely balanced, with his head tilted slightly back and to the left. His eyes were gleaming ... at the peak of intensity, the Dervish stopped spinning quite suddenly. He did not seem to be giddy at all. He just came to a halt, crossed his arms over his chest, and bowed deeply.
>
> *The Last Barrier*, pp. 115–16

When spinning, the Dervish allows the folded arms, as described by Feild, to open out from the body as the turning becomes faster and they are then held out, the left hand palm upwards to receive grace from God and the right hand palm downwards to convey this grace to the earth. As the Dervish spins, his mind is focused in meditation always upon God and upon the awareness that, in his spinning, he is turning with a complete stillness and steadfastness of intention always towards God ... always towards God.

## EASTERN AND WESTERN APPROACHES TO MOVEMENT

It is interesting to note the fundamental difference between the meditative approach to physical movement exemplified by the Dervishes, yogis and other Eastern schools of thought, and the approach popular in the West. In the West, physical exercise is seen primarily as a way of developing the body, of using muscles and joints. The nearest we come to recognizing mental or spiritual dimensions is when we talk of exercise as promoting relaxation and combating stress. This is a reflection not only of our materialistic approach to life, but also of the fact that Western religious thought has seen the body primarily as an obstacle to spiritual progress, something that must be rigorously subdued through asceticism, denial, and even the excesses of self-flagellation and mortification (remember that the root of *mortification* is the Latin *mortis*, death; death of the body and its desires).

This idea of punishing the body through physical exercise is so deeply engrained in the Western psyche that we still think that if it is to be of any use, exercise must hurt. From physical education lessons in school to the performance of Olympic athletes, the body must be driven hard, made to protest, pushed to the limits of its endurance, taught its place in life as the slave of the will. There is little real recognition that physical movement can at the very least be light and joyful, and at its best can be a way of meditation leading to psychological and spiritual growth. Even where the beauty of movement is emphasized, as in ballet, the practitioner is still put through a regime of mind-boggling physical intensity in order to attain the 'standards' which are demanded.

It's true that in the colder climates generally experienced by Western civilization, physical exercise serves to keep the body warm in a way unnecessary in, for example, India, the home of hatha yoga. But no-one doubts the need to keep warm in a country like Tibet, yet the Tibetans never shared the Western philosophy of movement as essentially a self-punitive activity. And even where, as in the Far East, training in the martial arts required great physical discipline and dedication, it was always accepted that there was a spiritual dimension that spoke of action in inaction, of stillness in movement. Even in the 'hard' martial arts such as kendo and karate, the practitioner was taught that the root from which action sprang was a total stillness of the mind. The practitioner concentrated in intense, thoughtless awareness on the opponent, ready to flash into movement in the split second before the latter did so.

Joe Hyams, an American who spent twenty-five years under

the guidance of leading martial arts specialists, quotes one of his teachers as telling him, 'You must learn to allow patience and stillness to take over from anxiety and frantic activity ... Between martial artists of the first rank there is room for only one mistake'. When watching two such martial artists face up to each other, Hyams writes that:

> I had gone expecting to see a magnificent display of flashing acrobats and whirling limbs. Instead I saw two men in fighting stance study each other warily for several minutes. Unlike boxing there were no feints, no tentative jabs. For the most part the masters were still as statues. Suddenly one of them burst into movement so quickly that I was unable to grasp what had happened, although I did see his opponent hurtle backwards. The match was over and the two masters bowed to each other.
>
> *Zen in the Martial Arts*, p. 50

C. W. Nicol, a Welshman who spent five years in intensive training in judo and karate in Japan, describes in similar terms the behaviour of the masters with whom he trained:

> In perfect stillness they exuded strength ... I thought of herons, poised above a pool, ready to spear a fish; of high soaring falcons ready to swoop; of a cat, sitting patiently by a mouse hole ... What my teachers demonstrated was ... strength in stillness, yet more, more. I try to pin it down with words and it eludes me. 'Perfect finish' ... 'remaining spirit' ... they will have to do.
>
> *Moving Zen*, p. 111

In addition to the absorbed concentration that lay behind this stillness, there was also, as in tai chi, an emphasis upon the direction of the internal energy, the ch'i (Japanese *ki*). Watch the stillness with which the karate practitioner waits before exploding into action and shattering a brick with the edge of the bare hand. In that moment of stillness, the mind is directing the energy towards that one instant of power. The movement comes from the stillness and a moment later, when the task is done, is absorbed back into the stillness.

It would be wrong to suggest that demonstrations of energy in the martial arts are an indication that the practitioner has achieved the deep stillness of the insight stage of meditation, the 'stopping' of which my Ch'an teacher spoke. Stillness here is the path, the method, rather than the fruit, the result, of the path.

However, if we think back to Dögen's teaching earlier in the chapter, we will recall that the path and the fruit of the path must not be seen as distinct from each other. In the stilling of the mind that takes place during the martial arts, the practitioner is also experiencing something of the stillness which contains all stillness, the fruit that gives birth to the path, the goal that is also the way to the goal.

## CONCLUSION

In stillness meditation, the emphasis is upon slowing the frantic activity of the mind, and thus on achieving tranquillity followed by insight into stillness itself. Stillness is the undifferentiated unity of which we all partake, and which is 'still' because there is no movement of one thing relative to another. All move as one, or are still as one, whichever way you prefer to put it. Of course, 'stillness' is only a metaphor for this, but it is a good way of referring to a state in which everything is already there, complete in itself and perfect in its completeness. There is nothing – no agitation, no confusion, no uncertainty – to disturb this state. How could there be? For there is nothing that is not this state.

If you are unhappy with the metaphor, no matter. It is only a metaphor. In the end, we must each choose our own metaphor. The moment we represent something in the human mind we limit it. And therefore our representation is not and can never be the thing itself. The metaphor, the myth, the legend, is simply what they speak of in the East as a finger pointing at the moon, a finger which must never be mistaken for the moon. This is yet another metaphor, but it is one that helps us, that prevents us slipping back into the dogma that claims it *knows*.

It is noticeable how the Buddha, that greatest of meditation teachers, avoided such dogma and taught in its place a practice, a way, in and through which we could find truth for ourselves. Try it, he said, and see what happens. If it works for you, use it. If it does not, discard it and look elsewhere. Meditation is that practice. 'Be still and know that I am God' is another way of speaking of it. And in a hectic, destructive world we cannot return to it too often.

# 5

## *Flowing Meditation I: Inner Voice and Compassion*

Flowing meditation differs from stilling meditation in that the meditator works with a sequence of stimuli rather than concentrating upon a single point of focus. It embraces, for example, the form of meditation in which the meditator opens him or herself to the 'inner voice', the chain of thoughts and ideas that lead deeper and deeper into the inner world until one begins to experience the insights – even to hear the voice – of what some traditions call God, others spirit guides or one's own higher self (terms which should not be regarded as necessarily referring to the same aspect of inner reality). It embraces also such practices as the loving kindness (compassion) meditations and purification meditations of the Tibetan Buddhist tradition.

Let's take the first of these two examples, the practice in which the meditator opens to the inner voice. Meditation of this kind is a feature of all the great theistic religions, such as Christianity, Hinduism and Islam, which personalize the life force as a heavenly father or mother. It is less a feature of Buddhism which – in theory at least – uses more abstract symbols for the life force such as Nirvana, or what we in the West translate as emptiness or the void. But we find it again in shamanism, that set of spiritual and mystical practices which once pervaded Asia and Europe and which still persists in various forms among African and American Indian cultures. And arguably we find it in Western spiritualism, in Brazilian spiritism, and even in the currently popular practice of 'channelling', in which the practitioner is claimed to act as a channel for the wisdom of some discarnate higher being (see, for example, *The Seth Material* and other published writings of Jane Roberts).

Before looking at the practices involved in inner voice meditation, a word of warning is necessary. Flowing meditation, in whatever form we find it, is not simply sitting down and indulging in free, undirected thinking. Such an exercise, akin to daydreaming, may prompt relaxation and lead to creative ideas and the solution of problems, but it is decidedly not flowing meditation. To be effective, flowing meditation is just as focused and disciplined as stilling meditation. It is quite definitely not a form of spiritual woolgathering, however sincerely intended. And perhaps of all meditational practices, it carries the greatest risk not only of slipping into the very mind chatter which meditation is designed to dispel, but also of mistaking the products of one's own thinking for profound and weighty insights from advanced 'beings' of one sort or another.

## THE PRACTICE OF INNER VOICE MEDITATION

Inner voice meditation, when properly practised, involves the same disciplined concentration and experience of tranquillity as all other meditational practices. Its primary difference is that it focuses upon a specific idea (such as 'God is love', or 'Allah is great') or upon a specific symbol (such as the cross) and allows insights, visions or ecstatic states of being to emerge in response to them. For this reason it is sometimes referred to as 'meditation with seed'. Just as in stilling meditation, the attention is returned firmly to this point of focus each time it gets lost in mental chatter. And just as in stilling meditation, the meditator may practise diligently for months and even years before the arrival of true insight.

This last point is particularly important. There is a particular risk on the inner voice path that the meditator expects God or the higher self or whoever to speak right from the beginning. It is this mistaken expectation that leads not only to the meditator accepting his or her own thoughts as the word of God, but also to lack of real progress. In any meditation, there is a golden rule against exalted expectations. One meditates, as Dögen (Chapter 4) implies, *because one is meditating*. High-flown expectations are simply mental concepts, and concepts are the very things that get in the way of insight. Such concepts are in fact prejudices (*prejudgements*), no more and no less, and most of us know all too well how prejudices prevent us from seeing things as they actually are in all walks of life.

So without prejudices, the meditator in inner voice meditation concentrates upon the chosen stimulus, and allows whatever eventually will arise to arise of itself. There is no sense in which he or she 'makes' it happen. Inner voice meditation is a form of 'waiting upon the Lord', as the Christians put it, and true insight when it appears is invariably registered as a gift of grace. You have not done it for yourself. It is given to you, in the same bountiful way that, without doing it for ourselves, we are given the gift of life.

The term *contemplation* is sometimes used for this form of meditation, and although for many people contemplation is a rather unstructured process, for the genuine meditator it represents a particular way of opening the self to revelation. Thus, for example, to contemplate the statement 'God is love' may enable you to obtain revelation into the real meaning of love, and into the way in which this love is an expression of God. And although you may not hear voices or see visions, you may nevertheless arrive at a sense of profound understanding, either gradually or with the sudden flash with which grace is sometimes received. This profound understanding will not simply be a formula, a form of words that can be conveyed verbatim to others, or a new dogma that can be imposed upon them in the name of God. Instead it will be, as the Christian mystics put it, 'a turning around in the deepest seat of consciousness', a profound change not only in what is understood by love but also in the way in which this love is actually *lived*.

A profound change which means in fact that you no longer have to rely primarily upon your own efforts in order to follow the spiritual path, with all the failings and the difficulties and the backsliding that your own efforts involve, but that the spiritual path is now lived through you. You become, in a real sense, an avenue through which God's grace flows into the world. There

**BOX 8**
**THE SELF**

In all the great religious traditions, there is talk of the need to 'lose' the self. One either loses it by total devotion to God or a divine principle (as in the theistic religions), or by looking within and seeing that it never really existed in the first place (as in Buddhism and in the Hindu Advaita philosophy).

But what is this 'self' that we are supposed to lose? And in losing it, do we give up our individuality, as might be implied by such statements popular in Hinduism as 'the dewdrop slips into the shining sea'? If we lose our individuality, either in this life or in the next, then surely this is tantamount to annihilation? If there is nothing left of 'me', then it looks as if there is no immortality (that is, nothing that is not of mortality).

The issues here are so profound that they cannot readily be answered, even if we had a language in which to do so. But they will be touched on many times in this book, particularly when I talk of 'formlessness', and of ultimate reality not being a diversity but a unity. However, some initial guidelines are helpful.

From a psychological as well as a spiritual viewpoint, the 'self', the set of qualities, characteristics, attitudes and so on that I come to recognize as 'me', is a learned construct. *Other people tell me who I am.* Parents and schoolteachers initially, and partners and friends later on. But their 'telling' does not contain any absolute truth. It is simply their view of me, coloured by their own prejudices, their own illusions and their own subjective view of life. And which 'me' in any event is the real 'me'? The one of my childhood, of ten years ago, of five years ago, of now?

Yet all of us come to identify with this small self, and spend a lot of our time − through fear and anger − defending it as if it had a real existence. And not only defending it but judging it, either with the pride or with the guilt which in their different ways simply serve to strengthen its illusory existence. Meditation, like the more powerful forms of psychotherapy, is a way of seeing through this small self, and ultimately of discarding it.

But what is left when it's gone? This is for you to find out. But in losing the self, you are in reality losing nothing. How can you lose something that never existed in the first place? You are simply dropping a set of concepts, the veil of ignorance through which you viewed your own being. The mystics talk in fact of a vast *expansion* of being when ignorance is discarded. An expansion which embraces everything in a profound realization of unity and love. 'It is not that I am nothing', says the mystic, 'but that I am everything'.

So take heart. The one thing of which we can be sure is that when enlightenment dawns, it will bring expansion, not loss.

is no longer a small grasping ego, concerned with personal power and self-aggrandizement and social status. The small self has disappeared, dissolved in the flow of grace to which the heart has been opened.

## INNER VOICE MEDITATION IN CHRISTIANITY

As this language suggests, inner voice meditation is a particular feature of Christianity. This is because of the intensely personal nature of the relationship that many Christians feel with God as expressed in Jesus Christ. However, with the exception of the Eastern Orthodox tradition and the Quakers, Christianity has not particularly encouraged meditative practices, at least among lay men and women, primarily from a belief in the role of the Church as the representative and interpreter of divine authority and thus as the intermediary between the faithful and God. It is the Church that, from the time of St Peter and by virtue of the apostolic succession, holds the keys of the Kingdom of Heaven. And it is the Church therefore that decides on what is to be believed and what is not, on what material should be included in the scriptures and what should be excluded, on who can be accepted into the Church and who must be expelled from it, and ultimately on who appears destined for heaven and who for hell.

## GNOSTICISM

It was not always thus. In the first two centuries of Christianity a different tradition, that of Gnosticism (from *gnosis*, knowledge) flourished side by side with the movement that in due course became the recognized Church. The gnostic tradition differed from the latter in that it held that each man or woman could have direct knowledge of God, and thus had no need for a priesthood to act as go-between. The only 'priests' in the gnostic tradition were those who, by the clarity of their own spiritual vision, attracted others to them for spiritual guidance and help. Even then, the relationship between guide and guided was a voluntary one, based upon value rather than upon authority. And far from imposing dogma or exercising power, the task of the guide was to assist people to the point where they were able to continue their spiritual journey unaided. There was no formality in the relationship, no structure, no hierarchy, and above all no punishment of one person by another.

Those who criticize Christianity for lacking a meditative tradition among lay people should blame the actions of those people who sought power over their fellows by claiming for themselves the authority that rightly belongs to the spirituality within each of us. There are various explanations as to why Christianity was taken over in this way, but the most plausible has to do with its adoption as the official religion of imperial Rome. Once it became so firmly an organ of the state, the Church replicated within itself the power structures of the state, using the authority that religion had over people's minds to bolster the authority that the state had over their bodies.

Gnosticism, the direct knowledge of God, was in these terms seen clearly as a threat. If men and women could find God for themselves they would have no need for the Church, and in that case what would happen to the Church's power? The only remedy to this threat was suppression. And this, with the efficiency almost of a secret police, the Church proceeded to do. There are no exact figures for the thousands upon thousands of people who perished down the centuries because of their unorthodox views. But those who are interested may like to look at the history of the Albigensian crusade, that outpouring of hatred and savagery with which the thirteenth-century Church, allied to the King of France, exterminated the resurgence of gnosticism in the Languedoc area of France (see, for example, Arthur Guirdham's *The Great Heresy*). At a conservative estimate, in the one town of Béziers alone, the crusaders put some 30,000 people to the sword, massacring them even within the sacred confines of the Roman Catholic cathedral of St Madeleine itself. And did so, what's more, under the eye of a local prince of the Church, the Abbé of Citeaux, who, when asked by the crusaders how they could distinguish between the heretics and the many good Catholics who lived in Béziers was reported as saying, 'Kill them all. God will know His own'.

With this massacre of gnosticism went a large part of the meditative spirit of Christianity. For the Church, meditation was not only unnecessary for the ordinary person, it was a downright invitation to heresy. Once people started to meditate, who was to say what subversive ideas they would come up with? No, meditation, like philosophical speculation and queries about the afterlife, was definitely not something in which the general public could be allowed to indulge.

It would be wrong to suggest that the Church had no saintly members. Assuredly it did. Or to suggest that the ideas spawned by the gnostic tradition within Christianity were free at all times from error and narrowness of vision. Assuredly they were not. What we can suggest is that Western Christendom is itself to blame for its lack of an appropriate meditative tradition. And things were little helped by the arrival within Christendom of the nonconformist sects, many of whom had their own brand of authoritarianism in which the Chapel, rather than the individual, replaced the Church as the arbiter of what must and must not be believed. (The exception to this was the Quakers, the Society of Friends, who from their foundation listened to the inner voice within the prepared stillness of the mind.)

This anti-gnostic, anti-meditative stance of the Church and Chapel that bear his name is at variance with the teachings of Christ, particularly if as recorded in the writings suppressed by the Church in AD 369 when the Church Fathers put together the New Testament from the much larger canon of scriptures then available (see, for example, Anthony Duncan's *Jesus: Essential Readings*). The four gospels, the heart of the New Testament, were only accepted as the sole reliable and authoritative account of Christ's ministry in AD 130; up to that time, and indeed to the end of the second century AD, there were a number of other gospels and related writings in use among the various Christian groups. It was only when men like Bishop Irenaeus and his followers were making pronouncements to the effect that outside the Church 'there is no salvation' that these other, more gnostic texts were condemned to be burned as heretical.

## THE NAG HAMMADI LIBRARY

Yet if we go back to these texts – and we are fortunate that sixty-one of them were rediscovered in 1945 near Nag Hammadi in Upper Egypt, where they had been buried between AD 350 and 400 in order to avoid destruction – we find that they reveal a Christ who, far from establishing an authoritarian Church, was concerned to lead His followers to a direct knowledge of God. These sixty-one texts are available in English translation in *The Nag Hammadi Library* (edited by James Robinson), and include the *Gospel of Thomas*, the *Gospel of Philip*, the *Gospel to the Egyptians*, and various texts attributed to Christ's followers such as the *Secret Book of James*, the *Apocalypse of Paul*, the *Letter of Peter to Philip*, and the *Apocalypse of Peter*. (For those without access to these original texts, a good introduction is given by Elaine Pagels in *The Gnostic Gospels*.) The dating of the texts is not an exact science, but many of them were in existence at least as early as AD 120, while the *Gospel of Thomas*, which is a collection of the sayings of Christ, may well be based upon a document that actually predates the four New Testament gospels (AD 60–110).

The implications of these early writings for Christianity cannot be over-emphasized. Victims of one of the first outbursts of censorship and book burning known to history, they supplement and enrich the orthodox canon of the New Testament. And particularly in the *Gospel of Thomas* and the *Gospel of Philip*, we have texts which stress the need for each of us to embark on our personal spiritual quest, and discover the divine spark within ourselves. A few quotations make this clear.

In the *Gospel of Thomas* Christ is recorded as saying:

There is light within a man of light, and he lights up the whole world. If he does not shine, he is darkness.

He who will drink from my mouth will become like me. I myself shall become he, and the things that are hidden will be revealed to him.

Whoever finds himself is superior to the world.

Similar examples occur in the *Gospel of Philip*, for instance:

You saw the spirit, you became spirit. You saw Christ, you became Christ. You (saw the father) you shall become father ... you see yourself and what you see you shall (become).

Many of the other recorded sayings of Christ in these gospels carry clear parallels with the teachings of religions with strong meditative traditions, such as Buddhism. What clearer teaching on the concept of emptiness, so central to Buddhist philosophy and meditation, could one find, for example, than Christ's symbolic description of the Kingdom of Heaven in *The Gospel of Thomas?*

> The Kingdom of the Father is like a certain woman who was carrying a jar full of meal. While she was walking on a road, still some distance from home, the handle of the jar broke and the meal emptied out behind her on the road. She did not realize it; she had noticed no accident. When she reached her house, she set the jar down and found it empty.

And what clearer parallel could one find with the Buddhist teachings that 'when the opposites arise the Buddha mind is lost' and 'life and death are the same', and (once again) with the Buddhist concept of emptiness than Christ's words in the *Gospel of Philip* that:

> Light and darkness, life and death, right and left, are brothers to one another. They are inseparable. Because of this neither are the good good, nor the evil evil, nor is life life, nor death death. For this reason each one will dissolve into its original nature.

There are also sayings in both the *Gospel of Thomas* and the *Gospel of Philip* which are similar to koans, those enigmatic statements that serve as the point of focus in certain kinds of Zen meditation (Chapter 8). For example, 'Blessed is he who came into being before he came into being' and 'Blessed is he who is before he came into being' are both reminiscent of the koan, 'Show me your original face before you were born' – as also is:

> When you see your likeness, you rejoice. But when you see your images which came into being before you, and which neither die nor become manifest, how much you will have to bear!

Another example of a koan-like statement from among the many that could be chosen is:

> From me did the all come forth, and unto me did the all extend. Split a piece of wood, and I am there. Lift up the stone, and you will find me there,

which is reminiscent of such statements as that of Tozan who, when asked to say what the Buddha is, answered, 'three pounds of flax'.

There are also koan-like statements which appear to warn of the dangers of the misuse of spiritual power, such as:

> Blessed is the lion which becomes man when consumed by man; and cursed is the man whom the lion consumes, and the lion becomes man,

or which warn of the need to unite the spiritual power inside one with the spiritual power of the rest of creation:

> That which you have will save you if you bring it forth from yourselves. That which you do not have within you will kill you if you do not have it within you.

There are also striking similarities with many of the concepts prominent in Hindu thinking. For example, in *The Thunder, Perfect Mind* (what a wonderful title!) comes a statement that always profoundly moves me:

> I am the silence that is incomprehensible, and the idea whose remembrance is frequent.

Here, in a single poetic sentence, are the Hindu concepts of the meditative states of *nirvikalpa samadhi* and *savikalpa samadhi*, states in which respectively one loses all sense of self and abides in the unity which is the unspoken ground of our being, and in which one retains a sense of oneself as the experiencer of this unity (see Chapter 9).

The importance of symbols, so central a part of meditation as stressed in Chapter 2, is emphasized in the *Gospel of Philip* when Christ is recorded as saying, 'Truth did not come into the world naked, but it came in types and images. One will not receive truth in any other way ... The bridegroom must enter through the image into the truth'. The place of gnosis, of the personal discovery of this truth, is referred to in the very next sentences:

> It is appropriate that those who do have it [i.e., the truth] not only acquire the name of the Father and the Son and the Holy Spirit, but that they have acquired it on their own. If one does not acquire the name for himself, the name will also be taken from him ... this person [who acquires the name] is no longer a Christian but a Christ.

In their emphasis upon gnosis as opposed to authority, the gnostic gospels are much in tune with the *Gospel of St John*, the most mystical of the four New Testament gospels and pure gnosticism in places. Elaine Pagels, in *The Gnostic Gospels*, suggests in fact that it was only the presence of the seventeen words, 'I am the way, the truth and the life; no-one comes to the Father but by me', in the *Gospel of St John* that persuaded the early Church Fathers to include it in the collection which in due course came to form the New Testament. In her view, the Church chose to interpret these words as meaning one can only find God through the historical Jesus and that therefore, by extension, one can only find Him through the Church which bears His name. However, when set alongside some of the above quotations from the gnostic gospels, these words can be interpreted as referring not to an historical person but to the Christ within each of us. 'The place which you can reach, stand there', Christ is recorded as saying in the *Dialogue of the Saviour*.

The gnostic gospels clearly deserve consideration as a supplement to the New Testament canon, and there is no doubt that, used in this way, they lend powerful support to meditation as the path to inner truth. They suggest, in fact, a Christ who taught not only the life of love and service (karma yoga) and of prayer and devotion (bhakti yoga) which so shines through the New Testament gospels, but also the life of meditation (rajah yoga) and of spiritual insight (jnana yoga).

## WOMEN AND INNER VOICE MEDITATION

The fact that many of the Christian mystics associated with inner voice meditation have been women – St Theresa of Avila, for example, Mother Julian of Norwich, Catherine of Siena, St Joan of Arc, Catherine of Genoa – raises the possibility that women and men differ in the forms of meditation to which they are most suited. Are women perhaps better at working with personal and emotional techniques than men, while men are better at ones that are more impersonal and abstract? I'm never happy about the clear divisions sometimes made between female and male psychological experience, especially when supported by the highly debatable argument that femininity is more linked to the right hemisphere of the brain, responsible for visual imagination, dreams and intuitive states generally, while masculinity is more linked to the mathematical, rational and spatial functions associated with the left hemisphere.

I'm equally unhappy about the cultural arguments suggesting that women are less drawn towards impersonal and abstract meditation practices than men because society has confined them to working more with people and with the practicalities of life. Perhaps rather more convincing is the argument that since the historical Christ was male, women are better able to envision him as the source of love and compassion than are men, and are also more drawn to the idea of the soul becoming wedded through the Church to Christ. Further support for this argument is that, at least in the Western world, women appear better able than men to enter the ecstatic states which sometimes arise in flowing meditation, and in which the meditator feels taken over and possessed by the divine figure upon whom the meditation is focused.

But whether any or none of these explanations is appropriate, men seem to take more readily to koan meditation, which on the surface looks suspiciously like an intellectual exercise but which is in fact designed to drive the mind into the space where the limits of intellect are exposed. Equally, women seem more disposed towards flowing meditation and the inner scenery and celestial visions to which it sometimes leads. But there are many women who practise koan meditation and many men who practise flowing meditation, so any attempt to be dogmatic on differences in meditative disposition looks misguided.

The best advice to all meditators, irrespective of sex, is to work over suitable periods of time with at least two or three of the different forms of meditation given in this book before deciding which is most suitable for your own needs.

## TECHNIQUES OF FLOWING MEDITATION

I've already mentioned that inner voice meditation typically takes as its point of focus an idea or a symbol, and allows this to carry the mind towards insight. In addition to the Christian examples upon which I've touched, meditation of this kind is

particularly associated with the Hindu tradition, where one of
the most widely used meditative practices is that of *japa*, repetition of the names of God. In itself, repetition of a particular
sound or of a particular phrase is usually seen as a part of
mantra meditation (Chapter 10), but in japa there should be, as
Patanjali reminds us, not just repetition of the sound but 'meditation upon its meaning'.

Swami Swahananda, in one of a series of practical essays on
meditation produced by monks of the Ramakrishna order
(*Meditation*), writes that japa 'is the easiest spiritual practice',
because 'any word which has for years been used in the spiritual
practice of holy men and women is charged with special power'.
Thus simple repetition, even if one cannot penetrate to its inner
meaning, brings rewards. But Swami Venanda and Christopher
Isherwood, in their commentary upon the *Yoga Sutras*, stress
Patanjali's admonition that in meditation, concentration upon
meaning is vital. Such concentration, they tell us, will lead

> inevitably into meditation. Gradually our confused reverie will give
> way to concentrated thought. We cannot for long repeat any word
> without beginning to think about the reality which it represents.
>
> *Yoga Sutras*, p. 42

In the Hindu teaching, the supreme word to be used in flowing
meditation is 'Om', pronounced 'aum' (with a long 'a' as in
'*a*rm'' pronounced at the back of the throat, 'u' as in 'c*oo*l'
pronounced in the middle of the mouth, and 'm' as in '*m*other'
pronounced behind the closed lips). 'Om' is probably the most
ancient word for 'god' in existence, and is said to be the primal
sound from which all creation springs, the 'word' that existed in
the beginning and which, as *St John's Gospel* tells us, 'was
God'.

But in order to ponder the meaning of a word, a Westerner
might prefer to take another of the symbols for God, such as
'love', repeating and concentrating upon the word on each out-
breath. Or one of the attributes of God, such as 'space' or
'eternity' or 'omnipotence'. But whatever the starting point,
whatever the 'seed' of the meditation, the meditator probes and
probes into its meaning. Not in a rational way, the way that
would provide a flat dictionary definition, but in a way that
holds the word at the centre of awareness and allows it in its

own good time to reveal itself not only as an emotion but as an intuitive feeling of understanding.

Should the mind begin to wander from the word – for example, by beginning to free associate to whatever mundane images or ideas are sparked off by it – it is brought gently but firmly back, just as in all meditational practices. And if the mind, suddenly captivated by a particular insight, wants the meditator to get up and write it down before it is forgotten, then once again the meditator resists the distraction and stays concentrated upon the word itself. It is the truth behind the word that leads the meditator deeper and deeper into inner space, and any distraction, no matter how important it may seem, serves only to disrupt this deepening process.

Those familiar with Carl Jung's *word association* technique will notice similarities here. In word association, the individual takes a word or an image – perhaps from a dream – which appears to have personal significance, and sees what arises from the unconscious in response to it. Unlike Freud's *free association* technique, in which the mind is allowed to go rambling off along the chain of associations set in motion by the original stimulus, in word association it is brought back to this stimulus after each association arises, so that it stays linked to the stimulus. Only in this way, Jung argued, can the insights which the stimulus represents be probed to their depths.

## LOVING COMPASSION MEDITATION

Flowing meditation can also be used for the development of specific qualities, as for example in Buddhist loving compassion meditation. In this practice, the initial focus is upon the suffering of others. In a careful sequence, the meditator thinks first of the suffering of parents and of loved ones and others close to him or her, and allows the emotion of empathy to develop together with the feeling of how wonderful it would be if these people could enjoy peace and enlightenment.

The meditation is then broadened to include people towards whom the meditator is neutral, and the same feeling of compassion and of the desire to see them free from suffering is generated. Next the meditation takes in people towards whom the meditator feels antipathy of some kind, and finally it takes in the suffering of all living beings throughout the various realms of existence. The meditation concludes with a visualization technique (see Chapter 7) in which Avalokiteshvara, the Buddha of Compassion, is imagined and petitioned to strengthen one's own loving compassion and that of all beings.

A meditation of this kind can lead the meditator to hear the inner voice of Avalokiteshvara, though as I indicated earlier, this 'inner voice' can simply be the product of one's own normal thought processes. Buddhism in particular warns against being misled by the activity of one's own thoughts into imagining that one is having some deep spiritual experience. It is not that such activity necessarily gives misguided information; simply that it can beguile the meditator into supposing an advanced state has been reached, and consequently hinder legitimate progress. Distinguishing between one's own thoughts and genuine insights is no easy task. For the beginner, it is best to accept that if there is a shadow of doubt as to where the 'inner voice' originates, it is probably from one's own thinking.

## THE SPIRITUAL EXERCISES

One of the most comprehensive guides to flowing meditation – one that embraces, in fact, the purposes underlying all the examples I've so far given – is *The Spiritual Exercises*, published in 1548 by the Spaniard St Ignatius Loyola, the founder of the Jesuit order. Bound by the traditional monastic vows of poverty, chastity and obedience, the main functions of the Jesuits were instruction, preaching and confession, and from their inception in 1534 they waged a spiritual 'war' against the sixteenth-century reformers both within and without the Roman Catholic Church. Part of the reason for their effectiveness as an organization was the fact that the members of the order received a rigorous grounding in meditation and self-discipline through the use of *The Spiritual Exercises*, a slim volume that takes the practitioner step-by-step through an examination of his (the Jesuits are exclusively male) own weaknesses, and then through a series of meditations on the major events in Christ's public ministry designed to help the meditator penetrate more deeply into the meaning behind them, and to feel within himself something of the love, the self-sacrifice, and the suffering experienced by Christ.

Some of the material contained in the *Exercises* has a dated approach, and its emphasis upon hell and damnation is out of keeping with modern thought. Certain aspects of the practices, such as self-flagellation, are even actively repugnant, as is the anti-feminism that surfaces from time to time. Nevertheless, overall *The Spiritual Exercises* remain a meditation manual of extraordinary power, incorporating in their short space many of the techniques to be found in more esoteric texts. Sixteenth-century Spain was much influenced by Moorish and Middle Eastern ideas, and St Ignatius, who had been a soldier in his younger days and who had also travelled in the Holy Land, clearly came under this influence and adapted certain of these techniques for Christian use.

The *Exercises* were not, however, intended for use by the general public, but only by those who had already sworn obedience to the Church. They were designed to be given, step-by-step, to the novice Jesuit on a four-week retreat, and used by him under the guidance of a spiritual director, with five one-hour meditations undertaken each day. But anyone who approaches them in the right spirit will find they are sufficiently self-contained to give invaluable help as a *set of techniques*. This is true no matter over what period they are used, and no matter whether the existing language and concepts are employed or whether the meditator adapts them to his or her particular spiritual beliefs.

Briefly, the *Exercises* stress certain general principles which I summarize as follows.

The meditator should:

● prepare for meditation with a prayer to encourage the right frame of mind,

● use visual imagination – for example, by visualizing the temple or the mountain top where he or she is most able to sense the spiritual presence upon which the meditation is to focus,

● summon up deep emotional involvement towards this spiritual presence,

- turn the mind towards the following morning's meditation as one goes off to sleep, so that it will be in a better state of preparation on awakening,

- turn the mind towards the morning meditation immediately upon waking, so that it will enter easily into meditation upon arising,

- visualize oneself with the qualities one wants to possess, and avoiding the behaviours one wishes to avoid,

- examine the effectiveness of a meditation session after it is completed so that one can identify where and why things went badly,

- make the visualizations as specific as possible,

- use the other senses to assist visualization – for example, by listening to what the people in the visualization appear to be saying to each other, smelling the fragrance of the flowers or of the incense which may surround them, touching the ground upon which they have walked,

- place oneself inside the visualization.

In particular, the guidelines on the use of visualization are among the best available in Western literature, and include many of the important features which occur in the mystery tradition and in the Tibetan Buddhist traditions (Chapter 9). So central, in fact, is visualization to certain forms of meditational practice that I devote a large part of the next chapter to it.

St Ignatius also instructs that when using a word as the focus of meditation, one should concentrate upon it for meaning, for analogies, and for spiritual comfort. In the case of a word like 'God' or 'Om', this would mean awakening insights firstly into what God *is*, secondly into what God *is like*, and thirdly upon the *emotional reactions* that these insights arouse.

Among the other valuable guidelines given in *The Spiritual Exercises* are those on how the breath can be used. To take once again the example of 'God' or 'Om', the meditator silently repeats the word on the in-breath, and then focuses upon the meaning of (or the analogies or the emotions aroused by) the word on the out-breath. Thus there is both a rhythm and a

discipline to the way in which one is using the word, a rhythmical coming and going of the word 'God' or 'Om' and of the
inner powers to which the word gives rise.

*An Example from The Exercises*   A single example from *The
Exercises* will illustrate some of the points I have been summar-
izing. It's taken from the meditation on the Nativity, and I have
paraphrased and supplemented the wording in order to make
the example, taken as it is out of context, as clear as possible. I
am also treating the meditator as if male or female. In this
example, as in the other exercises, the meditator goes through
certain preliminaries designed to put the mind in the right state
before proceeding to the headings under which the meditation
proper is presented.

*First Preliminary*   The meditation starts with a preparatory
prayer, asking God to direct the thoughts, activities and deeds of
the meditator to His service and praise.

*Second Preliminary*   The meditator deliberately recalls the
story of the Nativity, visualizing each detail as clearly and de-
voutly as possible. In particular, he or she pictures Mary, nine
months pregnant, setting out for Bethlehem on a donkey,
accompanied by Joseph.

The visualization is then deepened by seeing the road to
Bethlehem and the countryside through which it is passing. Is it
level or through valleys and hillsides? When the place of the
Nativity is reached, this is visualized in the same careful detail. Is
it large or small? How is it furnished? etc.

*Third Preliminary*   The meditator asks for deep-felt knowledge
of Christ, in order the better to follow and serve Him.

*First Heading*   The meditator now looks at the people present
in the visualization, Mary, Joseph, the infant Jesus, and then
sees him or herself present in the picture as a humble attendant,
looking after their wants 'in a spirit of complete and respectful
subservience'.

When this experience is stabilized in the mind, the meditator
then feels him or herself deriving spiritual benefit from being
present.

*Second Heading* The meditator listens to what the people present are saying, and then thinks of him or herself as deriving benefit from it.

*Third Heading* The meditator reflects upon what the people are doing, upon the long journey they have made and the hardships they are suffering in order to bring Christ to humankind.

He or she then reflects upon what lies ahead of Christ, the labours, the heat and cold, the hunger and thirst, the injustice and the insults, and finally the death on the cross. And all for the benefit of the meditator.

The meditator then feels him or herself deriving benefit from these reflections.

*Conclusion* The meditation finishes with the meditator thinking what to say to Christ or to Mary, and asking to follow and imitate Christ. Finally, the Lord's Prayer is repeated.

The care with which the visualization is built up, and the subsequent placing of oneself inside it, are integral parts of *The Spiritual Exercises* and of all flowing meditations of this kind, whether within the Western mystery and occult traditions or within those of Egypt and Asia Minor. More will be said about the latter traditions in Chapter 9, but a word of warning is necessary. In all work of this kind, once the meditator can construct and enter the visualization clearly, the events begin to take on a life of their own, as if the meditator has actually entered another world. And this can be both alarming and dangerous.

From an orthodox psychological viewpoint, we don't know what is happening at this point. We use the term 'vivid hallucinations', as if this label is an explanation. But we don't know why the mind has this creative power, why the visualization can become so 'real' and can have such a profound effect upon the visualizer. We do know, however, that these visualizations can begin to intrude into everyday life, threatening either to leave the meditator 'unworldly' and preferring to retreat into them than face reality (the exact opposite of what is required), or to cause alarm and fear. Either way, they can mimic psychotic states, and herein lies a reason for the warning sometimes given against 'dabbling in the occult'.

Used properly, the techniques taught by *The Spiritual Exercises* and by the mystery and other spiritual traditions are anything but 'dabbling in the occult'. But they are suitable only for the meditator who can keep the visual experiences they evoke firmly within the confines of controlled meditation practice. A further requisite is that the meditator follows the karma yoga of a moral life lived within the philosophy and self-discipline of a spiritual or humanistic tradition. Such a life will help ensure that the contents of the visualizations are of the benevolent kind. Until such time as these safeguards are in place, the meditator should choose the path of stilling meditation.

Finally, it is right to say that the content and tone of *The Spiritual Exercises* will in any case not appeal to everyone. Both Christians and non-Christians may reject their emphasis upon obedience to the Church, upon sinfulness, upon penance and the fear of damnation, and upon the powerful devotional element which is present throughout. But the sincerity and commitment of the author of the *Exercises* still sparkles after 400 years, as does his emphasis upon the need for gentleness and patience on the part of the meditation teacher (qualities that are not always associated in popular thinking with the Jesuits). What also sparkles through is the power of the meditational practices which the *Exercises* offer, and the realization that it is always such *practices* that count, rather than the dogma with which they inevitably become surrounded. The *Exercises* can still serve as an invaluable handbook for those ready to practise flowing meditation, and for all of us they serve as a reminder of the need for discipline and structure in meditation if it is to be truly effective.

# 6

## *Flowing Meditation II: The World of the Shaman*

The third example of flowing meditation with which I want to deal is *shamanism* (the first 'a' pronounced as in 'far'). The word 'shaman' comes from the Tungus people of Siberia, and is now generally used to refer to the indigenous spiritual practices and beliefs of a wide range of cultures stretching from Siberia and Tibet eastwards to the American Indians, Eskimos and Australian aborigines, and westwards to the African medicine men and to the pagan cults of Europe. Whether this ubiquitous use of the word is fully justified, since there are many important differences between the spiritual practices and philosophies of these cultural groups, is debatable. But certainly, running through all of them is the belief that the shaman is someone who has the ability to enter an altered state of consciousness in order to contact an inner source of knowledge and power, usually described as the spirit world.

As such, shamanism in its pure form and freed from the superstitions that adhere to it represents a sophisticated set of techniques which carry undoubted psychological power. The tragedy is that we in the West have come to realize this only when we have already done much to destroy the culture and the ways of thinking from which shamanism springs.

Much of the publicity that shamanism currently enjoys comes from the series of books by Carlos Castenada on the teachings of an old Yaqui Indian shaman called Don Juan (see *The Teachings of Don Juan* and seven subsequent publications), whom Castenada claims he first met while an anthropology student at the University of California. Over a period of years, first in Arizona and later in Mexico, Castenada allegedly served an apprenticeship with Don Juan, learning how to induce altered states of consciousness, first with drugs such as peyote and later with the power of the will alone.

Considerable doubt exists over the reliability of Castenada's accounts, both in relation to the actual existence of Don Juan and to the details he gives of his own experiences. The reader who works systematically through each of Castenada's books, noting how these accounts become more bizarre and far-fetched with each one, will make up his or her own mind. But before Castenada is dismissed, it is fair to point out that parts of his work are undoubtedly based upon a knowledge of actual shamanic practices, however this knowledge may have been acquired. Unfortunately, other parts appear to have misled some of his readers, and may have contributed to the rash of ill-considered books on shamanism that have appeared in recent years.

The reality is that genuine shamans (who could be male or female), even in the cultures which bred and sustained them, were few and far between. And their gifts were developed only after a lengthy training whose rigour and whose psychological and physical dangers are well beyond the scope of most people. Shamanism never was a way of spiritual development for the ordinary man or woman, any more than St Ignatius' *Spiritual Exercises* were intended for non-Jesuits or marathon running is a way for the ordinary man and woman to keep physically fit.

However, this does not mean that certain shamanic practices cannot be incorporated into your meditation if you find them helpful. As already stressed, meditational practices are not separated from each other as if in watertight compartments. Meditation is meditation, and the different techniques can feed and inform each other. Nor does it mean that, even if you don't actively use them, a knowledge of these practices and of the philosophy behind them is without value to you as a meditator. They are in fact useful for four main reasons. The first is that shamanism confirms once again the power of visualization; the second is that it places great emphasis upon the effectiveness of *sound* in inducing the meditative state; the third is that it provides us with a symbolic version of aspects of the meditative journey. And fourthly, and most importantly, because shamanism teaches a special relationship with the earth, a relationship that has been largely lost in the materially-minded West.

The first of these reasons, the power of visualization, is dealt with elsewhere, and I will come back to the third and fourth in due course. Let me first say something about the second, the effectiveness of sound. This is a topic which is touched upon in Chapter 10, but there is no doubt that the prolonged repetition of certain sounds – especially rhythmical sounds – can influence the physical rhythm of the brain in a way which assists the meditator to achieve the relaxed yet focused concentration which meditation demands.

But here yet again a word of warning is needed, and again it is to do with the meditator entering an altered state of consciousness in which touch with reality is lost. The altered state associated with sound is not dissimilar in some ways to the ecstasy which is a feature of the inner voice meditation of many of the mystics, and which is also seen in certain forms of yoga meditation as described by Krpälvanand in his *Science of Meditation*, mentioned in the last chapter. In these states, the individual loses sense of time, place or personal identity, and becomes caught up in the experience of ecstasy or of inner visions. Such states can be of great value and can mark a step on the path towards losing the limited ego, but for the inexperienced and the unprepared, they can be disorientating and unnerving, involving feelings of depersonalization which can be terrifying and psychologically dangerous.

For the shaman, however, these states are part of the realization that our habitual way of experiencing the world and ourselves in relation to it is only one way of doing so. And that for the shaman our way contains a number of false assumptions, in particular that this world is the only plane of reality, that there are impassable boundaries between realities, that it is impossible to commune with the departed or to make contact with the consciousness of animals or of other living things.

The rhythmical sounds used by the shaman to enter an altered state of consciousness come primarily from drumming, often accompanied by the shaking of a rattle and by repetitive and monotonous chanting on a single tone or with two beats on one tone and two beats two and a half tones lower (you can get the idea of this by chanting *Hi-a---wa-tha* in either of these ways). There are good reasons for this. Brain research reveals that a drumming rhythm of above 205 beats per minute has a strong effect upon the brain's own electrical rhythm, inducing both the alpha and the theta rhythms associated with meditation and altered states of consciousness. The steady sound of a rattle and monotonous chanting add to this physiological effect.

Against the background of this drumming the shaman begins the process of visualization that leads to the inner shamanic journey. In some shamanic traditions, in particular those of the North American Indians, fasting or physical pain were also sometimes used – particularly in the case of the apprentice shaman – to induce and speed entry into this inner journey. Physical pain increases the disorientation induced by the drumming and chanting, and since physical pain also stimulates the release of endorphins into the bloodstream (the hormones which deaden pain and which are in themselves responsible for a certain kind of psychological 'high'), the cumulative effect upon the mind is a particularly powerful one.

Isolation was another method, with the apprentice shaman spending a long period in solitude out in the forest, with all the emotional charges of loneliness and fear that such a period of isolation would induce in a young and impressionable mind, already filled with whispered teachings about power animals, spirit guides and spirit journeys.

In his or her subsequent initiation, the apprentice shaman would visualize the mouth of a cave or a chasm in the ground as the symbol of the entrance into the Lowerworld, the world of the spirits. If the long preparatory training had been effective, the visualization would assume a life of its own, in the way that I mentioned in the last chapter. The apprentice would then follow the pathway that opened up into the Lowerworld and there, as a final stage in initiation, sometimes experience a symbolic dismemberment at the hands of spirits or power animals (symbols of inner psychological forces) – the ritual death of the shaman – subsequently to be 'reborn' into the new life of the mature shaman (see, for example, John Halifax's *Shamanic Voices*).

**BOX 9**
**DRUMMING**

If, with the warning about depersonalization firmly in mind, you wish to experiment with drumming, you should use a single-headed 16–17 inch (45–47 cm) round frame drum, which can be ordered from a music store (you *can* make your own, but without some training on a craft course it isn't advisable). If you want a rattle as well, one of the dried gourd rattles available in ethnic craft shops is ideal. Alternatively you can buy a commercial maraca, but try out several and buy the one with the strongest, sharpest sound.

Initially, you'll need to work with two partners, one beating the drum and the other shaking the rattle (with a steady beat of not less than 180 a minute). See what effect it has upon you. Use your normal meditation practice against this background. If you're working with a visualization (as in inner quality meditation, Chapter 7), use a picture from nature like a tree or a waterfall. Focus upon it just as you did when using the picture of a spiritual teacher. When the visualization is clear, enter it and note how the scene takes on a life of its own. Do not be alarmed by anything or anybody you meet. Note it and pass on. After a prearranged time (for example, ten minutes) your partners should increase the speed of their drumming and rattling to signal it is time to return.

The spirits or power animals concerned would often have been encountered during the earlier training in visualization. Again, this training is similar in many ways to *The Spiritual Exercises*. The apprentice, frequently under the whispered guidance of the teacher, would visualize a scene in a deserted place – a forest or a mountain perhaps. He or she would then imaginatively enter the scene and find his or her personal power animal, which would subsequently act as a guide.

Often, the place visualized would be an actual location that the apprentice shaman knew well, so that the visualization became particularly clear. Later, the apprentice was sometimes left in solitude in that actual place, and the power animal would then be visualized as making its appearance in 'normal' reality. In this way the power animal would become increasingly real to the apprentice, and appear readily on entry into the Lowerworld. If the ritual death and dismemberment took place, this would seem equally real, and afterwards, when the body was re-assembled within the visualization, it would literally seem like a resurrection, a rebirth into a new, more powerful self.

## SHAMANISM AND GREEK MYTH

There are interesting parallels here with the Tibetan *chod* ritual, in which the novice monk is left in a burial ground, and there calls upon the spirits of the dead and wild animals to devour him limb from limb. Again there is the ritual death, this time with the added feeling of sacrifice, of giving one's body and blood in the service of others, followed by a rebirth into a purified and heightened consciousness.

There are also parallels, of particular value to the Western meditator, with the story of Orpheus, the son of one of the Greek muses. Like the shaman, Orpheus had a special relationship with the earth and could charm the trees and the wild animals and the springs and fountains with his music. After the death of his wife Eurydice, Orpheus descended into the Lower-world to rescue her, but failed because he broke the conditions of her rescue and looked back at her before she reached the daylight. Heartbroken at his loss, Orpheus ceased to worship the god Dionysius and for his disrespect was torn to pieces by the maenads, the female devotees of the god.

Jung pointed out that a study of myths and legends like that of Orpheus is of great psychological value, since they contain in story form eternal truths about our nature and the psychological tasks that we have to undertake on the way towards wholeness. The fact that these stories occur across cultures and across centuries indicates even more clearly that they carry this sym-bolic message. It is the common features of these myths and practices that are a guide to their psychological truth. All the great traditions have become overlaid with the prejudices, the bids for power and the misunderstandings of people who failed to nourish themselves by returning continually to the spiritual source from which these traditions spring. And it is only by looking for these common features that we are able to separate out the wheat contained in these traditions from the chaff.

Thus, in many of the Greek legends we see, in symbolic form, teachings which occur in traditions as remote from classical Greece as Siberian and American Indian shamanism. Orpheus is a shaman in that he has a special relationship with nature, and can speak its language and understand its secrets. Orpheus, like the shaman, descends to the Lowerworld to find his other half, his spiritual self symbolized by Eurydice. But Orpheus allows himself to be misled by his untamed emotions. Because he cannot contain his desire to see Eurydice he looks back, and loses her for ever. He becomes, in effect, a shaman who has failed his most important test, the control of self. Subsequently this failure destroys him because, after his ritual death at the hands of the maenads, his dismembered body does not undergo resurrection into a new life. However, in the legend his severed head continues to sing, symbolizing the promise that life is indestructible, and that the opportunity to reach enlightenment will occur again in a future life.

This brings me back to the third reason, given on page 99, why a knowledge of shamanism is of value to the meditator, the symbolic picture it gives us of the road to wholeness which the meditator must tread. This road leads deep into our own being, into the Lowerworld where our individuality, as we understand it, ends and we make contact with the psychological forces that are our common human heritage. In an attempt to find a label acceptable to Western science, Jung called this domain the *collective unconscious* (see Box 2). The label doesn't explain it, of course. 'Collective unconscious' merely indicates that across ages and cultures, we share this hidden reservoir of psycho-spiritual energy. Jung suggested we inherit it in our genes, a kind of mental blueprint analogous to the physical blueprint which gives us our common human form.

In order to enter *consciously* this Lowerworld of the collective unconscious we have first to discipline ourselves, through meditation, to control our wandering mind and wayward emotions. Once ready, we enter the Lowerworld and there find that our 'self', the person we think we are, has to be torn apart, dismembered as the shaman is dismembered, to be reassembled into a different consciousness, the consciousness of a 'liberated' person who knows who he or she really is. Or, in the language of the shaman, a man or woman of power. One is now free to move into what we might call the Upperworld, that part of the collective unconscious which is in communion with spiritual wisdom, or to remain in the Lowerworld, that part in contact with nature and natural forces.

The idea of entering a different consciousness, of being 'born again', is of course stressed by Christ, who emphasized that to experience rebirth we must first tread the path of discipline and preparation – that is, we must first leave home and family (not necessarily literally; these are symbols for turning the mind away from its usual concerns). We must then follow Him – that is, follow the path of spiritual growth. And only through subsequent rebirth do we fit ourselves for the next stage, the entry into the Kingdom of Heaven, the Upperworld of spiritual wisdom which is here and now, and not reserved only for a state beyond death.

There are other striking parallels with this idea of rebirth. In Egyptian mythology – another treasure house of psychological and spiritual truths – it takes the form of the story of the god Osiris. Osiris, the sky god, who symbolizes our full potential, is tricked and murdered by his brother Seth, symbolizing the distracting, corrupting side of our own minds, the side that destroys our chances of spiritual growth. Eventually, after a long search, Osiris' dismembered body is discovered by his sister Isis, who symbolizes our spiritual nature and the patient processes of spiritual practice, and is revivified through her love in order to serve as a symbol of enlightenment, redemption and immortality.

How interesting that the minds of the ancient Greeks and Egyptians, who clearly knew as much if not more about the deeper levels of human psychology as we do, chose to present this knowledge not as we present it – by psychological labels such as the conscious and unconscious minds – but in terms of gods and goddesses who could enter our world and take on at will human form or the form of the animals that symbolized the powers they represented. It's fashionable to pity these poor primitives with their heads full of fairy tales, and denied the benefits of modern science! And yet, which culture is nearer the truth? One that speaks of a Lowerworld and an Upperworld, and that gives us techniques to discover them and symbolic maps to help us find our way around within them; a culture that personalizes into gods and goddesses the forces found in these worlds so that, since their humanity represents our humanity, we can recognize aspects of ourselves in them and thus better understand and come to terms with these aspects? Or a culture that uses a barren term like the unconscious to cover these mysterious worlds, and that replaces the gods and goddesses with labels shorn of direct meaning, like 'drives' (instincts) and 'complexes'?

The question can't be answered by scientific truth. We must resort instead to poetic truth. Which means asking which set of cultural ideas moves us more when it comes to understanding ourselves? Which set of ideas more inspires us to explore our own minds? Which set gives us clearer directions for this exploration, and a clearer belief that it will lead us towards psychological wholeness and spiritual growth? A great psychologist like Jung was in no doubt of the answer (see, for example, his *Selected Writings*), and I share his certainty.

## SHAMANISM AND NATURE

The fourth reason given on page 99 why a knowledge of shamanism is of value to the meditator is that it teaches a relationship with the natural world based upon the realization that we are part of, not separate from, this world. A realization that it is this world that bears and sustains us, and is in a sense our mother, giving us what we need, renewing itself (if we let it) from its own horn of plenty. In Chapter 2 I talked about the four elements recognized by the ancients, earth, air, fire and water, and said that literally we are made from them. With the addition of the fifth element, ether (spirit), we are they and they are us. We are created physically from them and carry them inside us as gifts from the earth during our physical lives. At death, in gratitude, we return them to the earth, while the fifth element goes on to take another form in another place and another time.

Shamanism teaches that if we listen to our bodies, they carry the wisdom of the elements, the wisdom that gives us a love for natural things; for the beauties of lake and sky and forest, for the clouds piled high on the horizon, for the clear faces of the sun and the moon, for the whisper of the wind, for the rain, for wooded valleys and far mountains, for the joy of the river's song, for the beauty of blossom and flowers, for the sense of rightness, of belonging that sweeps over us when we stop what we are doing and look and listen and sense nature around and within us.

It is sad that only as children are we fully in touch with this wisdom. We begin to lose it at puberty, which is one reason why the Tibetan monk, the shaman and the sorcerer's apprentice all traditionally begin their training before adolescence, when they are still open to the wonders of being alive, and when their emotional energies are still at their height. Having lost contact with this wisdom, we have laboriously to relearn it later on, through practices like meditation. And it is sad too that only as children are we in touch with the wisdom of the fifth element, the spirit inside us, the wisdom that knows who we really are if we only take heed. The wisdom which also has to be relearned in adulthood by treading the path of meditation.

But the shaman never loses contact in this way. He or she lives and grows with natural wisdom, and walks always in a different reality from the rest of us. A reality to which, if in adult life we find our way back to it, we respond only with, 'Ah yes, of course; how foolish of me to forget'.

Filled with this wisdom, the shaman has always loved and understood nature and has scorned to inflict on it the senseless violence which, through our greed, we have made a callous habit. When you experience the empty, echoing, overwhelming space of the American plains you catch whispers of how the North American shaman understood the vastness of physical reality and the corresponding vastness of his or her own mind. And when you take part in the shaman's rituals you catch hints of how he or she so sharpened the concentration that outer and inner realities became one.

Once, huddled in a teepee during the American Indian sweat lodge ceremony, and joined in humble nakedness with a group of like-minded men and women, I understood how the shaman conveyed this wisdom to the rest of the tribe. He or she did it by bringing them to confront the elements and thus remember their own nature. With the ground under the bare skin, and the searing heat filling the lungs with fire and wringing the last drops of moisture from the body, one is stripped of everything except elemental being. Even the fear, born of that dark claustrophobic space and the unimaginable choking heat, evaporates. And afterwards, when the series of long stays in the sweat lodge is over and one lies submerged in the waters of a nearby river (the 'long man' of Indian tradition), there is nothing left but the sense of being one with everything, of dissolving separateness and of knowing oneself to be back in that place which in reality we none of us ever leave.

## MEDITATION ON THE ELEMENTS

In the sweat lodge, the elements are confronted directly, face-to-face. The element of fire from the scorching heat; the element of water from the scalding steam that rises as the shaman dampens the red-hot stones in the centre of the circle; the element of air from the burning in the lungs; and the element of earth from the ground beneath. There are no concepts *about* the elements, only experience of them, and then suddenly confrontation falls away and the elements outside and inside the body flow and merge with each other. Whether one wills it or not, thoughts also fall away, and everything comes together in the one-pointedness of an intense yet open and relaxed meditation.

But there are other, less dramatic ways of bringing the elements into meditation. In the shamanic tradition, the shaman sits with nature, poised in stillness with every sense focused upon a tree, or upon the sound of the wind or a river or a waterfall. He or she stares long into the leaping flames of a fire, lies on the ground until the body pressing against the earth becomes one with it, watches the soaring flight of a bird until the mind soars on the same wings, and studies intently the ways of wild animals in the forest until he or she sees and senses the world as they do.

Meditating upon nature in this way brings you relatively quickly to a sense of unity with the life and the energies around you. Sit in meditation in a place outdoors which seems right to you, focus upon the breathing until you enter the meditative state, then transfer your concentration to tree, wind, water, earth or whatever you please. Don't choose more than one focus of concentration at once; the mind, as always, must be one-pointed. Don't allow it to become distracted by other stimuli, however attractive or potentially helpful. And don't allow concepts *about* the tree or the wind or the water to intrude. Focus with a clear and open mind upon your awareness of the object of meditation. If it is visual, keep your eyes open as long as possible, blinking only when they become sore, and sit where you can see the whole of the object, so that there is no temptation to move your head or eyes to scan it.

If the object of meditation is auditory close your eyes and, again without allowing concepts to intrude, place your awareness upon hearing. Don't ask anything of it. Don't expect anything. Just listen. Similarly, if you are meditating upon the feel of the ground under you, don't start pondering whether it feels hard or soft, warm or cool. Concentrate upon the physical sensation. Feel it, and do not stray from that feeling.

Once you have developed this way of meditating, you can widen your concentration until it embraces both sight and sound at once, but do not hurry to do this. And do not allow your concentration to flick back and forth from one to the other. With practice, you will find that the mind is able to remain in the space filled by both, and you will come to know that this space is the mind itself, the space that unites outer and inner in an eternal unified game.

## MEDITATING ON THE INNER ELEMENTS

There are also techniques for meditating upon the elements within the body. These are more difficult, since the starting point is the creative imagination rather than the outer world, but they are equally rewarding. Choose one of the elements – astrologers say start with the element of your sun sign – and imagine you can feel it in your body.

Let us assume you start with water. Once your meditation is stabilized by focusing on the breath, switch your attention to the liquid element in your body. Imagine you can sense the blood flowing through your arteries and veins. Don't concentrate upon a throbbing pulse somewhere (that would be meditation upon a throbbing pulse) but imagine you are experiencing the actual sensation of movement. Start with the feet and hold the awareness there. Next move to the calves, then to the knees, then to the thighs, and so on upwards. Don't allow the awareness to *travel* through the body, as if flowing with the blood. This disperses the concentration and leads to inner questions such as, 'How fast is the blood travelling?'. Instead, concentrate at fixed points, and imagine the sensation of the blood flowing past.

Eventually you will feel a tingling at the points where your concentration rests, and once you have moved around the whole body, ending with the crown of the head, you will feel this tingling suffusing you in a pleasant sensation of vibrant, flowing energy. Don't concern yourself whether this is still your imagination or whether you are now experiencing something objective. The vital thing is that you are experiencing it, that it gives the body a sense of health and well-being, and that after regular practice with this meditation you will feel, both in and out of meditation, that you have something of the liquid grace of water itself. You will notice also that you gain a new affinity for water in all its forms, a fellow feeling for it, as if by sensing it inside yourself you have come to know it as a life companion, a generous brother or sister.

Similar meditations can be carried out with fire, earth and air. When working with fire, follow the same procedure as with water, feeling the warmth in your feet, legs, and so on. Don't *make* yourself hot by putting on thick clothes. Even if your feet, for example, initially feel cold, don't try and warm them. They *are* warm already. The blood inside them is at the same temperature as the blood in the rest of your body. If it were as cold as the outside air, your feet would literally be dead. So stay with a sense of warmth. Don't expect this immediately to warm the feet. This is not the point of the exercise (though it is a welcome side effect in due time). The point is to imagine the warmth inside the feet, the warm blood, the warm tissues. Don't be distracted by sensations of cold on the surface of the feet. Place the imagination inside the feet, and then allow the imagined warmth to spread out slowly from there.

When meditating upon air, start with the lungs. Don't focus on the sensation of the lungs expanding and contracting. Instead, imagine you can feel the air inside the lungs, then imagine this air being carried by the blood to every part of the body. The technique at this point is the same as for water, in that you station the awareness at chosen parts of the body and imagine the air (the oxygen) in the blood flowing past. Imagine it in whatever way appeals to you; as white light, as a gentle current, even as a stream of bubbles.

The important thing is that whatever you are imagining should contain the idea not of fluidity as with water but of lightness, a lifting quality that allows the body itself to feel light and free, purified of the burdens that have been holding it down.

When meditating on earth, imagine the solidity of the body, starting again with the feet. Imagine it as strength, or as power, whichever you prefer. But again don't be tempted to try and feel these things directly (for example, by tensing the muscles). Imagine it from inside, the weight of the body held safe by the pull of gravity, the strength in the muscles and sinews which move the body in response to the commands of the mind, the power of the body which shifts and manipulates physical objects.

As with water, meditations on fire, air and earth bring with them a different relationship to your body and to the environment. You feel the sustaining warmth in your body and the relationship of this warmth with the warmth around you. You feel the lightness of air flowing into you and lifting you; you feel the grounding solidity of your weight and strength. And with each element you feel your kinship with the humans and animals and plants that share it with you.

## WESTERN SHAMANISM

Much has been written about the pagan cults of Europe, and attempts made (with some success) to link them to the shamanic thinking carried westwards by migrating peoples from central Siberia. The best entry into the ways of thinking associated with this Western shamanism is not, however, through the literature on paganism. Instead, it is through the work of that strange, mystical, universal genius Rudolph Steiner, whose ideas have never received the full attention they deserve.

Steiner himself was partly to blame for this neglect, for frequently he makes difficult and obscure reading, and some of the commentaries on his work haven't made things easier. But his *Knowledge of the Higher Worlds: How is it Achieved?*

provides a short, straightforward and invaluable introduction to that part of his thinking which can be called shamanic. Steiner's knowledge and practice were both encyclopaedic and extended way beyond shamanism, and to my knowledge he makes no extended reference to it by name. Yet his meditation techniques are in places charged with a shamanism that arose from his intense nature mysticism and awareness of inner realities, both based on direct experience.

Steiner has another important link with the concerns of this book in that he placed great emphasis upon gnosis, upon the direct knowledge of God discussed in Chapter 5. For example, in *Knowledge of the Higher Worlds*, he writes that:

> Whoever rises through meditation to the point where human nature is united to the spirit begins to kindle to life that which is eternal in him, that which is not confined within the boundaries of life and death. The existence of this eternal reality can be doubted only by those who have not experienced it. Thus meditation is also the way which leads man to the eternal, indestructible core of his being. And only through meditation can this vision come to man.
>
> *Knowledge of the Higher Worlds*, p. 43

A few lines later, Steiner assures us that, 'In true meditation the path opens ... in all of us lie the faculties that can help us to recognize and contemplate for ourselves what genuine mysticism ... and gnosis teach'. And it is in his descriptions of 'true meditation' that Steiner gives evidence of his shamanistic understanding, for he speaks of meditating upon objects in the world around so that you become aware of their essential natures. In the course of such intensive meditation upon individual objects we become aware in due course, says Steiner, of feelings arising within us specific to the class of objects concerned. These feelings represent the intuitive awareness and reverence of the shaman for the created world. Such awareness and reverence differ in response to the mineral, vegetable and animal kingdoms, but in each case represent the faculty of seeing with what Steiner calls 'spiritual eyes'.

Later, Steiner recommends that the meditator focus his or her attention on a seed (I use a plum stone). Having become minutely aware of the shape, colour and texture of the seed, the meditator allows the thought to arise that from this seed a plant will grow.

A visualization of this plant is then built up by the creative imagination, and the thought allowed to arise that if one were meditating upon an imitation of the seed, its outer appearance would be the same but it would lack the power to produce the plant. The real seed therefore has 'secretly enfolded within it the *force* of the whole plant ... The real seed therefore contains something invisible, which is not present in the imitation'.

The meditator now directs attention to this invisible force, holding firmly to the thought that 'the invisible will become visible'. Such a thought, says Steiner, must be intensely *felt*, 'must be *experienced* with no disturbing intrusions from other thoughts ... And sufficient time must be allowed for the thought and feeling united with it to penetrate to the soul'. By meditating in this way, the meditator gradually becomes aware of an 'inner force ... (which will) create a new power of perception'. The seed may then be seen

> as if enveloped in a small luminous cloud ... Something formerly not seen is here revealed, created by the power of the thoughts and feelings that have been inwardly stirred into activity. The plant itself, which will become physically visible only later on, now manifests in a spiritually visible way.

Steiner emphasizes that this form of meditation has been:

> tested and practised since time immemorial ... Anyone attempting to turn to exercises which he has himself devised, or of which he has heard or read somewhere or other, will inevitably go astray and find himself on the path of boundless fantasy.

This is important, because meditations such as that described by Steiner raise again the issue of whether one is simply carrying out autosuggestion or whether one is experiencing something that has objective reality. My main examination of this issue comes later in Chapter 9, but Steiner warns the meditator against 'boundless fantasy', and stresses that 'the healthy reason which distinguishes truth from illusion must be continually cultivated'. During meditative exercises, the individual must

> practise the same reliable thinking that he applies to the details of everyday life ... it would be the greatest mistake if as the result of such exercises the pupil were to lose his mental balance; if he were to be drawn away from judging the affairs of his daily life as clearly and soundly as before.

In other words, the meditator must know exactly what he or she is doing. When visualizing in meditation, one is visualizing in meditation. When dealing with the objects and events of daily life, one is dealing with the objects and events of daily life. Such a warning is vital for all meditators, whatever the system of meditation being followed. But it is particularly important when working with visualization, whether as described by Steiner or as detailed by St Ignatius in *The Spiritual Exercises*. The meditator who uses visualization must recognize that life operates under several different sets of rules, none of which necessarily represents reality, but each of which represents a *model of reality in particular contexts and at particular times*.

The good scientist says much the same. He or she knows that when working at the subatomic level, it is incorrect to treat a brick as if it were a solid object. A brick, like everything else, is at the subatomic level almost entirely empty space. However, once outside the physics laboratory and back in the world of ordinary reality, the scientist knows a brick should be treated as a solid object, and that if anyone throws it at you the sensible thing to do is duck.

Similarly, when we use visualization in meditation (or whenever we exercise imagination), a different set of rules operates from those of everyday life. To the imagination, the object visualized seems real (in fact, it is important the meditator regards it *as if* it is real if success is to come). The thing being visualized is there, existing clearly and with apparent objectivity in the mind's eye. Of that there is no doubt. It is an object registered by the brain in much the same way that the brain registers an external object perceived by the senses. It thus has its own kind of reality. But we shouldn't assume it obeys the same laws as external objects, and continues to exist even when we are not imagining it.

However, since Steiner refers to a life force within the seed which manifests itself 'in a spiritually visible way', he is raising an issue additional to that of visualization. Namely, can we, through meditation, develop the ability to 'see' things which are objectively there in the outside world, but which are invisible to the physical senses and to the instruments developed by science? What would that mean in the case of the seed which Steiner proposes as the object of meditation?

If we are simply imagining the life force in the seed, then we would see exactly the same 'life force' if, unbeknown to us, someone substituted the imitation for the real seed. However, if the life force is objectively there, then we would recognize the difference between the two seeds. There are thus these two possibilities, and it is disappointing that, to the best of my knowledge, no-one has set up a controlled experiment with meditators trained in the Steiner tradition to see which is correct.

But there is a third possibility; namely, that a creative interaction of some kind takes place between the mind of the meditator (the meditator's life force if you will) and the life force in the seed. And that it is this creative interaction that produces the 'small luminous cloud' described by Steiner. This idea need not sound too far-fetched even to the most materialistically minded scientist. Think, for example, of how when a man falls in love, the woman of his fancy can become transformed for him into the most beautiful woman in the world. Her beauty in his eyes comes from the interaction between her presence and his love for her. To other people, she may appear as a woman much like any other.

If this third possibility is true, then two meditators both trained in the Steiner – or in the shamanic – tradition would both see the luminous cloud surrounding the seed, though the details of what they see would differ somewhat in accordance with the differences between their two minds. Both meditators would be able to distinguish between the real and the imitation seeds, though their descriptions of what they saw would differ more than would two descriptions of a concrete physical phenomenon.

For the moment, we must leave it there. But for those who practise shamanic meditation of the kind Steiner describes, the answer to the question of which of these three possibilities is nearer the truth is most likely to be found by working with a partner meditating in the same way. When both the partners are sufficiently advanced in the practice, they can compare notes and see what both have discovered. Whatever the results, the experiment will prove illuminating.

# 7

# Visualization: A Key to the Inner World

Both flowing meditation and objective meditation make particular use of visualization, an ability that modern Western psychology is only now coming to recognize can play a vital role in our inner lives. The work of authorities such as Herbert Benson (*The Relaxation Response*) has shown, for example, the role of visualization in producing relaxation and combating psychological and physical stress and the medical conditions associated with it. And specialists like Carl and Stephanie Simonton (*Getting Well Again*) have indicated the contribution visualization may make to healing the body even of serious physical conditions such as cancer, ulcers and arthritis.

The point is that visualization, when properly trained, is an enormously powerful tool for human growth and development across a wide (perhaps the whole) range of psychological and physical functions. The mind–body links have now been so clearly demonstrated within both psychology and medicine that few who have studied the subject doubt that the mind is responsible not only for psychological problems but for many physical ones as well. 'As we think so we are' is not far from the truth. And of all the activities of the mind, visual thinking – visualization – is among the most potent.

## WHY IS VISUALIZATION SO EFFECTIVE?

The immediate question is, why should this be so? What is it about visualization that gives it this potential for influencing the way things are? The answer is that it invokes the mind's creative power, that mental dynamo that produces not only great works of art, music and literature but also great works of science and technology. Everything men and women create in the world out there has its origins in the world in here. If we can visualize something, imagine it in our inner world *as if* it is happening in the outer world, then we have begun the process that may lead to bringing it about.

A clear example of this is the way we can use visualization in psychotherapy and psychological counselling. If, for instance, I am trying to help someone who is shy when speaking in public, or highly nervous about a forthcoming examination, I will put them into a relaxed state using techniques such as those detailed in Box 10, and then invite them to visualize, in as much detail as possible, an actual occasion which arouses the unwanted emotion. The next step is to prompt them to visualize themselves as operating effectively on that occasion and maintaining their mental and physical relaxation. Several repetitions of this exercise, over a period of days or weeks, leads to a marked decrease in the emotion concerned and a marked increase in positive states of mind. When stressful real life situations actually present themselves, the person copes with them much more calmly and effectively.

---

**BOX 10**
**RELAXATION MEDITATION**

All meditation, with the possible exception initially of koan meditation (Chapter 8), has a relaxing effect upon mind and body. Research shows it can produce deeper states of relaxation even than sleeping itself. Many meditators find that once their practice is established, they need less sleep and feel much more alert and wide awake during the day.

But if you are particularly tense for some reason, the meditation techniques covered in this book can be adapted for the specific purpose of relaxation. For example, you can use the techniques of objective meditation to visualize relaxing and calming energy streaming from your spiritual teacher to you. Or

**BOX 10**
RELAXATION MEDITATION

you can focus on the breathing as in vipassana and feel yourself drawing in calming energy on each in-breath and exhaling tension on each out-breath, or filling the body with white light on the in-breath and expelling grey light on the out-breath.

But one of the most effective forms of relaxation comes from flowing meditation, as follows:

- Lie flat on the floor or on the bed. Close your eyes and focus upon the breathing. Once concentration is established, allow awareness to sweep the body, from the toes upwards, checking for centres of tension. When you find them, say 'let go' silently, and feel the muscles relax.

- Now imagine yourself lying in long grass or on a sandy beach, whichever you prefer. Strengthen the imagination by feeling the grass or sand under you. Listen to the waves, or the birds. Hear the sigh of the wind. See the blue sky, like infinity, above you.

- On each out-breath, repeat 'floating at peace'. With each repetition feel the body becoming lighter and lighter, so that soon it is so light that you seem to float up into the blueness above you.

- Experience immeasurable peace, as if you are dissolving into space so that you become one with the sky, flowing onwards and outwards beyond time, beyond distance, into a state where there is only peace.

- When you feel ready, gradually experience yourself returning into your finite floating self, bringing with you in every fibre of mind and body the relaxation just experienced.

- Now gently drift down until you are once more lying on the grass or the sand. Then feel this surface gradually changing into the comforting solidity of the floor or bed. Finally, tell yourself to open your eyes and be back in your own room.

- Open your eyes, and stay for a few minutes in this relaxed position.

Another example of the use of visualization occurs in the Alexander Technique, that re-education in bodily use that brings so many benefits (see, for example, Wilfred Barlow's *The Alexander Technique*). Having manually adjusted the client's faulty posture and physical movement, the Alexander teacher instructs him or her from now on consciously and frequently to direct the body to follow the corrected pattern of bodily use. Thus, at its simplest, a client who has been slumping badly may remind him or herself to 'think up'. No heroic attempt is made to hold the body in the correct position. The mind gives the instruction, and little by little the body absorbs the message. The process of absorption is greatly speeded up if assisted by visualization. The client silently repeats the direction 'think up', and at the same time visualizes him or herself standing or moving in the correct way. From within, the client is visually identifying the physical space that the body should occupy and the body, over time, moves into this space.

Another example is the way an artist will visualize the effect he or she wishes to capture on canvas, or an architect visualize the outlines of a completed building, or an inventor a piece of functional machinery. The creation is first of all seen with the mind's eye, and then translated into concrete reality. There is nothing 'unscientific' about this. It is simply how the creative mind, for many people, actually works. We don't know the precise psychological processes involved, or where this marvellous gift of imagination (non-visual as well as visual) comes from. But we know that it exists, and that it is responsible for the greater part of the changes, good and bad, that men and women have wrought in their environment.

## EVERYONE CAN VISUALIZE

You may say this is all very well, but that you personally can't visualize. You close your eyes but fail to summon up a clear picture of even the most familiar object, such as your car or your kitchen or your favourite picture. The visualization is vague and ill-formed and instead of staying at the centre of awareness, slides maddeningly away to one side or the other. No, you conclude, visualization is beyond your reach.

The response is that you can in fact visualize very successfully indeed. The fact that you recognize your car, your kitchen or your favourite picture the moment you set eyes on it shows you carry very accurate visual images of these things in your memory. Your problem is not an inability to *visualize*, but an inability to do so *consciously*. A further example of your powers of visualization is provided by your dreams. In dreams the conscious mind sleeps and the unconscious takes over, building such lifelike visual images that mostly we aren't even aware we are dreaming and imagine we are participating in real events. And before you protest that you never dream, let me say that even the most inveterate 'non-dreamers' report vivid and detailed dreams if awakened in sleep laboratories when changes in brain activity show that dreams are taking place. We all of us, such research suggests, have five or so quite lengthy episodes of dreaming each night. The only problem is that some of us fail to remember even fragments of these episodes – though the situation can be remedied with training of the kind that I described in my book *Dreamlife: Understanding and Using Your Dreams*.

Both the sorcerer's apprentice in Western occult traditions and the novice monk or nun in Tibetan Buddhist training were required to develop their conscious powers of visualization. Such powers were seen as essential requisites for progress on both the magical and the spiritual paths. Through visualization, the acolyte started the process of psychological and spiritual training that led towards adepthood and inner transformation. And for today's meditator, the same principle holds good.

## TECHNIQUES OF VISUALIZATION

As already indicated, the guidance in visualization given by St Ignatius in *The Spiritual Exercises* is still amongst the best available. In the summary form in which it appears in Chapter 5, it bears reading and rereading, and then putting into practice in whatever modified form you feel appropriate.

But excellent guidelines are also given elsewhere. Kathleen McDonald in her introduction to Buddhist meditation, *How to Meditate*, stresses that before visualization the mind must be put into the correct state – relaxed, clear and open. Too much effort leads to tension, which inhibits results. At the same time, however, the mind must be concentrated, just as in all forms of meditation. My own guidance to people is that they should start by focusing upon the breathing, and only when mind and body have calmed and concentration is established should visualization be attempted.

Kathleen McDonald also warns the meditator not to try and

visualize *with the eyes*. The visualized image should appear within the mind, in its own space. My own advice is to focus on the point between and just above the eyes, the so-called 'third eye' in Eastern and occult traditions. Concentrate lightly but firmly, redirecting the attention once the meditation is established from the breathing to the site of this 'third eye'. Don't strain. Imagine you are looking at this point from some little distance further back (that is, from inside your head).

Register at first simply the darkness you 'see' there. Allow yourself to feel comfortable with this darkness. It is objectively there, a fact of experience. Register its quality. Is it black or do you have some impression of colour, however faint? What is the quality of the darkness or of the colour – for example, is it hard or soft? Notice how still this visualized space is.

You need do no more than this during the first visualization session and the ones that follow. Use this darkness as the focus of your meditation, and continue to do so until you feel it has 'stabilized', that is, until your mind is not constantly distracted from it or your concentration constantly straying to your closed eyes. We are so orientated towards the sense of sight that we find it difficult to escape the idea that visualization must somehow be done with the physical eyes.

When your concentration is reasonably well stabilized upon the 'third eye', whether in the first visualization session or in subsequent ones, allow an image to appear there. Start with a simple geometrical shape. An open white triangle is usually best. Allow this triangle to appear. Don't expect it to be sharp and clear, or to stay firmly fixed in the imagination. *Don't struggle to make it something it is not.* It may only be a vague shape, and may even appear to be more the *idea* of a triangle than an actual triangle itself. So be it. This is perfectly acceptable to begin with.

Use this triangle for several meditation sessions. Don't be impatient at any lack of progress. Even if your powers of visualization don't appear to be developing very quickly, you are in fact gaining excellent training both in visualization and in concentration. Instead of focusing upon the breathing, you are now focusing on something much more subtle, located in inner space, and the value of this for the development of meditative concentration is incalculable.

However, should you consider more help is needed, draw an equilateral triangle with a white marker on a sheet of black paper, making each side 3 inches (7.5 cm) long. If these materials aren't to hand, a dark triangle on a white background will do. Fix the sheet of paper to a blank wall 3 to 4 feet (1 metre to 1.3 metres) away, making sure it's at eye level when you're on your meditation cushion or chair. Then sit and focus upon it, only blinking when the eyes become uncomfortable.

You will notice a curious thing. The mind keeps wanting to pull away from the image. Having inspected it, the mind becomes bored and wants something else to stimulate it. Resist the temptation either to move the eyes away or to start scanning the triangle in the way the mind habitually does when looking at an object. This is why it's important not to make the triangle too big. The mind must be able to take it all in at one go, without shifting the point of gaze. If you find this particularly difficult even with a small triangle, place a dot in the middle of it and keep that at the centre of focus.

Having gazed at the triangle for at least a minute, close your eyes as if you are taking a snapshot of it, and try to keep the image clear in your mind. If and when it begins to fade, open your eyes and gaze at it again, then close them once more and attempt to hold on to the mental image. It may take you several sessions before you can do this effectively, but with practice improvement will come. The ability to visualize is already there, as I pointed out earlier. All you need is the practice to bring it into conscious awareness.

## VISUALIZING IN COLOUR

If you've had no need to draw a picture of a triangle, but have concentrated from the start upon pure visualization, you will soon feel ready to introduce colour. I recommend using green, which is neutral and has a grounding quality. Imagine a green triangle on a white background. Keep the triangle open – three green lines against a white space. Work with it, over several sessions if necessary, until it is stabilized at the 'third eye' point in your mind, then convert it into a solid green one. Now keep switching between solid and open triangles. Coordinate this switching with the breathing, so that on the in-breath the triangle is solid, and on the out-breath it becomes open.

The next step is to proceed to other geometrical shapes and other colours. Use an open circle first, then go on to a solid green circle on the in-breath and an open green circle on the out-breath. Next repeat the process with a blue triangle and then with a blue circle. Follow this with a square, a cross, and a five-pointed star, working each time with open and closed shapes. Now use other colours with each of the shapes; red, orange, yellow.

At first it is best to use one shape and one colour during each meditation session, but once you are sufficiently well on with the practice, switch from one shape to another and from one colour to another during the same session. However (and this is very important) decide on what form this switching will take *before* you go into meditation. Don't try to think what to do while the session is actually in progress. Decide, for example, on a sequence of triangle, circle, square and star, all in green, then the same sequence in blue, then in red, then in orange and then in yellow. Decide also at what point you are going to switch from one shape to the next. Use the breath to help you. Decide to switch after every ten in- and out-breaths for example. With practice, progress to switching on each out-breath, or to using each in- and out-breath to go from solid to open shapes.

The next step is to use combinations of shapes. Once more, decide on this combination before the meditation starts. Go from a triangle inside a circle to a circle inside a triangle. Then place both of them inside a square, and so on. Use other shapes as well. Israel Regardie, in *The Tree of Life*, recommends use of the *tattvas*, the Hindu symbols for the elements. These are five in number and are combined to give thirty elements and sub-elements. The five consist of a yellow square (*prithivi* – earth), a horizontal silver crescent (*apas* – water), a red equilateral triangle (*tejas* – fire), a blue circle (*vayu* – air) and a black oval (*akasa* – ether). All five symbols are visualized as solid forms and can be combined with each other in any way which the meditator chooses; a red triangle superimposed on a blue circle, for example; a yellow square on a red triangle; a black oval on a silver crescent, and so on. (Don't change the colours, by the way; keep each colour identified with its own specific shape.)

## WHY USE GEOMETRICAL SHAPES?

The advantages of using geometrical shapes when training in visualization are twofold. Firstly they are clear and simple. Secondly, and more compellingly, they carry symbolic meanings, as evidenced by the extent to which the great religions of the world have made use of them, from the cross of the Christians to the wheel of the Buddhists (see J. C. Cooper's *An Illustrated Encyclopaedia of Traditional Symbols* for a thorough examination of the religious meaning of the major symbols, or see my own discussion in *The Elements of Meditation*). As stated in Chapter 2, the cross, the circle, the square and the triangle are archetypal shapes, with a particular appeal to the unconscious because, like all archetypes, we appear to inherit a special predisposition towards them. Psychologists have noted how these shapes make their spontaneous appearance as the first identifiable scribbles of very young children, and by virtue of their innate presence in our unconscious, they have a special ability to act as keys to the mental powers which it possesses.

Depending upon the individual, it can take as little as two or three weeks or as much as five or six months of regular practice before the visualization of these shapes in all their various colours and combinations becomes fully established. The golden rules are daily practice and a large measure of patience. Impatience impedes progress in all aspects of meditation. Remind yourself frequently that the more impatient you are, the longer it is going to take, and the more patience you are ultimately going to need.

## PICTORIAL VISUALIZATION

When you can visualize geometrical shapes with clarity and can stabilize your visualization for a minimum of fifteen minutes, move on to pictorial visualization – the visualization of objects, people and places. Start with familiar objects, the simpler the better (a vase, a chair, a garden tool, a lighted candle), and make sure they do not arouse strong emotions or associations which get in the way of concentration. Once you are successful with these, proceed to more complex objects. In all cases, allow the

**BOX 11**
**YANTRAS AND MANDALAS**

The symbolic power of geometrical shapes is seen particularly in the *yantra*, a design employing typically an outer circle (or sometimes a square) with inner squares, triangles and lotus petals. Such yantras represent in a visual form the concentrations of energy (the visual equivalent of the *mantra*, discussed in Chapter 10) which go to make up the cosmos. Transpersonal in meaning, they symbolize ultimate truth, formlessness emerging into forms.

In meditation, yantras also focus the meditator's energies, not only by acting as a point of concentration but also by operating upon the unconscious through the symbolic meaning of the shapes they contain. The meditator gazes initially at the yantra, with eyes held open as long as is comfortable, but once it can be visualized in all its intricate details it is summoned as a mental image within the inner world.

There is no clear distinction between a yantra and a *mandala*, but the latter term is usually used for designs that incorporate physical forms as well as geometrical shapes. These can be of a general kind, like the Buddhist wheel of life which depicts the various realms that animate beings are said to inhibit, or they can be specific to a certain spiritual being. In the latter case, they are used as a way of invoking the being concerned (that is, awakening in oneself the spiritual quality which he or she represents), often in conjunction with the repetition of his or her mantra.

Jung took the view that mandalas and yantras arise spontaneously from the human unconscious, and thus are innate symbolic ways of representing psychospiritual truths. In his therapeutic work, he found that at certain stages in the journey towards healing, his patients would often dream a mandala or yantra, which he would then encourage them to draw. By meditating upon this personal representation of the inner world, the patient would be further helped towards wholeness.

When using a mandala or a yantra in meditation, it is important – unless initiated into its precise use – not to attach conscious meaning to it. Simply place it at the centre of concentration and allow it to communicate directly with the unconscious. Later, during the meditation or spontaneously when the mind is working on other things, sudden insights into its 'meaning' may emerge into consciousness. But there is a sense in which these insights are of less importance than the transformation taking place at an unconscious level, a transformation which manifests itself in a greater sense of inner harmony and wholeness, followed by a growing awareness of spiritual development.

visualization first to form in its entirety, and then concentrate upon clarifying specific details of it. Look closely at shape and size. Investigate colours and proportions.

If, for example, you have progressed to a complex object such as your car, decide on the angle from which you are going to see it, and then try and bring to mind the exact proportions, the exact shape of the windows and wheels, the exact position of the door handles, the exact shade of colour. Next, change the angle of focus. Look at the car now from the front, taking in all the details with the same care. Now go round to the back, and afterwards to the other side. Don't rack your brains for details which you can't clarify from your visualization. Work with the visualization itself; see what is actually there. Don't rationalize. If a detail refuses to clarify itself, leave it and go on to another one. Afterwards, when the meditation is over, go and look at the car and check *visually* for the detail or details that were unclear. Look at them long enough to commit them to the visual memory. Don't use words. Take several 'snap-shots' by concentrating closely and then shutting the eyes and holding the image there mentally.

If difficulties of memory continue to be a problem, visualize an object physically present in the room. A lighted candle is particularly effective. When the need arises, open your eyes and focus on it, keeping this as part of the meditation in that you apply the same concentration to the actual object as you did to the visualization. After a moment, close your eyes and reproduce it again in your imagination.

## VISUALIZING PEOPLE

Once you can work well with familiar objects, go on to imaginary ones. An imaginary car, an imaginary flower, an imaginary pair of shoes. When you are reasonably happy with this work, go on to people. Again, avoid the distracting effect of strong emotions or associations. Choose an acquaintance or a casual friend rather than someone to whom you feel very close or for whom you feel strong antagonism (these can be used in connection with loving compassion meditation, as discussed in Chapter 5).

Again start with the general picture, and then look for details – the colour of the eyes, the shape of the face, the hairstyle, the curve of the lips. Don't attempt to take in the whole body. The face is enough at first. Next, as with objects, go from the real to the imaginary. Decide before the meditation begins on the *quality* you want the imaginary person to represent. Choose a positive quality – love, comradeship, trust, humour, strength, wisdom, purity, innocence, courage – then focus upon the quality once the meditation is established and allow a face that symbolizes it to form.

At this point, notice the creative power of the mind. If you have worked through each of the visualization exercises I've given, mastering one before going on to the next, you will find that, as in dreams, the mind creates the face for you without conscious effort on your part. And as in dreams, you will meet with surprises. Wisdom, for example, may not be represented by an old man or woman, but by a young child. Purity may be represented not by a nun or monk but by a nude figure. Sometimes an animal will appear rather than a human. Sometimes the faces will have a mythical quality reminiscent of the symbols used in the representations of the Egyptian gods. Don't concern yourself with whether these images come from your own memories or whether they represent some universal symbol-making quality of the human unconscious. Simply note them, and focus upon clarifying all the details associated with them.

Should a frightening image emerge even though you are concentrating upon a positive quality, don't be alarmed. In many of the symbolic languages of the world, the important qualities (or forces) in the human mind are symbolized in two ways, benign and wrathful. Thus purity could be symbolized by a Vestal Virgin or by the fire that consumes the corruption that stands in the way of purity. However, if an image particularly disturbs you, banish it by enclosing it in a white circle, then allowing the circle to get smaller until it shrinks into a dot. Then allow the dot to disappear and visualize a cross (or whatever symbol you prefer) in its place, in whatever colour seems best. Stay with this visualization until you feel comfortable again. Provided you have worked carefully through the earlier visualization exercises using geometrical shapes, you will have no difficulty with this routine.

## VISUALIZING SCENERY

The final stage in visualization is one which many people mistakenly try right from the start; visualizing a scene. This is more difficult than one thinks, simply because it is hard to take in all the details of something so complex. You may succeed even in the early days of visualization practice in conjuring up an impression of a particular view, but this isn't good enough. For visualization to be effective, it must take in everything, or nearly everything. So leave the visualization of scenery until your practice is well established.

As with objects and people, start with a familar place. Perhaps a parade of shops that you know well. Take in the overall picture first, then look for the details. Read the names above the shops, seeing the writing as boldly as in real life. Look at the displays in the windows. If the scene spontaneously becomes a moving picture, allow it to do so and watch the people passing by and entering and leaving the shops. Focus on the colours, and try and see them sharply and clearly. Resist the tendency for the attention to rove over the scene. Instead, concentrate upon taking it in in its entirety, as you did with the geometrical shapes, then upon one of the shops, inspecting it minutely. Then move on to the next and the next and so on until you have been down the whole row.

Once you can work effectively with a familiar scene, create an imaginary one. Again decide *before* the meditation starts on the overall details of the scene – perhaps hills or mountains, a river, woodland or the seashore, perhaps an unknown city from the present, past or future. Decide on the scene, then allow it to develop of its own accord by focusing upon the idea of 'hills' or 'river' or 'seashore' or whatever once the meditation is established. If the scene refuses to come, don't try something else just yet. Focus instead on the empty inner space where, in its own time, the scene will appear – perhaps in this session, perhaps the next. If nothing has happened after three sessions, try a different scene. The original one may not have sufficiently stimulated your creative imagination, or deep down it may have long-forgotten painful associations for you which are blocking its entry into consciousness. Leave it for the present, and resolve to return to it at a later date. One day, in its own time, it will be there.

If, as is more likely, the intended scene does appear but unexpectedly changes into something else (mountains turn into the roofs of a city, a river becomes a lake or an ocean, as happens in dreams), allow the changes to happen and see where the meditation leads. You are now at the point where the creative imagination is well and truly established, and some exploration of it is of value for its own sake. But don't become carried away. You are not meditating just in order to embark on enchanting imaginary journeys. And make sure that even on the occasions when you do embark on them, you also work with a more grounded meditation practice (such as watching the breath, the bedrock practice), so that the concentration and self-discipline which you have done so much to establish do not begin to weaken.

## GROUNDING MEDITATION

In fact, whenever you are using visualizations in your meditation, it is advisable to use a grounded meditation in conjunction with them. If you are meditating twice a day, a good balance is to use a grounded practice in the morning and flowing meditation in the evening. If you are meditating once a day, spend three consecutive days on one practice, then switch to the other for the next three days. Even if you are using visualization in flowing meditation, don't use it exclusively, because all too easily one can become entranced by the scenes that present themselves – long, winding pathways disappearing into the hills, rivers and woodland of indescribable beauty, towering castles and cities perched high in the snows. All too easily the mind bcomes beguiled into following the visions, which ultimately is of no more value than becoming distracted by the free association of your thoughts. It certainly is not what visualization, as a meditation practice, is actually for.

## PUTTING VISUALIZATION TO USE

Which brings us to the question, what exactly *is* visualization for? I have spoken of its power in bringing about psychological change, but how precisely is this done? The answer is that it depends what kind of meditation you are using. Some of the uses of visualization can wait until objective meditation is discussed in Chapter 9, but visualization is an important feature of flowing meditation not only because it can set the scene in the way taught by St Ignatius in *The Spiritual Exercises*, but also because it can act as a visual adjunct to the inner voice. For example, when using the word 'Om' as the seed in flowing meditation, you can at the same time visualize the Sanskrit symbol for Om (see Figure 2). Lama Anagarika Govinda, in *Creative Meditation and Multidimensional Consciousness*, describes in great detail how shapes and their associated colours can be used in mantra meditation (Chapter 10), with the meditator visualizing the appropriate symbol as he or she recites each word of the mantra.

Using a visualized symbol along with the repetition of 'Om' (or whatever seed word you use) rapidly deepens the concentration, since the meditator is now focusing with both aural and visual imagination at the same time. But it is also said that both a sound like 'Om' and the visual shape associated with it are expressions of eternal creative forces – or of the archetypal powers of the unconscious – and thus that in and of themselves, if concentrated upon sufficiently intently and regularly, they have a special ability to take you into the inner world where we may all be linked to each other, to the history of our race, and to the spiritual forces recognized by the great religions.

But in flowing meditation visualization can also be used on its

Figure 2. *Om Symbol (Sanskrit)*

own as the point of focus. You can, for example, use the symbol for 'Om' instead of the sound. Or you can work with one of the images that has arisen in response to meditation on qualities like love or wisdom or peace. Or you can focus on a place which symbolizes these qualities for you — a temple or a clearing in the forest or towering mountains. This time, don't allow your visualization to take you away from this place; keep your concentration on the point of focus. Allow the meaning of the particular quality the place is symbolizing to arise. If the quality is love, what is love? If the quality is peace, what is peace? Don't pose these as questions. Allow them to arise of their own, bringing with them their own special insights.

## DISSOLVING YOUR VISUALIZATIONS

At the end of the meditation — and this applies to all meditations using visualization — dissolve the point of focus, with a feeling of gratitude towards it, back into the space from which it arose. Don't simply open your eyes and end the meditation. Failure to dissolve the object of your meditation may leave you attached to it, a prisoner of it, as Lama Govinda puts it, 'as a man possessed by his possessions'. No bad thing, you may say, since the visualization is symbolizing a positive quality. But you have to live in the real world, where the conscious mind must turn its attention to everyday matters. Meditation should be a way of sharpening this concentration, not of leaving you in a dreamy, otherworldly condition where you become less, not more, proficient at coping with the world out there. Your meditation will continue its work at an unconscious level even after you come out of it, rest assured. Gradually the quality upon which you have been meditating — its meaning in your own life — will manifest itself more and more within your nature, influencing your conscious behaviour by changing what you are, rather than by intruding between you and the things of daily life.

So be sure to carry out the dissolving routine by allowing the visualization to become fainter and fainter, until it disappears into emptiness. If this should prove difficult, use the strategy I mentioned earlier and enclose it in a circle, gently and lovingly allowing the circle to become smaller and smaller until it is the merest dot and then disappears altogether. Next, return to your grounded meditation practice. Bring the mind to the breathing or to your usual point of focus, and stay with this for at least ten out-breaths. Finally (this need not be done in great detail) visualize the familiar, safe friendly environment that will greet your eyes when you open them. Hold the visualization for another ten out-breaths, then open your eyes and be back in the present moment.

# 8

## Subjective Meditation: Knowing Your Own Mind

In introducing this chapter and the next, something must be said about the relationship between the two topics covered, *subjective* and *objective* meditation, the former sometimes referred to as 'self-power' and the latter as 'other power'. The difference between the two paths brings me back to the question raised in Chapter 1; namely, what in meditation is 'me' and what is 'not me'? For example, if the object of focus is God or the Buddha, are these beings immanent or transcendent, inside me or outside me? Or, to broaden the question, is the spiritual power which they represent inside creation or outside creation? Within Christianity, those who argue it is inside accuse those who say it is outside of making God in their own image, personalizing Him as an old man in the sky making decisions about people's lives as an employer makes decisions about his workforce. On the other hand, those who argue it is outside accuse those who say it is inside of impersonalizing God into a blind force that sustains life but neither knows nor cares anything about it.

Whichever side of the argument we choose to take, there is no doubt there are problems. If God is transcendent and outside creation, then He is neither infinite nor omnipotent, because if God's creation is separate from Him then He fashioned it from something other than Himself, which means there is a substance – call it matter – which is not part of God, just as the clay under the potter's hands is not part of the potter. The view that God is immanent in everything that exists avoids limiting Him in this way but raises difficulties of its own. Our minds cannot grasp the idea of the limitless God implied by immanence. Any statement we make about such a God inevitably cannot include everything, with the result that anything we say about Him is limiting and therefore necessarily wrong. (The Buddha was very wise in refusing to make statements about ultimate truth!)

The individual has to make up his or her own mind where they stand on transcendence and immanence, but like Jung, I take the view that when we move into this kind of debate, the test of 'truth' is usefulness. Any concept which helps our inner growth is 'true' until we progress to a point where something more useful is needed. By this token, the only 'true' concept of an unlimited God must hold Him to be both immanent *and* transcendent, as containing both the personal and the impersonal (with, at a level beyond our rational understanding, no difference between the two). An unlimited God is not *confined* to this immanence and transcendence, but as a symbol of limitless being, immanence plus transcendence will have to do. And so will a refusal to limit God to masculinity. Any symbol of limitlessness should contain femininity as well, God as both He and She, with, again at a level beyond rational understanding, no difference between the two.

In terms of this symbolic interpretation, God is both inside and outside, both immanent and transcendent, both masculine and feminine. And since, until we reach enlightenment, there is no doubt that *we* are very limited creatures, it is up to us to decide whether we want to relate to the immanent or to the transcendent aspect, the masculine or the feminine (or to all four). This is indeed one of the reasons why each race creates its own picture of the gods.

In talking about 'God' I may now be puzzling Buddhists, who do not recognize the idea of a supreme creator god in the way that Christianity and other theistic religions do. I may also be puzzling readers who, although concerned with inner growth, do not think about spirituality in terms of a 'God'. But all our human concepts, as I have just pointed out, are limited. 'God' is a way of referring to spiritual force, and used in this way I have not found that most Buddhists have difficulty with it.

D. T. Suzuki, one of the prime interpreters of Buddhism, uses
the term extensively. In any case, I hope that the similarities
between the ways in which the great traditions conceptualize
spirituality will become apparent as I go along. Many of the
seeming *dissimilarities* between these traditions have more to do
with the difficulty of putting spiritual realities into words than
with differences in actual spiritual experience.

## CONCEPTS OF GOD

When facing this difficulty, the Hindu way of talking about God
can be particularly helpful. It speaks of God in three different
ways. Firstly, there is God with both form and attributes. This
aspect is transcendent and is represented both by the symbols
men and women have devised for God and by the great spiritual
teachers. The next aspect is that of God without form but with
attributes, the immanent aspect symbolized by God as perfect
love, wisdom and power, and as dwelling within us as the
potential to express these attributes. The third aspect is that of
God without form or attributes, and this is the aspect beyond
both transcendence and immanence. This is the Godhead of the
Christian mystics, the Brahman of the Hindus, the Ain Soph of
the Hebrew Kabbalists, and the Nirvana of the Buddhists. The
God about whom nothing can be said, the God who must be
experienced rather than discussed, the God who is known only
by being known.

   None of these three aspects of God is necessarily 'wrong' or
inferior to the other two. They each have their place in the life of
the devotee. And if God is indeed limitless, He/She in any case
can be thought of as containing all three. In the lives of many
people it is necessary to move 'upwards' through the three
aspects, out-growing, for example, the idea of a Heavenly
Father when this becomes too much like an old man in the sky,
and moving on to the idea of God as perfect love and wisdom
and power, only to outgrow this in turn when it seems too
limiting for the boundless nature of ultimate truth. But when
this ultimate truth is approached, one realizes that the first two
aspects are still contained within it as symbolic representations
of it, and as ways of leading people towards it.

So in dealing in this chapter and the next with meditation on the immanent spiritual power within (subjective meditation) and the transcendent spiritual power without (objective meditation), I am not drawing a boundary between the two. Each is a way of approaching the one truth, and many meditators use both paths rather than regarding one as superior to the other. Indeed, in my own experience across the traditions, I have found that the best teachers are those who do not exalt their own teachings (and, by implication, themselves) above the teachings of others. Having travelled far in their own development they have left behind such narrowness, and are able to see truth wherever it is to be found. Nor are they averse to criticizing their own traditions where such criticism is justified. They live in openness and freedom because they are not bound by the dogma that gets in the way of wisdom.

## THE NATURE OF SUBJECTIVE MEDITATION

Subjective meditation works on the principle of examining one's own mind, thus seeing into oneself and the real nature of consciousness. Of all the great schools of thought, Zen Buddhism is probably the best example of this subjective, mind-examining, 'self-power' approach to meditation, and accordingly it is on Zen Buddhism that I shall now concentrate. Let me set the scene.

Imagine a man or woman sitting cross-legged in a still, silent room, the eyes focused but half-closed. Only the slight, almost imperceptible coming and going of the breath, deep down in the abdomen, tells us that he or she is not a statue. Is this, the non-meditator may wonder, 'examining the mind'? Surely examining the mind must involve taking part in paper and pencil or computer tests of some kind, showing off intellectual skills, demonstrating powers of reasoning or problem solving.

Next, imagine the same man or woman walking through the countryside on an open, summer day, gazing with pleasure to left and right, taking in everything, concentrating upon the sights and sounds and smells of nature, the sensation of the cool grass brushing the legs, the stirring of the breeze, the murmur of insects, the sun on the back of the neck, the dappled shadows under the trees, the song of the birds. How, the non-meditator now wonders, can this also be described as examining the mind? Surely the man or woman is simply enjoying being idle. A pleasant enough pastime, but even less to do with examinations than sitting quietly on a cushion.

In these examples, we see the errors that the non-meditator, looking on, is making. To him or her, an examination has to do with comparisons between your condition and that of other people, with achieving standards and perhaps obtaining certificates and diplomas. Only a fellow meditator knows that examining the mind is done by what the Zen Buddhist calls *mindfulness*, focusing with clarity and precision upon what is occupying the mind at the moment, whether in meditation or the activities of daily life.

## MINDFULNESS

Mindfulness means that instead of allowing the attention to be scattered amongst 101 things, it is directed to the experience that is registering *now* in the mind, the experience of being alive *now*, *here*, in the successive instants of existence which are all we actually have. For, although we think of our lives as having a history that stretches back to our birth and a future that stretches ahead, in point of fact all we ever have is the present moment, and in the twinkling of an eye we have lost it and are experiencing the moment after, and then the moment after that and the moment after that. And each moment, as it recedes into the past, is as far beyond reach as the moment of our birth.

But why practise mindfulness? Why not allow life to go past in a daze of preoccupation, with our minds always somewhere other than where we actually are? The answer is, of course, that it is up to the individual to decide. But for those who wish to know reality, then a start must be made by knowing where we are now, by knowing reality as it arises moment by moment and passes away. Without knowing this, we cannot hope to know the greater reality which lies behind the arising and passing away of our immediate experience.

Does this mean we should never be lost in thought, or planning for the future or remembering the past? No, it does not. It means that when we *are* planning for the future or remembering the past we should know what it is we are doing. We should plan or remember as a deliberate decision of the mind, and not slip constantly into it as a way of avoiding the reality of *now*. In Buddhism, the teaching is that the mind, or rather the self-centred and egotistical part of the mind, dominates us as a way of inflating its own importance and tricking us into believing it is who we really are. We create this egoism and allow it to grow inside us, like a cuckoo in the nest. We spend our lives pre-occupied with it, feeding it with attention, defending it against the assaults we feel are made upon it, grasping the things we imagine it wants and avoiding the things we imagine it doesn't want. It becomes our life's work, and in serving it we forget what this work should really be.

It is not for nothing that so many of the great traditions repeat over and over again the call to wake up, to open our eyes, to be born again. What we are being told is that if we choose to go through life half-asleep, then all we will know are the delusions, the fantasies and the nightmares of our childish daydreams.

## ZEN BUDDHISM

For Zen Buddhism, mindfulness is quite literally allowing yourself to see what is going on. The two examples I gave of the person sitting in a still, quiet room or walking through the summer landscape, with the mind intent upon what is actually being done, illustrate this. For whether sitting in formal meditation or walking through the countryside – or the busy street – the mind of the Zen practitioner is placed firmly in the action itself. When the Zen practitioner eats, he or she is eating. When working, he or she is working. When sitting, he or she is sitting. The sanctity, the sacredness of the moment is always observed. Life is too precious not to notice it, too holy to ignore, too fascinating to turn away from.

The Japanese word 'Zen' is a derivative from the Chinese 'Ch'an', which by way of the Pali 'jhana' comes from the Sanskrit 'dhyana', which simply means meditation. But Zen is meditation set within the profound philosophy of psychological and spiritual growth stemming initially from the teachings of the

Buddha and re-stated by a long line of Zen patriarchs stretching back to Bodhidharma, who brought Buddhism to China in AD 520.

Bodhidharma taught that all men and women are Buddhas from the very beginning. 'Buddha-nature', the enlightened mind, is always there inside us and the only reason we don't realize it is our ignorance. (I remember the first time a Buddhist teacher told the group of which I was a member, 'You are all Buddhas', I caught myself thinking, 'He means everyone except me'. My subsequent realization of the ignorance of such a thought was a profound moment of illumination for me.) Zen is the act of discovering this enlightened mind, our 'original nature'. It is the act of dropping our ignorance, of discovering ourselves, and thus of living a life of dynamic immediacy. However – and this is often hard for Westerners to accept – this involves recognizing that an important cause of our ignorance is the intellectual, rational mind. Or rather, the way in which we *use* our intellectual, rational mind. Our mistake is that we assume it is the means towards an understanding of life's mysteries, whereas left to itself all it does is lead us round and round in circles. Use the rational mind by all means (in fact, of all the great religions, Buddhism probably makes most use of it), but recognize that it is merely a tool, powerful and of great value within its own frame of reference but a hindrance when misapplied.

This teaching on the limits of the rational mind is in fact so obvious that it's strange we need to have it pointed out to us. Can one use the rational mind, for example, to explain – or, more pertinently, express – our love for our children or for a partner? Can the rational mind explain and express our feeling for poetry, for art, for music? Can it explain or express our joy and sadness, the inspirations and aspirations that motivate our lives? Can it explain or express the pleasure we take in nature – the moon on a frosty night, the thunderclouds under a yellowing sun, the scent of incense, the satisfaction of working with flowers and animals? Can it even explain the medium upon which the rational mind itself depends, namely thought and consciousness? Hardly.

In that case, it is absurd to expect it to explain our lives to us, or help us understand our spiritual longings, or tell us what happens when we die. And it is the tragedy of Western culture that, since the dawn of scientific materialism, we have assumed that it can. The rational, logical mind is a splendid gift, but like any gift it is an embarrassment to us if we don't know where in our lives it properly belongs.

## THE THREE PILLARS OF ZEN

Zen has from the first sought to put the rational mind in its place, and the meditation techniques Zen teaches are very much devoted to this end. But for these techniques to be successful, Zen practitioners must cultivate along with them three qualities of mind, the three foundations on which Zen rests (see, for example, Kapleau's *Three Pillars of Zen*). These are *great faith, great doubt* and *great determination*. Great faith doesn't mean blind belief. The Buddha himself was at pains to tell his followers not to believe the things he said simply because it was he who said them. These things should be tried and tested, and only retained if they are found to work. Great faith means essentially that we look at the life of the Buddha (or the life of the spiritual teacher we choose to follow) and know that that is the person we wish to be like. It is a faith based on the acceptance that if the Buddha put his advanced humanity down to something called 'enlightenment', then that enlightenment is what is necessary for us as well.

Great doubt – Suzuki in his *Essays in Zen Buddhism* offers the alternative term *great spirit of enquiry* – refers to the burning question of why suffering exists. If there is such a thing as enlightenment or if, as Christianity says, God is love, why should people suffer? Why? There must be an answer. And so *great doubt* means that the wish to be like the Buddha is not just for one's own sake, but because through attaining the enlightenment of a Buddha we may understand and alleviate the suffering of others as well as of ourselves.

*Great determination* speaks for itself. *Great doubt* will not take us far unless we have the determination to resolve this doubt. Without great determination, our doubt turns to despair. Great determination is what drives us forward. It is what allows us no rest from the question, 'why?'. Why should there be greed and selfishness? Why should the innocent suffer? Why should the guilty go free? Why should there be hatred and jealousy and deceit and exploitation? Why?

The answer to the question 'why?' isn't a theoretical statement that the world is really perfect, and that obstacles are put there just to test us. Try telling that to someone dying of starvation, or someone senselessly maimed by the aggression of fellow men and women, or someone in the shock of bereavement, or someone told they are terminally ill. No, the answer to *great doubt* is an inner realization of spirit, a 'knowing' which comes not through belief but through direct experience. And once that inner realization is attained, the suffering of others is helped not by telling them to be strong but by giving them one's own strength, in the way the Buddha and Christ gave their strength.

## SAMADHI, SATORI AND KENSHO

How does Zen describe this inner realization? The terms used are *samadhi, satori* and *kensho*. Because Zen is outwardly so simple, eschewing the dogmas that have gathered around so many other religions, and because the word 'Zen' has passed into the popular literature, the real meaning of these terms in their Zen context is often misunderstood. For example, people talk about a 'Zen state' when they are so engrossed in an activity that they have forgotten themselves. Or they speak of samadhi and satori as if they mean the same thing, or argue that samadhi isn't a term associated at all with Zen.

In fact, as Sekida makes clear in one of the best available manuals on Zen (*Zen Training*), there are two types of samadhi in Zen and both of them are different from satori. Sekida calls them *positive samadhi* and *absolute samadhi*. Positive samadhi occurs when we are indeed absorbed fully in an activity, whether it be painting or a martial art, or a Zen koan or the breathing. In all of these, some small consciousness of self does remain. Absolute samadhi on the other hand occurs when, in Sekida's words, we *become* the work of art or the koan or the movements of the muscles in breathing, and all consciousness of self is lost.

Both positive and absolute samadhi must be mastered, says Sekida, and both can lead to kensho, one's first experience of satori, enlightenment. But satori is continuous with absolute samadhi, and hence absolute samadhi is the goal of Zen training (or rather the *gateway into this training*, since the word 'goal' implies reaching an end). In absolute samadhi the reflecting action of consciousness ceases, and in Sekida's words one comes to:

> notice nothing, feel nothing, hear nothing, see nothing. This state of mind is called 'nothing'. But it is not vacant emptiness. Rather is it the purest condition of our existence. It is not reflected, and nothing is directly known of it ... The experience of this Great Death is no doubt not common ... Nevertheless, if you want to attain genuine enlightenment and emancipation, you must go completely through this condition, because enlightenment can be achieved only after once shaking off our old habitual way of consciousness.
>
> *Zen Training*, p. 94

When you emerge from this state, Sekida tells us:

> you find yourself full of peace and serenity, equipped with strong mental power and dignity. You are intellectually alert and clear, emotionally pure and sensitive. You have the exalted condition of a great artist. You can appreciate music, art and beauties of nature with greatly increased understanding and delight.
>
> *Zen Training*, p. 95

And once having attained this state, simple things in the outside world like the sound of a stone striking bamboo or the sight of blossom can have an impact 'so overwhelming that the "whole universe comes tumbling down"'.

In other words, once satori has been realized, the simplest of experiences can propel you into it again, because satori is 'nothing more nor less than your recognition of your own purified mind ... emancipated from the delusive way of consciousness ...' In satori, you *become* the sound of the stone on bamboo, or the sight of blossom, instead of being aware of yourself experiencing them. And in this moment of becoming, you recognize your unity with creation. You are *in* creation along with the sound and the sight, and creation is in you. Creation is continuous, without breaks, not a collection of isolated dots like a newspaper photograph.

In discussing the two main sects of Zen Buddhism, Rinzai Zen and Soto Zen, Sekida writes that although both contain positive and absolute samadhi, Rinzai Zen tends to emphasize the former and Soto Zen the latter. Kapleau puts it more broadly in that Rinzai Zen, with its frequent use of koan meditation, emphasizes equally all three pillars of Zen – great faith, great doubt and great determination – while Soto Zen, which makes more use of *zazen* ('sitting in awareness' meditation), places most stress upon great faith, knowing that as one sits in meditation satori will reveal itself in its own time, like a seed ripening. To work with great doubt and great determination upon one's koan implies, says Kapleau, that there is an element of self-awareness, an awareness that *someone is working upon something*, and the corollary is a positive samadhi which may lead *into* an absolute samadhi. When meditating primarily with great faith on the other hand, this self-awareness is less strong, less positive, and (although the path is more difficult) the corollary is absolute samadhi, which may then allow one to experience positive samadhi.

---

**BOX 12**
ZAZEN

In some ways zazen is the most difficult form of meditation, because the focus of awareness is thinking itself. Instead of allowing thoughts to pass in and out of the mind without attending to them, in zazen the meditator watches his or her thoughts, though still *without becoming distracted by them*. As each thought arises it is seen for what it is, a temporary creation of the mind, and allowed to pass away without clinging to it, no matter how attractive, and without repelling it, however unpleasant.

An analogy is to think of a spectator standing on a motorway bridge and watching cars speeding past below. No car is delayed or helped on its way by the spectator. All are regarded with the same objectivity. No judgements are passed, with one car seen as more attractive than another. All partake of the same quality, namely motion, and all come from one direction and pass away in another.

Watching the thoughts helps your examination of the mind in three main ways.

1. By distancing you from your thoughts, so they no longer trigger off the overwhelming emotional reactions that lead to suffering. (This doesn't mean you also cease to feel pleasant emotions; but it does mean that these emotions arise more from experience than from merely thinking about experience.)

**BOX 12**
**ZAZEN**

2. By allowing you to recognize what thinking actually is – a succession of words or pictures fleeting as snowflakes falling on a fire. Surely the mind is more than these?

3. By enabling you in due course to see the emptiness from which thoughts arise and into which they disappear.

'Emptiness' is a vital concept in Buddhism, and refers to that formless potential from which creation is constantly streaming and into which it constantly disappears. In a way, *emptiness* (or the *void*) isn't a good word for this, for it suggests a vacuum, annihilation, whereas what we are talking about is infinite potential.

One of the practices often used in zazen to sharpen the examination of one's thinking is to identify each thought as it arises. Some thoughts are 'memories', others are 'hopes', 'anticipations', 'nostalgia', 'doubts' and so on. Similarly emotions are also identified ('anger', 'fear', etc.). Yet the meditator never identifies *with* any of these temporary phenomena, or passes judgement on them. They are what they are, transitory episodes on the surface of the mind.

As zazen proceeds, there comes a point where thoughts arise less often. The spectator is still there, but the motorway is now quiet. This stillness is watched with the same detached awareness as were the thoughts. And with this stillness comes deeper insight into emptiness.

## TESTING SATORI

After the first experience of satori (kensho), there is a period of *maturing*, during which the practitioner brings his or her new understanding into harmony with inner thoughts and emotions and outer behaviour. For Zen isn't an escape from the world; many of the greatest Zen teachers have been lay men and women. Rather it is a way of living life in its richness, whatever the circumstances. During this process of maturing, even the Zen monk or nun would sometimes go out into the world and travel from one monastery to another to test the genuineness of their satori with other Zen teachers, or take up a lay role to test it against daily life. Once this testing reveals that satori is genuine and can be re-entered, the period of maturing is over and the task now becomes to rebuild the whole person in the light of satori. How can life be lived so that satori is ever-present? How can one live in a world of multiplicity, knowing that in reality it is a world of unity? Only when the practitioner has completed this task is he or she recognized as a *roshi*, someone competent to teach others. And in the Zen tradition this recognition can come only from other roshis, who are themselves in the direct line of transmission through the Zen patriarchs back to Bodhidharma himself.

The point is not that only roshis understand Zen, but that roshis – assuming they have been given the title properly and not from some spurious group claiming to represent Zen – are fit people to test the satori of others. Without such testing, it is all too easy to delude yourself into thinking that the experiences you have had in meditation – even though of value in themselves – are what Zen means by satori. And in order to be put to the test, Zen teaches that it is important you submit fully to the teacher, putting your 'great faith' in him or her as someone who has achieved satori, and following his or her instructions as closely as you can.

This does not mean you surrender your right to question and ultimately reject the teacher if you wish. Such surrender is highly dangerous in any system, and can lead to the unthinking obedience upon which dictators and cult leaders prey in their followers. It means that if you decide to work with a particular teacher, you must play fairly. You must accept that the teacher can only be properly tested (since you are testing him or her as surely as they are testing you) if you follow the method he or she is offering. Follow it and see what happens. If you give the teacher a fair trial – which means following them *as if* their rules will work for you – and they prove to be no help after a reasonable time, then discard them and seek another teacher.

## THE KOAN

One of the most intriguing aspects of Zen meditation is the use of the koan. This isn't exclusive to Zen Buddhism. All religions (and all psychologies) true to the name contain koans. Koans arise automatically as you begin to ask the questions fundamental to the inner life. 'What is love?' 'Where does life come from?' 'Why is there suffering?' 'What is birth?' 'What is death?' And – the koan at the heart of all koans – 'Who am I?'.

The difference is firstly that Zen approaches these koans head on, and secondly that it rephrases them in apparently nonsensical language. Why head on? Because a direct assault upon the mysteries at the centre of life is more effective than philosophical debates which risk going round in circles. Why nonsensical? Because the answer to these mysteries is 'nonsensical'; that is, not discoverable through 'common sense'. As I explained earlier, the rational, conscious mind cannot provide the answers to many fundamental questions. These answers come as intuitions from deep in the unconscious, as if they are things we already 'know' and simply have to remember. They are not the result of looking outwards, in the way of science, but of looking inwards in the way of the mystic, the poet, the artist.

Zen thus plays a trick on you. It provides you with a question which cannot be solved by your rational, linear, analytical, either–or thinking. The more you try to solve it thus, the more elusive the answer becomes and the more infuriating the question. You work on the question both in sitting meditation and in daily life, and each time you hit on a solution you hurry to tell the roshi, only to have it rejected and be sent back to your search. And then suddenly the answer comes, often with total unexpectedness, and it is all very clear and very simple and very, very funny. How could you have been so foolish as not to see it straight away? This time when you go to the roshi he or she smiles and acknowledges your success. And gives you another koan on which to work!

In my own experience, people either accept koan meditation the first time they hear about it, as if something within them answers a preliminary koan 'What is a koan?', or they find the whole thing rather foolish. I once gave a lengthy talk on the koan to a particular meditation group, only to be met with incomprehension and dimissive comments such as, 'It all sounds very intellectual'. 'Intellectual' is the one thing a koan definitely isn't, and after ruefully registering the bruises this inflicted on my ego, I had to admit that the fault lay in the way I presented my topic. It is much more appropriate to give a koan than to talk about it.

And yet we are children of our culture. We are so used to verbal presentations that we ought to be able to identify merit no matter how disguised behind a smokescreen of words. So in spite of the inadequacies of my presentation, the nature of the koan should have been apparent to anyone who wanted to see it. On other occasions, it usually is. But the experience told me, as only experience can, that koan meditation isn't for everyone. This doesn't mean those who reject it are less effective meditators than those who accept it. It means that the koan either makes its own crazy sense to you the first time you meet it, prodding you with its own version of the great doubt, or it doesn't. You are either held by it, in spite of the promptings of your rational mind, or you find it a distraction that disturbs the inner stillness with which you are trying to work.

The koan most frequently given to the beginner is 'Mu'. When giving it, the roshi will tell a short story. And never has a story so short led to so much inner struggle by so many people! The story is that a monk one day asked the ninth-century Chinese Zen master Joshu, 'Has a dog Buddha-nature?', to which Joshu answered, 'Wu'. Now 'wu' ('mu' in Japanese, the form in which the koan is usually given) is a word meaning literally 'not' or 'none'. So on the face of it, Joshu answered with a negative. On the face of it. Yet in the best known collection of commentaries on the koans, the *Mumonkan* ('The Gateless Gate'), the thirteenth-century Zen monk Mumon has this to say about 'Mu'.

In order to master Zen, you must pass the barrier of the patriarchs. To attain this subtle realization, you must completely cut off the way of thinking. If you do not pass the barrier, and do not cut off the way of thinking, then you will be like a ghost clinging to the bushes and weeds. Now, I want to ask you, what is the barrier of the patriarchs? Why, it is this single world 'Mu'. That is the front gate to Zen. Therefore it is called the *Mumonkan* of Zen ... Wouldn't you like to pass this barrier? Arouse your entire body ... summon up a spirit of great doubt and concentrate upon this word 'Mu'. Carry it continuously day and night. Do not form a nihilistic conception of vacancy, or a relative conception of 'has' or 'has not'. It will be just as if you swallowed a red hot iron ball which you cannot spit out even if you try. All the illusory thoughts and delusive ideas accumulated up to the present will be exterminated, and when the time comes, internal and external will be spontaneously united. You will know this, but for yourself only, like a dumb man who has had a dream. Then all of a sudden an explosive conversion will occur, and you will astonish the heavens and shake the earth.

*Mumonkan*, p. 29

So 'Mu' is not to be taken at face value. Seven hundred years later another great Zen teacher, D. T. Suzuki, gives us similar guidance.

There is no doubt that [you are] not to think about ['mu'], for no logical thinking is possible. 'Mu' does not yield any meaning inasmuch as it is to be thought of in connection with the dog, nor for that matter with the Buddha-nature either; it is 'Mu' pure and simple. The koan neither denies nor asserts the presence of Buddha-nature in the dog, although Joshu used the 'Mu' on being asked about the Buddha-nature. When the 'Mu' is given as a koan to the uninitiated, it stands by itself; and this is exactly what is claimed from the beginning by Zen masters, who have used it as an eye-opener.

*Essays in Zen Buddhism, Second Series*, p. 126

But surely, if 'Mu' does not mean what it says it means, then the koan is more like an eye-*closer*? Indeed, in a sense it is. To answer it we must close our eyes to one way of seeing before we can open them to another. But why on earth couldn't Joshu say what he meant by 'Mu'? The answer is that had he done so, that would have been Joshu talking, not you. And the answer would have become so many empty words. Joshu was too kind a teacher to allow that to happen.

---

**BOX 13**
**MORE ABOUT KOANS**

There are many collections of koans. One of the most readily available is *Zen Flesh, Zen Bones*, by Paul Reps. The most extensive collections are the *Mumonkan* ('The Gateless Gate') and the *Hekiganroku* ('The Blue Cliff Record'), both of which are translated and edited by Sekida and Grimstone. The most controversial is the *Gendai Sojizen Hyoron* ('A Critique of Present-Day Pseudo-Zen'), available in an edited translation by Joel

**BOX 13**
## MORE ABOUT KOANS

Hoffman. This last is the most controversial because although the *Mumonkan* and the *Hekiganroku* contain comments by Zen masters on the koans, the *Gendai* actually gives solutions.

At one time there was great opposition to the inclusion even of comments in koan collections, and some Zen masters burned these if they fell into their hands. They need not have worried. The comments are as baffling as the koans themselves. However, giving solutions is a different matter, because it is the path towards the solution that is important for the meditator, rather than the solution itself. The latter is simply the evidence that he or she has travelled this path. Furthermore, the 'correct' solution may not be the same for all Zen students, and in any case, as soon as a solution is produced the master will test the student with another koan and then another and then another, sometimes in rapid succession. This allows the master to see whether the pupil's 'correct' answer was genuine or was simply being parroted.

However, it can be argued that attempting to see *why* a particular solution is 'correct' may be of as much value as working on the koan itself, or as working on the comments to a koan by one of the great masters. Try for yourself. Firstly, here is a koan from the *Hekiganroku*, with Zen master Setcho's comment.

A monk asked Joshu, 'All the *dharmas* (truths) are reduced to oneness, but what is oneness reduced to?'. Joshu said, 'When I was in Seishu I made a hempen shirt. It weighed seven pounds.'

Setcho's comment: You brought a piece of logic
To trap the old gimlet,
But do you know the meaning
Of the seven-pound hempen shirt?

Now I have thrown it away
Into Lake Seiko
And sail before the wind
Who will share the coolness with me?

Secondly, a koan from the *Gendai*, with its answer.

*Master*: The main pillar of the house, what does it preach?
*Pupil*: The Zen master wakes up early in the morning and takes care of his pupils. In an ordinary house the father, from early morning, raises his voice and looks after his family's affairs.

## MEDITATING ON A KOAN

The best way to work on a koan is to be given one by a Zen teacher. In fact, it is sometimes said that we should not select a koan for ourselves, even from revered collections like the *Mumonkan* or the *Hekiganroku*. The teacher gives the koan that is right for the student at any particular moment, and is the best person to say whether the student's answer represents true understanding or not. But Grimstone, in his Introduction to the *Mumonkan*, concedes that authentic Zen teachers are few in number. In that case, we may have to work on our own, and Grimstone assures us that 'much can be done without [a teacher's] help. There are numerous instances of Zen students who have found their own way to enlightenment'.

If you want to try koan meditation and have to work on your own, first choose a koan from the *Mumonkan* or the *Hekiganroku*. The koans in both collections can be taken in any order, but most Zen teachers give 'Mu' as an opener, so let us assume you are working with 'Mu'. The best written summary that I know by an authentic Zen teacher is that given by Sekida. In his *Zen Training: Methods and Philosophy* Sekida plots our course for us like a wise friend gently but firmly checking we have understood each detail, and I personally have found his guidance as useful as some of the direct teaching I have received on koan meditation. In summary, this is what Sekida says.

*Stage 1*  After taking your meditation seat, attend to your breathing. Begin by breathing through the mouth, with the breath expelled forcibly through the slightly parted lips. This helps to build up some tension in the respiratory muscles, and helps control wandering thoughts. At this stage, the breath can either be counted, with the count taking up the whole of the exhalation, or you can begin saying 'Mu' silently to yourself.

*Stage 2*  Having established concentration, the breathing is now switched to the nostrils, and should be quite rough, even audible, as a way of further deepening concentration. Your eyes, which should be open in Stage 1, can now be closed if you prefer. Although koan meditation is traditionally done with the eyes open to help prevent drowsiness, closed eyes assist the meditator to direct attention inwards, thus rendering the eventual experience of absolute samadhi more possible.

Even if in Stage 1 you were counting your breath, 'Mu' should now accompany each exhalation. 'Mu' means 'nothing', but do not suppose you are investigating the meaning of nothingness. Your teacher will ask you 'What is Mu?' or 'Show me Mu', but this is not an invitation to engage in conceptual speculation. You must *experience* 'Mu', and to do this you have to take 'Mu' simply as 'the sound of your breath and entertain no other idea'. Keep saying 'Mu' without any philosophical speculation, and one day you 'will come to realize that the answer is already given, and you will clap your hands and burst into a great shout of laughter'.

Sekida is telling us that koan meditation is really a rather fierce business. And it's certainly true that some people sweat profusely when working on their koan, as if engaging in intensive physical activity. But this doesn't mean tranquillity will not in due course arise. It simply shows us that we are still at the concentration phase of meditation, and Sekida is intructing us how to deepen this concentration, how to chew upon the koan as if our lives depend upon it.

If Stage 2 is proceeding as it should, the first levels of positive samadhi begin to develop, and these are accompanied by certain changes of sensation in the body. The first of these, Sekida tells us, is a loss of awareness of individual joints and muscles, and in their place a generalized feeling of pressure, 'as if the body is clad in heavy armour'. A traditional Zen phrase to describe this state is 'silver mountains and iron cliffs' (Zen always falls easily into poetry), but as samadhi develops it is replaced by a second sensation in which all physical feeling dies away. This is the 'falling off' of body and mind. As Sekida puts it, 'There is something existing there it is true, but one cannot say what it is'.

*Stage 3* The breath now loses its roughness and becomes almost imperceptible. The pauses between breaths become longer, with the gap between in-breath and out-breath as long as one minute. No conscious effort is involved here, the process takes place on its own. Occasionally, as the reserves of oxygen are used up, the body will compensate by taking a very long in-breath. One is now able to enter absolute samadhi. Even the repetition of 'Mu' ceases. All is stillness and silence. Not a thought enters the mind, and there is a bright illumination there, as if the mind is illuminating itself 'and the whole universe is stretching boundlessly around you'.

Stage 3 thus represents both tranquillity and insight, insight of the deepest kind in which the mind is no longer exploring itself but has *become itself*.

## CONCEPTUAL EXAMINATION OF 'MU'

However, in spite of the warning not to examine 'Mu' conceptually, you may nevertheless feel a strong urge to do so, especially in the early stages (and this is true of all koans). Sekida concedes that it is acceptable to obey this urge provided you recognize that you are now 'reciting Mu with your head instead of pushing it down into your abdomen'. The best way to carry out this conceptual examination is by asking inwardly and repeatedly, 'What is Mu?'. But be careful. Don't be misled by the idea of conceptualization. You are still not trying to *define* 'Mu', to replace it with another word or set of words. Look at 'Mu' from all angles, as if you are examining a flower or a sunset. Don't be trapped by the rationalization that your mind will try to produce.

And remember Sekida's warning – 'Do not suppose that you are investigating the meaning of nothingness'. How can 'nothingness' possibly be 'investigated' or have a 'meaning', in the sense in which we usually understand the terms? And don't be tempted to meditate on the word 'nothingness' instead of 'Mu'. 'Mu' has particular value for Westerners in that, although the knowledge that the English equivalent is 'nothing' helps to add to the great doubt with which we approach the word, 'Mu' in and of itself is just a sound, and therefore stripped of the associations that usually set the mind woolgathering.

Conceptual examination of 'Mu' is less likely to take you into absolute samadhi, says Sekida, than is the non-conceptual approach, but it may take you more quickly into positive samadhi. And since one must achieve samadhi at both positive and absolute levels, my own interpretation is that we should use both the conceptual and the non-conceptual methods. In any case, when you are working intensively on a koan conceptual examination occurs spontaneously when you are going about your daily life, and this should be encouraged. It would be wrong to leave your 'hot ball of doubt' in the meditation room.

A Zen master quoted by Suzuki puts it that you should keep this hot ball of doubt by devoting

> yourself to your koan day and night, whether sitting or lying, whether walking or standing ... Make resolute efforts to keep it always before your mind. Days pass, years roll on, but in the fullness of time when your mind is so attuned and recollected there will be a sudden awakening inside yourself – an awakening into the mentality of the Buddhas and the patriarchs. You will then, for the first time, and wherever you may go, never again be beguiled by a Zen master.
>
> *Essays in Zen Buddhism*, p. 99

That is, no Zen master will be able to test your enlightenment and find it wanting. You will have *achieved* nothing, because there is nothing really to achieve. Since you are already standing in the right place, where else is there to go? All that has happened is that for the first time, you now know that place. And once you have that knowing, how can it be taken from you? Where would it be taken *to*?

## IS 'MU' SIMPLY A MANTRA?

The best balance between the non-conceptual and the conceptual methods of working on a koan is to use the former in sitting meditation and the latter when going about daily life, returning to it repeatedly, often in a playful, relaxed manner, curious yet not curious, keeping in mind always that the solution (or rather the *resolution*) will inevitably come, all in its own good time. And when it comes, as Sekida says, there is the feeling that 'the answer is already given'. There is an old Zen saying, 'I thought I had a long way to go, until I looked back and saw that I had passed my destination many years before', and it is a useful one to remember in connection with the koan.

People who use mantra meditation sometimes ask how

working non-conceptually upon 'Mu' (or any other koan) differs from mantra meditation (Chapter 10). There is the same repetition of a sound, the same emptying of the mind. So where is the difference? In meditation systems, differences are always more apparent than real, and begin to dissolve the deeper one goes. But there is an important initial distinction in that, when working on the koan, your state of mind contains the great 'ball of doubt', a ball of doubt which can be increased, Zen master Hakuin advises, by telling oneself that, 'This body of mine is the "Mu" itself, and what does it all mean?'. The koan carries a meaning, and it is this meaning that will eventually lead to insight.

In mantra meditation, on the other hand, you focus on the repetition of the mantra, and it is the mantra *itself* that takes you into insight. When true insight arises, there is no difference between what your koan reveals to you and what your mantra reveals. You may use different words to describe it, but true insight involves experiencing the unity that is already there and in which we live and move and have our being. Provided they give us the space and the stillness in which to recognize who we really are, the different meditation paths cannot lead in different directions.

## THE ENLIGHTENED STATE OF MIND

What words does Zen use to describe this true insight? Or rather, since there is no gap between the insight and the state of mind in which it arises, how does Zen describe this state of mind? Listen to Zen master Han Shan's words, as translated and summarized by Lu K'uan Yu. Having first trained in the Buddhist Pure Land sect, which meditates by repetition of the mantra of Amitabha Buddha ('Namu Amidha Bhutsu'), Han Shan encountered Ch'an in his twentieth year, and was given the koan, 'Who is meditating on the Buddha's name?' (a variant of the 'Who am I?' koan). Eight years later, in meditation, he 'suddenly felt as if his body had vanished', and in his experience of absolute samadhi a few days later:

> ... his body and mind disappeared and were replaced by a great brightness, spheric and full, clear and still, like a huge round mirror

containing all the mountains, rivers and great earth. Thereafter he noticed a still serenity inside and outside his body, and met no more hindrance [in meditation] from sounds and forms.

*Practical Buddhism*, p. 48

On another occasion, in his own words, Han Shan says that:

All that had been in tumult in the great void was now as still as when the rains had passed and all the clouds dispersed. The air seemed thoroughly cleansed and everything was perfectly tranquil without a single appearance of shadows and images. The mind was empty and the surrounding objects were still; the resultant bliss was without compare.

*Practical Buddhism*, p. 49

As a further way of describing his state of mind, Han Shan quotes words from the Surangama Sutra:

In utter purity, the bright light pervades all,
With its shining stillness enfolding the great void.
Worldly things, when closely looked at,
Are but illusions seen in dreams.

These lines don't imply that worldly things don't exist, but that they don't exist *in the way in which we usually experience them*. We see them as separate, static, fragmented, isolated, cut off from each other by boundaries sharp as knife blades, when in reality each thing is a moving, dynamic, everflowing manifestation of the one life force, the one unity. Nothing can be added to or taken away from that unity. Each one of us is indispensable to it, just as is every tree, every mountain, every insect. And since there are no boundaries between us and it, we in a real sense *are* it. Our minds contain the whole world, or as William James, one of the founders of modern psychology and one of its greatest spirits, wrote at the turn of the century, 'to know any one object in its entirety is to know the whole world'.

Zen, perhaps more than any other tradition, finds a way to represent this unity. Let me give a further example of an experience of this state, taken, coincidentally, from another of Lu K'uan Yu's works *The Transmission of Mind Outside the Teachings*. This time the words belong to one of his pupils, a Westerner, who had been working for a long time on the koan, 'All things return to the One, to where does the One return?'.

At first the mind was crowded with thoughts but gradually a change took place until I was able to clear my mind of all but the koan. Then I could go no further . . . I felt useless and lost. But I was determined and I withdrew to solitude in the mountains . . . all the while keeping the koan in my mind. Then one day I stopped by a river and sat exhausted. Suddenly I heard, not with my ears it seemed, the sigh of the wind in the trees. Immediately I passed from my state of exhaustion into one where I was so relaxed I felt open to total flow . . . Everything was dripping with white-hot light or electricity (although there were no objects as such) and it was as though I was watching the whole cosmos coming into being, constantly, molten. How can there be so much light? . . . All is illumination. The dominant impression was of entering into the very marrow of existence – no forms, no personalities, no deities, just bliss. (pp. 19–20)

## DESCRIPTIONS ARE ONLY HALF THE PATH

But Lu K'uan Yu implies the same distinction as does Sekida between positive and absolute samadhi when he writes, of descriptions such as the above, that, 'If a meditator can describe what he has realized, it is not the absolute, but is still the relative state'. It is 'half of the path'. There is still a distinction between the person who is realizing and the thing that is being realized. The next stage on the path is the disappearance of this distinction, so that one *becomes* what one really is, instead of just observing it.

The experience, says Hakuin,

is beyond description and can never be transmitted to others. It is those who have actually drunk water that know whether it is cold or warm. . . . the past, present, and future are concentrated in this moment of your consciousness. . . . no joy is ever comparable to this.
Quoted by Suzuki, *Essays in Zen Buddhism*, p. 196

## SOTO ZEN

Suzuki, in *The Field of Zen*, refers to Rinzai Zen with its koan meditations as the *activity* aspect of Zen, and Soto Zen with its zazen ('sitting in awareness') as the *quiet contemplation* aspect. This does not imply that the two aspects are separate from each other. In fact, one of the most liberating experiences I had when I first began to study Zen was the discovery of the oneness between the two sects. Indeed between all the Buddhist sects, and between Buddhism *for its own part* and other religions. It is true that more recently I have found a rejection of this openness amongst some Western converts to Buddhism (for such is the way of we Westerners). But I have never found it amongst those reared within the pure Buddhist traditions themselves. For these people, the different sects of Buddhism and the different religions themselves simply represent different paths up the same mountain.

Thus Rinzai Zen uses both activity and quiet contemplation, and places more emphasis upon the former, while Soto Zen uses both activity and quiet contemplation, and places more emphasis upon the latter. Lay men and women are perfectly free to train in both schools, and such cross-fertilization is usually encouraged. Even the great Zen masters of the past had the habit, during their training, of going from one teacher to another, receiving wisdom wherever they could find it. And one of the greatest masters was of course Dögen.

*Zen Master Dögen*   I made reference to Dögen, the thirteenth-century Zen master responsible for founding Soto Zen in Japan, in Chapter 4. The two main points of Dögen's teaching are firstly that there is no gap between meditation and enlightenment, and secondly that right daily behaviour is Buddhism itself (see, for example, *Zen Master Dögen: An Introduction with Selected Writings*, by Yuho Yokoi and Daizen Victoria).

Both these points illustrate the fact that one does not meditate or manifest right daily behaviour in order to achieve enlightenment, but because these are what enlightened people do. They are a manifestation of enlightenment, rather than a way towards it. This does not mean we can be complacent, imagining that provided we meditate a little and behave properly no further effort is needed. The teaching is much more subtle than that. Our mind is originally one with the Buddha's, in the sense that it contains the essence of the same enlightenment, but our enlightenment will not reveal itself without strenuous practice. However, as soon as we start to practise correctly we are, according to Dögen, already manifesting shallow enlightenment and this, with devout and wholehearted practice, will eventually become deep enlightenment.

Koans are little used in Soto Zen because Dögen taught that Buddhist training itself (meditation, veneration of the Buddhas, adherence to the precepts) is the supreme koan. However, the Soto Zen teacher is not averse to giving a pupil a koan if it is going to be helpful. And in the *Shobogenzo Zuimonki* (a collection of Dögen's brief talks to his followers, translated by Masunaga), Dögen himself gives answers to one of the most famous koans, *Nansen and the cat*. Nevertheless, Dögen's emphasis was upon sitting in meditation with the mind fully composed and thus allowing enlightenment the space in which to manifest itself, and he gave clear instructions on how this should be done.

In Soto Zen meditation, the practitioner usually sits facing a blank wall (as opposed to Rinzai Zen, where the practitioner normally sits facing out into the meditation hall). The practitioner is instructed by Dögen to take up the full or half lotus, with the left leg on top of the right, and the left hand in the palm of the right. Then:

> With your eyes kept continuously open, breathe quietly through your nostrils... Take a deep breath, sway your body to left and right, then sit firmly as a rock. Think of nothing. How is this done? By thinking beyond thinking and non-thinking. That is the very basis of zazen.
>
> *Shobogenzo*, p. 46

Dögen then goes on to explain that zazen is not step-by-step meditation.

> Rather it is simply the easy and pleasant practice of a Buddha, the realization of the Buddha's Wisdom. The Truth appears, there being no delusion. If you understand this you are completely free, like a dragon that has obtained water or a tiger that reclines on a mountain. The supreme Law will then appear of itself, and you will be free of weariness and confusion.

The reader is entitled to say that this may be 'simply the easy and pleasant practice of a Buddha' as far as Dögen is concerned, but for we lesser mortals it is anything but. Dögen, of course, recognized this and reminds us elsewhere that even Buddha Shakyamuni (the historical Buddha) had to spend six years in zazen before he achieved enlightenment, while Bodhidharma, the founder of Zen, had to spend nine years (and is reputed to have cut off his own eyelids to stop himself falling asleep).

Yet Dögen is reminding us once more of the paradox at the heart of all meditation; namely, that once enlightenment is achieved, it is seen to be so absurdly simple that one is justified in describing the way to it as 'easy'. It is as easy as opening the eyes and seeing something that has always been there in front of you. As easy as being alive. As easy as taking your next breath. It is not something 'out there' to be grasped, like learning a foreign language. It is simply recognizing the reality of what you already know.

Yet until one *has* realized this, nothing seems more difficult. In a sense nothing *is* more difficult, because it is we ourselves who create the difficulty. We are like a man standing on his own foot and wondering why he can't walk. Until we realize that one foot is trapping the other, we are never free to take a step, or to recognize that our pain is self-inflicted. But once realization dawns and we step off our own toes, then we laugh at how absurdly simple it all was. We were already free, and always had been.

So Dögen's teaching is enormously helpful, although its profundity is often not apparent at first sight. Whatever the tradition within which we practise meditation, he is telling us that although we delude ourselves to the contrary, we are in reality never separate from enlightenment, never separate from grace. All that is required is that we open ourselves to it.

## CONCLUSION

Some people, although they see the value of subjective meditation as a way of discovering what is going on within our own minds, reject it as a path of spiritual growth because to them it smacks of hubris. I hope I have helped dispel this mistaken impression. Subjective meditation isn't self-aggrandizement; rather, it is a way of realizing that the ego, the 'self' as we understand it, has no real existence. It is a learned construct, a way of thinking about your life that you have mistakenly come to believe really *is* your life.

All paths of spiritual growth speak of the need to negate the self, whether this is described as losing the self, or acting without thought of self, or humbling the self. Zen, and Buddhism generally, goes further by pointing out that in losing the self we aren't really losing anything at all. How can we lose what we never had? The self isn't a 'thing' at all. Can you say what it is? Try. At most, you will come up with a set of dull descriptions which in no sense do justice even to who you think you are, far less to who you really are. And even those descriptions are subject to constant change. Your age, your job, your marital status, your opinions and attitudes, your likes and dislikes, your moods, your life goals, your beliefs, all change as the weeks and months go by. The person you are now is very different from the person you once were. Except in one way. And that one way is the fact of your awareness, the observer who has no name and who looks on at the passing pageant of life and of the self you imagine is living this life. Lu K'uan Yu reminds us that one way Ch'an symbolizes this is to talk of the *host* and the *guest*. We are in reality the host, yet in our delusion we identify with the guest.

Zen tells us to wake up to this, and to realize that in losing the illusory small self we experience the totality of being. Let's quote another embodiment of the truth; 'He that findeth his life shall lose it: and he that loseth his life for my sake shall find it'.

---

**BOX 14**
'TELL ME WHO YOU ARE'

There's another way of working on a koan. I'll take 'Who am I?' as an example.

You need to work with a partner, agreeing to take the role of questioner and respondent in turn. Sit facing each other. It is up to you whether you maintain eye contact or not but after the session is over, examine whether you found it difficult to do so, and if so why.

Focus on your breathing until a state of calm concentration is established. Your partner watches you, and when he or she judges the moment is right, says, 'Tell me who you are'.

Don't think about or force an answer. Simply say what comes into your mind. If nothing comes, stay silent until it does. If your partner judges the silence has gone on for long enough, he or she can say again, 'Tell me who you are'. When you do speak, your partner accepts whatever you say without comment or judgement.

**BOX 14**
**'TELL ME WHO YOU ARE'**

After five minutes have elapsed (you can set a timer for this or your partner can glance at a watch) the roles are reversed. Now it is your turn to ask, 'Tell me who you are', and the turn of your partner to respond.

The exercise can continue for thirty to forty minutes, with the roles changing every five minutes. At the end of the exercise you can discuss your feelings with each other, but again without judgement. Feelings may be shared empathically (and often are) but should never be rejected or trivialized.

Often in this exercise, both you and your partner will come up initially with labels – your name or your occupation or your domestic status. But as the exercise persists these labels are left behind, and it is for you to see what arises then.

I return to this question 'Who am I?' in Chapter 10, and of course you can work on it on your own, as with any koan. The advantage of the duo exercise (as an addition to working solo, not in place of it) is that the presence of another person can help break down some of the barriers we erect inside ourselves to prevent self-knowledge. A partner helps to give us confidence, and once the exercise is under way and trust is established, we can often say more to someone else than to ourselves.

This and similar exercises are discussed in more detail by John Crook in *Space in Mind*.

# 9

## *Objective Meditation I: The Mysteries of Life and Death*

As discussed in the last chapter, objective meditation differs from subjective in that it takes as its point of departure the idea of a spiritual power 'out there' with which the meditator can make contact, and from which he or she can seek and obtain help. At its simplest, this involves concentrating upon an awareness of presence, whether visualized or felt, but it can include the imaginative construction of a highly detailed picture of the being at the centre of the meditation, and then visualizing the actual transmission from him or her to us of the personal qualities which we wish to develop.

Before looking at the techniques for doing this, it should be said that sometimes the sense of meditating upon a being 'out there' is only the start of the practice. As the meditator progresses, there comes a point where the boundaries between the spiritual power 'out there' and the spiritual power 'in here' dissolve. The Christian mystics put it that God is realized as being both without and within. The Kingdom of Heaven is not a country above the clouds but a living reality here in our hearts. It is we ourselves, not frontier posts and border guards, who through ignorance exclude ourselves from it. In these terms, whether we start with subjective or with objective meditation, we eventually come full circle. Look inwards and ultimately you find you are also looking outwards. Look outwards, and ultimately you will find you are also looking inwards.

## THE TIBETAN BUDDHIST APPROACH

Objective meditation practices find some of their clearest expression in Tibetan Buddhism, with the use of the immensely detailed visualizations described below. After prior training in visualization (see Chapter 7), the meditator studies one of the very intricate *rupas* (statuettes) or *thankas* (pictures) of the Buddha or bodhisattva who is to be the focus of attention, noting the exact position of the hands (each gesture or *mudra* carries a specific meaning), the presence of any symbolic object carried in the hands, the details of the clothes, of the facial expression and so on. Each of these features will then be reproduced exactly in the visualization.

There are two reasons for all this detail. The first is that it immeasurably improves the power of visualization itself. By the time you can visualize a rupa or a thanka in all its minute detail, you will be a very powerful visualizer indeed. The second reason is that even the smallest detail carries a symbolic meaning of profound psychological and spiritual benefit to the meditator, even if he or she is unaware of its exact meaning.

In some practices, the visualization process is assisted by the meditation teacher reciting the details of the Buddha or the bodhisattva while the meditation is in progress, thus enabling the meditator to build each detail in turn into the visualization. For monks, nuns and experienced meditators the teacher will chant this recitation at great speed, knowing that it is so familiar to the listeners that they will build up the visualization with the facility of a child completing a much loved and practised picture puzzle.

Examples of the kind of descriptions that the lama will recite are given by Kathleen McDonald in her book *How to Meditate*. But if you are working on your own, the best idea is to start with a simple picture that carries special meaning for you – usually but not necessarily that of a spiritual teacher. Place it in front of you, at eye level as you sit, and gaze steadily at it, blinking only when necessary. Take in every detail. When you feel you have the picture fixed in your mind, close your eyes as if taking a snapshot of it. When the image begins to fade, open your eyes and gaze at the picture once more. As when visualizing geometrical shapes, don't scan the picture with your eyes. Absorb the whole picture first of all, then move deliberately to specific areas in turn and focus on each until you have it clear.

Working in this way, take in also the symbolic meanings that the picture is intended to convey. It will contain an overall symbolism – such as love or compassion or serenity – but identify what it is *specifically* about the picture that conveys this. What are the details that represent this love or compassion or serenity? You may notice, for example, that the eyes seem to radiate the quality concerned, as if giving out rays of invisible light. Then you may notice that one hand is stretched towards you, in a gesture symbolizing giving. Then you may become aware of a slight, reassuring smile on the lips, conveying the message that ultimately all is well. Next you may see that the soft folds of the clothes carry an almost tactile impression of warmth and gentleness, while the colours, perhaps white and blue, suggest purity and spirituality respectively. Then you may notice the delicacy of the hands, which symbolize a sensitive, loving touch, and so on.

By studying the picture you will see how it conveys its message to you, how it comes alive through symbols, and how through your response you have helped bring it to life and shared with the artist the act of creation. You will thus see how and why the picture plays a special role in your experience.

This process of symbol identification will further develop your powers of visualization, and these powers can be assisted still more if you tape your own description of the picture and play the tape back in meditation, just as the lama recites the qualities of the rupa or thanka to the listening monks or nuns. In recording your description, include all the symbols you have identified. For example, for a Christian a description of a picture of Mary might be as follows (I am using Fra Angelico's painting of the Madonna and Child):

Mary's head is surrounded by a halo of golden light, symbolizing her spirituality and the radiation of this spirituality to the whole world. She looks directly at me, and her eyes are full of the love she has for all men and women. Her face is beautiful, and she has the calm smile of one who knows that God's grace is given to all. Her right hand is raised, palm facing outwards and thumb and first finger touching, in a gesture symbolizing reassurance and fearlessness. Mary's outer robe is a rich blue and falls in gentle folds to her feet, and her inner robe, revealed at her throat, is the red colour of sacrifice. Cradled in her left arm against her heart is the infant Jesus, symbolizing the love between parent and child and the entry into the world of Christ's power to transform the hearts of men and women.

Once the picture is built up in your mind, whether you use a tape recording to help you or not, hold it there clearly and steadily throughout your meditation. If you have particular problems in life or particular aims and goals with which you need assistance, ask for help with them and then imagine this help flowing from the visualization into you in the shape of beams of light. In the Tibetan Buddhist tradition, this is usually seen as white light radiating from the forehead of the visualization, red light from the throat, and blue light from the heart, symbolizing the elimination respectively of all obstacles of body, speech and mind.

The final stage of the meditation is to dissolve the visualization into yourself. This is important for two reasons. The first is that, as mentioned in Chapter 7, failure to dissolve the visualization can mean you become attached to it. True, you may believe in the objective existence of Christ or Mary or the Buddha or whoever, and the idea of being 'attached' to the visualization may therefore be an attractive one. But the visualization itself and the picture upon which it is based are creations of the mind, and must be recognized as such. This doesn't mean that the help the visualization appears to give through the rays of light is necessarily clever autosuggestion, a way of building the confidence needed to overcome the obstacles in your path. Your belief system may well embrace the idea that the visualization opens up an actual channel between you and the spiritual power which it represents. But nevertheless, a representation is only a representation. Become attached to it and you will make the mistake of taking the symbol as the real thing. Spiritual power is much greater than the method which takes you towards it, and the two must never be confused with each other.

The second reason for dissolving the visualization into yourself is that in so doing you are symbolizing the incorporation into your own being of the qualities which it represents. It is like – in prosaic language – meditating upon a role model of the person you wish to resemble, and then imagining that person becoming one with you – a powerful psychological technique for bringing about personal change, quite apart from the much deeper spiritual meaning which the practice may have for you.

Dissolving the visualization is done by imagining it moving from in front of you until it is situated above your head, then turning until it is facing the same direction. Then it is visualized as dissolving into light, and descending through the crown of your head until it comes to rest in your heart. In the Tibetan Buddhist system the Buddha or bodhisattva visualized will have a particular colour associated with him or her, into which they dissolve and descend into your heart. In the absence of a specific colour, the symbol of white light can always be used, but if you are meditating upon Christ or Mary or one of the Christian saints, you may wish to associate them with a special colour in your imagination. Blue perhaps, which is a universal symbol of spirituality. Or gold, the symbol of royalty. Or red, the symbol of courage and sacrifice. Or green, the symbol of creativity, fruitfulness, and earth energy. Or violet, a strongly mystical colour.

There is often no need to make a conscious decision on which colour to use. First practise the visualization as dissolving into white light, and then watch to see whether, after a period of time, a colour appears spontaneously within the visualization. But however you arrive at the colour, it is an important aid to your practice. Colours are easy to visualize, and when the meditation is over you may find you carry the impression that this colour fills your heart and sustains you as you turn your attention outwards. This is not the same thing as being attached to your visualization, because the colour now symbolizes the quality inside yourself which is being developed and turned to practical use by the meditation.

## THE WESTERN MYSTERY TRADITIONS

Visualization practices such as this raise again the question discussed in Chapter 3, namely in what sense are the experiences to which the meditator gains access 'real'? The power of visualization may develop to the extent that Christ or Mary or the Buddha is experienced as intensely as if they were physically present, and the power of their love objectively felt. Charles

Seymour, one of the leading authorities on the Western mystery traditions – which also work extensively with creative imagination techniques – records that initially he found it almost impossible to distinguish between pure fantasy and the genuine results obtained by the correct use of the creative mind. Later, after years of experience, he discovered that a cross-checking system (which involved comparing details of experiences with fellow practitioners) allowed him to tell the difference between the two with a 'fair degree of certainty'.

Seymour writes that the transition from fantasy to genuine results depends upon the meditator acting *as if* the images are real, and without worrying about the 'whys and wherefores of the human reasoning mind'. This suspension of disbelief frees the imagination to move from fantasy into genuine creativity. Seymour argues that a follower of the mystery traditions (a magician, to use the term in its original, proper sense) is *what* he believes himself to be and *where* he believes himself to be. Those with more orthodox religious beliefs will see parallels here with faith and the power of faith. *Believe* that you can have direct experience of Christ, and you will be able to move the mountains of doubt that metaphorically separate you from Him.

Some of the material upon which Seymour based his cross-checking is given by Alan Richardson in his *Dancers to the Gods*, and the most extensive collection of Seymour's written work is presented by Dolores Ashcroft-Nowicki in *The Forgotten Mage: The Magical Lectures of Colonel C. R. F. Seymour*, surely one of the best books of its kind.

My own longstanding interest in the Western mystery religions came from two inter-related sources; firstly, my concern to identify the psychological systems in use by men and women in earlier centuries, and secondly, a wish to look across the various spiritual traditions to identify any underlying similarities. Later, when as a postgraduate student I studied Jung and learned the importance he attached to the magical traditions in his exploration of the human unconscious, my interest was further inspired.

For the mystery religions, and the Western alchemical and magical traditions associated with them, were originally systems of inner psychological and spiritual growth. The term 'magic', which in its present debased context covers stage conjurors on the one hand and would-be dabblers in the supernatural on the other, comes in fact from the same root as the ancient (probably Sanskrit) word 'magi', the term for followers of Zoroastrianism, the ancient religion of Persia, represented at the birth of Christ by the wise men (or magi).

Magic in its pure form therefore has nothing to do with either stage conjuring or with spells, charms and potions. Certainly in the process of inner development the magician may find he or she develops what the Hindus call the *siddhis* (see Box 15), the extrasensory powers whose existence modern parapsychological research has demonstrated beyond reasonable doubt. But the development of the siddhis was incidental to and not the aim of magical practices, just as it is incidental to any system of meditation. The degraded attempt by spiritually immature individuals to use the siddhis for gaining power over their fellow men and women was in fact the origin of so-called black 'magic', an inversion of the true aim of the magical traditions in that the practitioner sought to call *down* higher powers to gain advantage on earth, instead of raising him or herself *up* to these powers where the inner nature properly belongs.

## ESOTERIC AND EXOTERIC ASPECTS

The terms 'mystery' and 'occult' mean secret or hidden. The mystery religions (like all religions) had both an esoteric and an exoteric side to them, the former available to those prepared to undergo the extensive training needed in order to gain *gnosis*, direct knowledge of spiritual power, and the latter available to those content to accept the outer forms of spiritual observance. But a feature of the mystery traditions was the strength of the esoteric side. In his or her initiation into the 'mysteries', the inner secrets, the practitioner came face to face with the gods, as Apuleius tells us in *The Golden Ass*, and penetrated 'to the boundaries of death ... the threshold of Persephone' and only 'after being borne through all the elements' returned to earth. This was in fact an initiation into death and the world beyond from which, like the shaman (Chapter 6), the initiate returned knowing the secret wisdom which dissolves fear and leaves the individual in certain knowledge of his or her immortal nature.

**BOX 15**
**THE SIDDHIS**

I mentioned when discussing the collective unconscious in Chapter 2 that it is probably at this level that extrasensory powers (*siddhis*) operate. Such powers, whether involving telepathy (receipt of other people's thoughts), clairvoyance (receipt of information about the environment) or precognition (receipt of information about the future), do not function through normal conscious channels. They emerge as 'hunches', 'intuitions', 'feelings'. Often the recipient does not know whether the information concerned is accurate or not, nor may he or she be able to receive it to order. Laboratory research, in addition to the spontaneous experiences of everyday life, indicates the existence of these extrasensory powers, but tells us little about the processes involved or how to train them.

Patanjali, in his *Yoga Sutras* (see Chapter 4), offers an impressive list of such powers, from walking on water to flying to invisibility. The Western reader is unlikely to be convinced by the grandest of these claims, but the interesting thing is that Patanjali links each siddhi to a particular point of focus in meditation. Thus, for example, by focusing upon the distinguishing marks of another person's body one gains telepathic knowledge of their mind; by focusing on the radiance at the back of the head, one develops the ability to see celestial beings; by focusing on the relationship between the ear and the ether, one obtains supernatural powers of hearing. These practices Patanjali lumps in with more credible ones such as focusing upon friendship in order to develop friendship or on compassion in order to develop compassion, as if there are no real differences between the two sets of powers and the two sets of techniques needed to produce them.

But like all spiritual teachers, Patanjali warns against deliberate cultivation of the siddhis – 'By giving up even these powers, the seed of evil is destroyed and liberation follows'. The reason for relinquishing them is that one risks becoming sidetracked by them into the exercise of personal power, which strengthens the ego – the small self that stands between us and progress on the meditative path.

However, even if you do not deliberately seek them, by putting you in touch with the wellspring of your unconscious, meditation does open many people to extrasensory experiences. At first these may involve picking up random snippets of information during meditation which one could not know by normal means, but which later check with the facts. Or seeing sudden images or pictures which also check out. Later, they may arise in daily life,

---

**BOX 15**
**THE SIDDHIS**

so that 'coincidences' become increasingly frequent, or you
seem to pick up other people's thoughts or details of their lives.

Unless you are particularly gifted in this direction or are a very
intense meditator, these powers are unlikely to amount to much.
But you are nevertheless advised only to note them. Don't
pursue them. Don't feel proud of them. They demonstrate
something of the mysteries of the mind to you, which is good,
but they are not the reason why you are meditating.

---

## THE ORIGINS OF THE WESTERN TRADITION

The Western magical tradition traces its roots back to the
mystery traditions of Asia Minor and the Near East (see
Joscelyn Godwin's *Mystery Religions in the Ancient World*), all
of which may have had their origin even further east. One of
these roots is the Kabbalah, that great system of Jewish mysticism which also exists in a Christian form, and to which I return
in due course. Another is the ancient Egyptian tradition which
predates the pyramids and is sometimes broadly referred to
as the Hermetic tradition after its mythical founder, Hermes
Trismegistus (Hermes 'Thrice-Greatest'), claimed by some to be
Thoth the ancient Egyptian god of wisdom, and by others to be
Adam the primal man himself. It is in *The Emerald Tablet* of
Hermes Trismegistus that the famous maxim 'Whatever is
above is like to that below, and whatever is below is like to that
above' (*as above, so below*) is given, a maxim which sees
humankind as a microcosm of the universe. The teaching behind
this maxim is that we are made in the image of God and carry
the divine spark which enables us to enter into a direct relationship with the cosmic forces that sustain all creation, both animate and inanimate.

Israel Regardie, another noted interpreter of the Western
magical tradition, when writing of its origins in ancient Egypt
has it that:

The myths and legends passed down to posterity by the Egyptian
priests concerning the Gods were not mere idle inventions by

ignorant ... men who having nothing else better to do, occupied themselves in story telling and in weaving pleasant and unpleasant fictions about the figments of their minds ... Primitive man did not 'create' the Gods ... What he really did, perhaps unconsciously, was to apply names (and even these names were significant) and quasi-human faculties to these 'powers' or great forces of Nature which he so accurately observed, and which he believed rightly enough to be manifestations or symbols of the divine.

*The Tree of Life*, pp. 86–7

Therefore, far from dismissing these early traditions as childlike attempts to explain the forces of nature, the mystery religions should be respected as stemming from profound experiences of inner being and of its relationship with creation. As when looking at Hinduism, we should not make the mistake of seeing the 'gods' of the mystery religions as individual beings, but as ways of symbolizing aspects of the one creative force, or as different channels leading to that force, rather in the way that the saints are often conceptualized in the Christian religion and the bodhisattvas in Buddhism.

Regardie's statement that even the names given to these 'gods' in the Egyptian tradition were significant is also of great importance, and raises again the subject of the power contained in certain sounds. Such sounds in fact symbolize at the auditory level what geometrical designs do at the visual. Their repetition therefore appears to provide keys to the unconscious in a way denied to other sounds. The example of 'Om', the so-called primal sound, was given in Chapter 5 and the names of the Egyptian gods carry the same sonorous, echoing quality. *Horus*, the falcon-headed lord of the skies and symbol of the link between matter and spirit; *Thoth*, the ibis-headed moon god of knowledge; *Isis* (pronounced 'Eeziz'), the goddess of magical power, and the symbolic mother of Horus; *Nephthys*, her sister and protector of Kings; *Anubis*, the jackal-headed lord of the sacred land and protector of the soul in death; *Osiris* (pronounced 'Ozeeriz'), brother of Isis and Nephthys, and lord of the afterlife. Each name can be used by the meditator in the same way as 'Om'.

Indeed, the names in one sense go further, since each provides a visual symbol as well as an aural one. Surviving funerary papyri depict the pantheon of Egyptian gods in similar, if less elaborate, detail to the buddhas and bodhisattvas of the Tibetan rupas and thankas, and the meditator can make use of these images accordingly. As in the Buddhist pantheon, each symbol represents a particular positive quality. Thus, Horus represents the indwelling divine spirit soaring into the heavens, Thoth the enlightenment and wisdom that awaits us on the spiritual path, Isis the power of love and compassion, Nephthys the protective nurturing strength that cares for us, Anubis the destruction of fear and the provision of a safe passage through death, and Osiris the resurrection into a new life once this passage is completed.

And before we rebel at the idea of symbols which contain reference to animals, we should remember that in the West we use the symbols of both the lamb and the fish to refer to Christ, while the lion (courage), the donkey (slow-wittedness), the mule (stubbornness), the dog (devotion), the dove (peace) and many others are idioms of everyday speech. The Egyptian animal symbols serve to remind us of the qualities of spiritual power – its soaring nature, its fidelity, its gentleness, its wisdom, its compassion. The Hindu pantheon makes similar use of animal symbols, for example in the monkey-headed god Hanuman (the symbol of devotion), and the elephant-headed Ganesh (the symbol of steadfastness and spiritual strength).

## MEDITATION IN THE MYSTERY TRADITIONS

We have no surviving accurate details of the meditative practices used by the mystery traditions. But there is no doubt they involved both intensive visualization and the repetition of sacred names. Thus, for example, in meditating upon Isis the meditator would in all probability sound her name on each out-breath, while at the same time building up her image in the way discussed earlier.

There would also appear, particularly in the lesser mysteries (which had to do with Isis, the moon and the earth) and perhaps also in the greater mysteries (which had to do with Osiris, the sun and the next life) to be journeys not dissimilar to those undertaken by the shaman (Chapter 6). Thus the meditator would accompany the visualized god into inner realms, and there be shown secrets which he or she would take an oath not to disclose to the uninitiated. The power of the practice was helped by taking the meditator into secret inner rooms in the temple, and sometimes by the ritual discarding of garments (symbols of ignorance) at each point, so that the meditator arrived naked in the inner sanctum (study the legend of Ishtar's descent into the Lowerworld, on which the so-called 'dance of the seven veils' is based).

It is also possible that the meditator 'transferred' his or her consciousness, as is done in certain Tibetan Buddhist practices and Western magical traditions to this day. This involved building up a clear visualization of oneself, sitting in front of one and wearing ceremonial robes. Once the visualization was strongly formed (which could take much dedicated practice), the meditator visualized him or herself as inside the visualized image and looking back towards the physical self.

Once consciousness was thus transferred into the visualization, the meditator was said to be able to travel at will in this 'astral body' to places in this or in other worlds, often being physically seen by other individuals. It may be that this practice was combined with the journey into the realms of Isis or of Osiris, or that the latter took place only in the inner world of the mind.

Western psychology has in recent years become increasingly interested in this alleged transfer of consciousness as manifested in so-called OBEs (Out of Body Experiences), in which individuals feel that they leave their physical bodies and observe them from somewhere in space. Such experiences happen most frequently in the face of some crisis or in the moments between clinical death and resuscitation in hospital. Controversy rages as to whether consciousness actually leaves the body on these occasions or not, but there is evidence that the individuals concerned are able at times to gather information which they could not have obtained from the location of their physical bodies (see, for example, Michael Sabom's *Recollections of Death*).

One thing seems certain. The initiate into the mysteries was in no doubt that the experiences he or she gained were those of death and the afterlife. It is said that such initiates lost all fear of death from having journeyed first through the border country that divides the visible from the invisible world, and then entering into the bliss that lies beyond. Paul Brunton quotes one of the few surviving fragments from the little that was written about the mysteries, to the effect that:

> The mind is affected and agitated in death just as it is in initiation into the Grand Mysteries; the first stage is nothing but errors and uncertainties, labourings, wanderings and darkness. And now, arrived on the verge of death and initiation, everything wears a dreadful aspect; it is all horrors, trembling and affrightment. But this scene once over, a miraculous and divine light displays itself ... perfect and initiated they are free, crowned, triumphant, they walk in the regions of the blessed.
>
> *Search in Secret Egypt*, p. 183

Anyone familiar with the *Tibetan Book of the Dead*, a manual read by the lama to the dying in order to give them a map to the country they were about to enter, will find the above description strangely familiar. The parallels between the 'dreadful aspect' seen in the mysteries and the fearsome 'wrathful deities' detailed in the Tibetan text clearly point to a common experience, as do those between the 'miraculous and divine light' of the mysteries and the 'clear light' which heralds the dawning of true wisdom for the departed Tibetan.

## HINTS OF THE OLD GODS

It is not difficult, even in present-day Egypt, to catch hints of the symbolic power of the old gods. Study their 5000-year-old replicas in paint and stone in the museums and ruined temples. Enter the darkness of the Great Pyramid at Giza. Go out into the countryside where people still farm the land as they did when the gods were known. Sit by the Nile and meditate on a visualization of Isis or on the sound of her name. Watch the clear crescent of the moon in the velvet night and meditate on Anubis or Osiris. Egypt still whispers its magic, as if a memory on the brink of recall stirs in the depths of one's soul.

This is true not only of Egypt. Notice how, as you travel through foreign lands, the local gods become credible in a way that remains with you long after you return home. It is as if each god comes into symbolic being in obedience to that third possibility I mentioned when discussing the reality of Steiner's life

force in Chapter 6; the possibility that they are created through
the union of the minds of a particular people with the creative
power of the universe. Each human race and its way of seeing
the world is in many ways a product of the climate and terrain
which provide its environment. So not surprisingly each race
symbolizes divine reality in its own way. But it would be as
wrong to say that these symbols are therefore mere human
creations as it would be to say that stones are human creations
because it is we who fashion them into our towns and cities.

## THE KABBALAH

The meditation practices involved in the mystery traditions
demand intense mental and emotional concentration allied to
highly developed powers of visualization and a rigorous inner
discipline, the whole assisted by rituals to sharpen further the
awareness and the concentration. By means of such techniques
the practitioner ascends step-by-step through the various levels
of spiritual realization until he or she passes beyond the symbols
of divinity and arrives at the final goal of union with the absolute. Regardie expresses it poetically:

> Arrived at the Crown, the Magician is no more. There still exists,
> however, that supernal consciousness of Eternal Life which is the
> real individuality of the Magician – that real part of him of which,
> perhaps, he was rarely conscious during his former lives on earth –
> that primal universal spirit, pulsing and vibrating unseen in the core
> of the heart of all.
>
> *The Tree of Life*, p. 246

Regardie's use of the symbol of the *Crown* introduces that
important element in the Western magical tradition mentioned
earlier, the Kabbalah. I have to say that although I have
attended both theoretical and practical teachings on the Kabbalah,
and am familiar with much of the extensive literature on the
subject, I do not claim to understand the full intricacies of the
system. Such understanding demands years of intensive study
which, orthodox Jews tell me, no-one should undertake until
past the age of forty and mature both in worldly experience and
religious knowledge.

At its simplest, however, the Kabbalah can be thought of in terms of the ten *sefirot* (singular, *sefirah*) (see Box 16), the constituents of the so-called 'Tree of Life', a symbolic representation of the ten forces that make up not only the psychological and spiritual life of the individual, but also the blueprint of creation itself. A full discussion of the Tree of Life would take up too much space – Gershom Scholem's *Kabbalah* is a standard work for those who want to explore further – but of particular relevance is the fact that the ten sefirot comprising the Tree of Life relate also to the levels through which the meditator ascends as he or she progresses on the spiritual path.

Charles Poncé, in his *Kabbalah: An Introduction and Illumination for the World Today*, draws interesting parallels between these levels and the yogic teachings of the ascent of kundalini (see Chapter 4), and between the individual sefirot and each yogic chakra. Poncé speaks of the union of the energy contained in the exiled feminine principle residing in Malkuth, the lowest sefirah, and the male energy contained in Kether, the highest. Through this union, the energy dissipated in the slumbering world of our passions becomes united with our spiritual energy, a 'mystical wedding' between the two forces within the human being takes place, and enlightenment dawns.

This 'mystical wedding' also lies at the heart of another aspect of the magical tradition, namely alchemy, in which the 'base metal' of the self is transmuted into the 'gold' of enlightenment; it is fascinating to note the extent to which this symbolism occurs and re-occurs in the magical tradition in general. Behind this symbolism lies Hermes Trismegistus' maxim mentioned earlier, 'as above, so below'. The material energy of the body is not eternally different in kind from the spiritual energy of the soul. Both stem from the same creative source. This material energy – our 'base metal' – can be raised up and transmuted into spiritual energy – into 'gold'. When the union takes place we know in a burst of illumination who we really are, and henceforth instead of living in the limited world of our material energy we live in the boundless world of the spirit.

In a sense we thus become as gods, since spiritual wisdom and power now act through us without impediment. And for certain of the alchemists, the belief also was that once we have transmuted the base metal of material being into the gold of spiritual

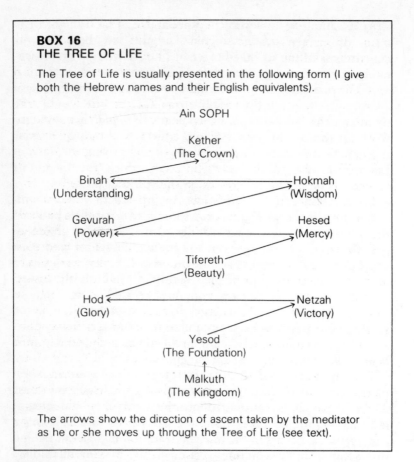

**BOX 16**
**THE TREE OF LIFE**

The Tree of Life is usually presented in the following form (I give both the Hebrew names and their English equivalents).

Ain SOPH

Kether
(The Crown)

Binah                                    Hokmah
(Understanding)                          (Wisdom)

Gevurah                                  Hesed
(Power)                                  (Mercy)

Tifereth
(Beauty)

Hod                                      Netzah
(Glory)                                  (Victory)

Yesod
(The Foundation)

Malkuth
(The Kingdom)

The arrows show the direction of ascent taken by the meditator as he or she moves up through the Tree of Life (see text).

being – and have thus found the symbolic 'philosopher's stone' – we gain similar powers of transmutation over the natural world. We can in consequence turn the base metal of other people and even of our environment into gold, in the same way that contact with an enlightened being is said in the Eastern traditions to produce enlightenment in the mind of the devotee. The philosopher's stone can thus be put to use in both the spiritual and the material worlds. Again, 'as above, so below'.

For Poncé, the mystical wedding of matter and spirit within us also depends upon a balance between the two outer columns of the Tree of Life. He compares these two columns to ida and pingala in the yogic tradition, and likens the central column, up which the energy of Malkuth ascends on its way to Kether, to the yogic sushumna. However, he then differs from yogic teaching in arguing that spiritual energy, in its ascent from Malkuth to Kether, can pass up the two outer channels as well as through the central one. Direct passage through the central channel is the quickest root to enlightenment, but there are few who can take it. A surer if slower root is to move up in turn through each sefirah, acquiring the spiritual powers it contains as one proceeds.

Nevertheless, the extent of the difference between this teaching and that of yoga is more apparent than real. For the philosophy of the Kabbalah holds that energy must not ascend *directly* up either of the outside channels. It must alternate between them as shown in Box 16, passing in turn through each sefirah, including those in the centre channel. In this way perfect balance is maintained within the system. Should energy ascend only through one of the outer channels this balance would be lost, with the disastrous results described shortly.

In order to understand the meditative techniques involved in this ascent through the sefirot, a qualified teacher is needed. But if my understanding of these techniques is correct, and if my own meditations upon the Tree of Life have any meaning, they follow the pattern common to the flowing meditations looked at in Chapter 5. The meditator thus experiences — and uses as the focus of concentration — the principal quality associated with each sefirah in turn, allowing the unconscious to reveal the true meaning of this quality, and in doing so to free its potential within him or herself.

So the meditator focuses initially upon Malkuth, the Kingdom, the body itself, either through meditations such as that on the elements described in Chapter 6, or through the scanning techniques used in vipassana (Chapter 4). Once insight is obtained at this level he or she moves to Yesod, the Foundation, the link between body and mind, working here on looking into the real nature of thoughts and emotions and seeing that these do not represent one's true identity. The next focus of concentration is Netzah, Victory, as one now gains victory over the thoughts and emotions that previously controlled the inner world. As a result Hod, Glory, emerges, the stillness and the space that are consequent upon the attainment of Netzah.

Next comes Tifereth, Beauty, the entry into the bliss of the spiritual realms, followed by Hesed, Compassion, characterized by infinite unselfish love. After Hesed comes Gevurah, Power, power over the heart and mind and over the hearts and minds of others. After Gevurah comes Hokmah, Wisdom, the all-seeing wisdom of the spiritual adept that allows him or her to see into the true nature of reality. Hokmah is followed by Binah, Understanding, the understanding of *why* reality is as it is, the understanding of creation itself, followed finally by Kether, the Crown. And in achieving Kether the mystical wedding takes place, material and spiritual become one, and the meditator attains to full enlightenment.

I say followed 'finally' by Kether, but there is one more stage, if it can be called a stage, where one leaves behind even the Tree of Life itself and ascends into Ain Soph, the absolute, the godhead, the ground of our being, the experience beyond experience where all distinctions disappear, the experience about which nothing is known until we *become* it.

To ascend thus through the Tree of Life the meditator must complete successfully the task contained in each of the sefirot before proceeding to the next. We can see now why it is dangerous to ascend through just one of the outer channels. To ascend exclusively through the left-hand channel and attain Hod, Glory, without first proceeding through Netzah, Victory, would lead to spiritual pride, inflating rather than diminishing the ego. To attain Gevurah, Power, without first knowing Hesed, Mercy, would be to use spiritual forces for personal gain (the temptation of Christ in the wilderness). And to attain Binah, Understanding, without Hokmah, the Knowledge which is to be understood, would be impossible.

Similarly, to ascend exclusively through the right-hand channel and attain Hesed, Mercy, without Hod, Glory, would mean that one's love would be of the emotional, personal kind, and thus not entirely unselfish, while to attain Hokmah, Wisdom, without first attaining Gevurah, Power, would mean that one's wisdom would be purely theoretical, unsustained by direct experience of the spiritual powers of which one speaks. By ascending through one or other of the outer channels the meditator would also miss out Tifereth, Beauty, the entry into spiritual reality. He or she could, however, ascend exclusively through the centre channel, the fast track so to speak, going directly from Malkuth, the Kingdom, to Yesod, the Foundation, to Tifereth, Beauty, to Kether, the Crown. But as I said earlier, this is a difficult path, probably impossible for all save great natural mystics.

But how does one know whether one has completed the task at each sefirah? In formal Kabbalistic training, a teacher is on hand to assess progress. But in one sense the progress is automatic in that when the task is completed at one sefirah, the task contained in the next appears of itself ('when the student is ready, the teacher appears'). The sefirot are thus not simply a set of stepping stones, they are a map of the stages through which any meditation must pass as the meditator progresses. A good teacher will ensure you do not delude yourself about your own progress, and will assist that progress by giving you a metaphorical nudge if you appear to be stuck, but ultimately the meditator rises as a result of his or her own efforts and developing spritual energy. A useful metaphor is a bubble. As it grows bigger, so it moves through successive obstacles in its path until ultimately it breaks surface into the light of day.

In some Kabbalistic teachings the meditator is encouraged to use the Hebrew letters for each sefirah as a visual focus in meditation. The letters are themselves claimed to hold symbolic value, much as do geometrical forms. In other teachings, and in particular in Christian Kabbalism (the Kabbalah was adapted to Christian use during the sixteenth and seventeenth centuries), the Tarot cards can be used as an adjunct, with each card associated with the path from one sefirah to the next. The Zodiac can also be used, with each sign of the Zodiac similarly associated with one of the paths. Poncé, for example, gives directions on how this is done. But although the Tarot cards, which are rich in symbolism, can be useful aids to meditation in and of themselves, helping the meditator develop powers of visualization and make contact with the unconscious, there is little justification in linking them with the Kabbalah, and the same goes for the signs of the Zodiac. Both of these attempts at establishing links have an artificial quality about them, and are elaborations by the nineteenth-century French occultist Eliphas

Levi. Neither of them appears to have any real basis in the original Kabbalistic literature.

## THE HINDU TRADITION

The hatha yoga aspects of the Hindu tradition were dealt with in Chapter 4, but as mentioned at the time there are four other principal yogic paths: bhakti yoga (the yoga of devotion), karma yoga (the yoga of good works), rajah yoga (the yoga of higher meditation), and jnana yoga (the yoga of knowledge). Taken together, the yogas present a complete path and in whatever tradition one is working, it is valuable for the meditator to reflect on whether each of these five paths is contained in some form in his or her life. The level at which each of the paths is engaged need not be of equal intensity. Normally one or two will be emphasized above the others but none of them should be completely neglected.

Thus, for example, the serious meditator pays attention to the body, the temple of the spirit, ensuring that it is not over-indulged on the one hand or neglected on the other (hatha yoga). He or she also pays attention to actions, attempting to do good and refrain from evil (karma yoga). Likewise he or she will have feelings of veneration and respect towards the spiritual teachers whose tradition he or she is following – or at the very least towards meditation itself (bhakti yoga), will wish to learn as much as possible about this tradition and its meditation practices (jnana yoga), and will want to put these practices into consistent effect (rajah yoga).

Whichever of the five paths you wish to emphasize, and whichever tradition you follow, you owe a debt to the sages of northern Indian who, 3000 years ago, mapped out the inner world of the mind and developed meditation techniques for its exploration. This surprises many people who trace their spiritual practices back the 2000 years or so to the birth of Christ. But as Seymour is quoted as saying (*The Forgotten Mage*, p. 107), 'God has never left Himself without witness, or His world without light'. Indeed, why should He? To do so would deny His own creation.

In historical terms, much in the spiritual philosophies of the

Western world can be traced back to the worship of Mitras by the Aryan peoples who arrived in northern India in the second millennium BC. Mitras is mentioned in the Hindu *Rig Veda*, one of the oldest known scriptures, and over the centuries his worship took on increasing importance amongst the Western branch of the Aryans who settled in what is now Iran. Mitras, or Mithras in his Iranian form, was seen as the life of the visible world, the saviour of mankind, the intermediary between the spirit and the flesh, the son of the Absolute Creator, Ahura Mazda.

With the subsequent emigrations of the Aryan peoples – northwards through Asia Minor and along the Danube as far as Britain, westwards into Spain and northern Italy, and southwards into Lebanon, Babylon, Palestine and Egypt – the cult of Mithras spread through much of the known world. It influenced Greek, Roman and Egyptian thought (where Mithras is in many ways identified with Horus), and probably served as the origin for all the mystery cults discussed earlier. In the Zoroastrian religion of Iran, Mithras was symbolized as the good shepherd, the protector of the poor, the guide through the valley of the shadows between this world and the next, the defender of righteousness, the bringer of light. In the words of Ahura Mazda in the Zoroastrian scriptures, he was 'as worthy of prayer as myself'.

As mentioned earlier, the wise men from the East at the birth of Christ were Zoroastrians, and it is likely that to them Jesus was the incarnation of Mithras, fulfilling by his birth the hopes of both East and West. Legend has it that Christ studied with the Zoroastrians during the lost years between his appearance in the temple at age twelve and the beginning of his ministry some eighteen years later. Certainly much of the symbolism used in his teaching was closer to Mithraism than to Judaism, and his message encapsulated all that was best in the spirituality of his day, from east of Jerusalem as well as from west.

The techniques of meditation which Mithraism brought from the East, and which permeated the mysteries, are still taught in India from where the Aryans migrated, and are an essential part of Hinduism. I say 'Hinduism', but in fact Hinduism is so vast and culturally and spiritually profound that it would be more accurate to speak of the *Hindu religions*, were it not that

Hinduism, with its deep understanding of spirituality, does not fragment and categorize humanity on the basis of localized differences in the expression of this spirituality. For the devout Hindu, all religions are an attempt to achieve union with the Absolute, and individual differences between them are simply the result of individual differences within humankind. Because a person follows one particular form of spiritual observance does not mean that other forms are therefore wrong. And a Hindu will be almost as likely to have an image of Christ or the Buddha on the family shrine as an image of Krishna or the many Hindu symbols of the one spiritual reality.

The form of Hinduism best known in the West is Vedanta (which simply means it places emphasis upon the early scriptures of the Vedas). There are many reasons for this, but the most important is that Vivekananda, a young follower of the Hindu saint Ramakrishna, arrived in North America in 1893 to attend the Parliament of Religions in Chicago. Apart from short breaks, the rest of his life until his early death in 1902 was spent in the West, teaching not a narrow dogma but a vision of God and man so majestic and complete in its scope, yet at the same time so human and immediate, that anyone who studies it cannot but feel it contains the essence of all that is best in humankind's attempts to walk and talk with the divine.

Such was the impact of Vivekananda's teaching that he attracted followers who carried on his work after his death, inviting other influential Vedantic teachers to the west. The movement (if such it can be called, for Vedanta is not a proselytising religion and is more concerned to help you live your life than to convert you into calling yourself a Vedantist) continued to grow, and during the 1930s prominent writers such as Aldous Huxley, Gerald Heard and Christopher Isherwood identified with it, and brought it to the attention of the general public. From my personal experiences in Vedanta, I can say that no-one who cares about the inner life can fail to be helped by studying Vivekananda's life and teachings (see, for example, *Inspired Talks*), and the same can be said in even greater measure for his teacher, Sri Ramakrishna.

The Hindus have a term 'avatar' which refers to those rare people who embody such spiritual power that they are expressions on earth of those qualities which we associate with God.

For the Hindus, such individuals are more than saints, they are
direct incarnations of God. Since this may be difficult for the
Western mind to accept, we can speak of them as perfect symbols of God. Such rare individuals manifest in their lives what
the rest of us can become. They are without sin and without self,
acting as channels through which spiritual power pours unim-
peded from the inner to the outer world, from the spirit to the
flesh. Just such a person was Sri Ramakrishna. Although he
wrote nothing himself, his teachings were carefully noted down
by his followers, as for example in *The Condensed Gospel of Sri
Ramakrishna*, recorded and translated into English by Mahen-
dran Nath Gupta.

Sri Ramakrishna taught that, for the people of the modern
age, the best blend of the yogic paths is bhakti (devotion) and
jnana (knowledge). Bhakti devoid of jnana, he makes clear, can
lead to empty sentimentalism, while jnana without bhakti can
become mere dialectic skill. But when the two are harmonized
and balanced, life becomes 'sweet, majestic and sublime'. In
both bhakti and jnana, meditation is the essential practice. Men
and women must have direct experience of ultimate reality, by
whatever name they call it. Dogmas, creeds, rituals, book learning, scholarship are of no use unless one also practises the inner
path that brings a full realization of one's own being and of the
source from which it springs.

And here Ramakrishna presents us with a gift that, if we
choose to accept it, puts an end to those conflicts between and
within the great religions that have caused so much suffering
over the centuries. For, over a period of time, he himself followed
intensively and in turn not only the major spiritual paths within
Hinduism but also those of Islam, Christianity and Buddhism,
and demonstrated through his own life that each led to the same
enlightenment. Writing of Ramakrishna's direct experience of
the inner truths of other religions, Swami Ghanananda puts it
that:

> He had traversed the vast and wealthy domain of Hinduism and
> would now travel outside for a while. . . It was not idle curiosity that
> prompted him to do so; he had attained a remarkable catholicity of
> mind and breadth of vision by the practice and realization of the
> Advaita – the crowning glory of the Vedanta, the rationale and
> science of religions and philosophy. This looks upon all paths and all

creeds as but different approaches to the one indivisible Brahman, the Absolute, into which the Personal God, however conceived, merges. Advaita regards the followers of all religions, irrespective of caste, creed or colour, as pilgrims, more or less conscious, bound for the Temple of Truth, to which the religions of the world are but so many roads.

*Sri Ramakrishna and His Unique Message*, p. 88

The Advaita is a philosophy of non-dualism, teaching that ultimate truth is the unity to which I have made so many references in this book. And Ramakrishna's realization of this truth through Christianity, Islam and Buddhism as well as through Hinduism demonstrates Advaita at practical as well as theoretical levels. Ramakrishna thus stands as a symbol of divine unity, a man poised at the meeting point of all paths.

Yet Ramakrishna had another gift for us, one which resolves the dispute between those who argue that ultimate truth is personal and best symbolized by a personal God, and those who hold it to be an impersonal Absolute. For Ramakrishna's direct experience of the unity under all diversity did not lead him to reject the idea of the personal God expressed in theistic religions such as Islam and Christianity. To be whole, Ramakrishna taught that we must have bhakti as well as jnana, love as well as wisdom. The personal God is an emanation from the Absolute that helps humankind develop this love, while the Absolute itself is approached through wisdom. Thus bhakti is associated with the personal God, and jnana with what lies beyond the personal. If our path is to attain the Absolute, it should therefore include realizations at both the personal and the impersonal levels.

I spoke in Chapter 8 of the three-level Hindu conception of God, namely God with form and attributes, God without form but with attributes, and God without form or attributes. It is given to very few to experience the ultimate level of this conception, the reality beyond both form and attributes – Brahman to the Hindus, the Ground of our Being to the Christian mystics, Nirvana to the Buddhists, Ahura Mazda to the Zoroastrians, On to the Greek and Amoun to the Egyptian mystery religions – without first experiencing the two preliminary levels. In Kabbalistic terms, we must ascend through all the sefirot if we truly wish to attain to Kether and experience Ain Soph. In particular, we should avoid ascending just through the path leading to wisdom without also passing through the path containing love.

Let me illustrate this by examples from Buddhism. In Buddhism there are two main schools of thought, the *theravadin* and the *mahayana*, the former prevalent in Sri Lanka and south east Asia, and the latter in Tibet, India and the Far East. Theravadins claim to be faithful to the original teachings of the Buddha, which offer a practice stripped of gods or heavenly realms, and which stress self-discipline, moral norms and renunciation of the world as the only way towards enlightenment. Mahayanists, on the other hand, claim to be faithful to the Buddha's later teachings, which detail wider opportunities for enlightenment, and refer to a pantheon of celestial beings available to help the efforts of mortals.

With its emphasis upon salvation through one's own efforts, theravadin Buddhism holds the Buddha to have been a mere mortal like the rest of us, and although it reveres and respects him, it lays no great stress on bhakti. This failure to recognize the need for bhakti as well as jnana produces what some regard as a 'dryness' in the theravadin path absent from the mahayana. The latter, although also a powerful jnana practice, has a strong bhakti element through its devotion to the Buddha and the various cosmic beings who, though different in theoretical terms, are in practice treated much as the personal gods or saints of the other great religions. The absence of bhakti is seen most clearly in the theravadin ideal of the *arhat*, the individual who achieves enlightenment for him or herself and enters Nirvana alone, while its presence is most apparent in the mahayanist ideal of the *bodhisattva*, the person who has achieved enlightenment but who, through pure compassion, returns to the world in countless incarnations until all can enter Nirvana together. The former path retains elements of self, while the latter is perhaps the purest symbol of selfless altruism available to the human mind.

The bodhisattva is in fact the embodiment of the bhakti path as defined by Ramakrishna, namely the path of 'communion by love, devotion and self-surrender'. The counterbalance it provides for jnana is clear when we study Ramakrishna's definition of the latter as the path leading to realizations that:

I am not the body, gross or subtle. I am one with the Universal Soul, the Being Absolute and Unconditioned. Not being the body, I am not subject to the necessities of the body – e.g., hunger, thirst, birth, death, disease, grief, pleasure, pain, etc.

*Condensed Gospel of Sri Ramakrishna*, p. 194

Jnana, by itself, can thus lead to indifference to our own suffering and the suffering of others, since they, too, are not the body. It can lead to that indifference to physical welfare which is the great failure of the East, and even to a lack of reverence for the material world and the things within it. We need an awareness of the personal God to develop this reverence, just as we need neighbours if we are to learn to love them as ourselves.

For Ramakrishna, the realization of the personal God in meditation is *savikalpa samadhi*, a samadhi in which the meditator retains some sense of individuality contemplating divinity, while the realization of ultimate reality is *nirvikalpa samadhi*, in which individuality is absorbed without trace into this divinity. Both, said Ramakrishna, should be realized, and ultimately no distinction exists between the two.

Ghanananda, in his commentary on Ramakrishna, emphasizes this absence of distinction when, speaking of the personal and impersonal aspects of God, he writes that:

The formful and the formless aspects of God are like the obverse and reverse of one and the same coin. If you say that you want a coin with only the image of the Queen and not the design on the other side, you will not even have the side with the Queen, because you cannot have a coin with only one side. Formless God is the basis of God with form. The illustration of the ocean is useful. As the ocean, water has ... no form; but as waves, [it] has form ...

*Ibid.*, p. 51

The parallels between savikalpa samadhi and nirvikalpa samadhi on the one hand and the positive and absolute samadhi of Zen meditation (Chapter 8) are too obvious to need comment. In his own practice, Ramakrishna took as the personal God the feminine principle of creation, Kali the divine mother, but while practising Christianity he meditated constantly upon Christ, and while practising Islam upon Allah. In connection with his Islamic practice, Ghanananda reports Ramakrishna as refusing to enter a Hindu temple and as saying subsequently:

... I used to repeat the name of Allah, dress myself in the fashion of Muslims, and recite Namaz regularly. All Hindu ideas being wholly banished from the mind, not only did I not salute the Hindu gods and goddesses, but I had no inclination to visit them.

*Ibid.*, p. 89

In the final stage of this practice, Ramakrishna experienced first Allah with form and attributes and finally without either. A similar realization came to him through Christianity, and he said afterwards of Christ, 'This is the Christ who poured out His heart's blood for the redemption of mankind and suffered agonies for its sake. It is none else than ... the embodiment of love'. When told that the Buddha was called an atheist, Ramakrishna replied:

Why atheist? He was no atheist – only he could not speak out his realizations. Do you know what 'Buddha' means? To become one with 'Bodha', the Supreme Intelligence, through deep meditation, to become pure Intelligence itself.

*Ghanananda*, pp. 92–3

On another occasion Ramakrishna remarked that, 'There is no difference between the doctrines of the Buddha and those of the Vedic *Jnanakanda* ... Being and non-being are modifications of Prakriti [mind stuff]. The Reality transcends them both'. (Ghanananda, p. 93)

I remember once the monk leading a Buddhist meditation retreat I was attending saying that the 'mistake' of the Hindus was to search for the self, whereas Buddhists recognized that the self was simply the temporary creation of the mind. The monk, in this case a highly educated Westerner who had entered the Tibetan *gelupa* sect, was a sincere and good man, who genuinely believed what he was saying. Yet if he had taken the trouble to study Hinduism even fleetingly, he would have found that what Hindus refer to as the 'Self' is not the learned, transient human ego to which like Buddhists and Westerners they give the term 'self', but the ultimate reality to which I have made so many references, and which the Buddhists call Nirvana.

He would have learned too that for the Hindu, *Atman* – which is our own enlightened mind – is ultimately one with *Brahman*, the impersonal absolute mind, in the same way that the Buddha-mind to which he himself kept referring is ultimately one with Nirvana. The difference between the Hindu and Buddhist positions on these matters is one of semantics, born of the attempt to express in language what is in fact inexpressible. No wonder that the Buddha kept silent when asked questions about ultimate reality, and preferred instead to encourage people to follow the practice by which it can be attained.

I wondered afterwards why the monk had not paid Hinduism the attention it deserves before making reference to its beliefs. In a similar way I wonder why individuals don't even study the different branches within their own tradition before dismissing them. (On my return once from Soto Zen teachings, a follower of Tibetan Buddhism remarked, 'Then he's not a Buddhist', when I told him the Abbot giving the teachings had referred to 'the Eternal'.) Why must we fragment ourselves over the terms we use, when the experiences of which we are trying to speak defy definition?

Sometimes it is enough just to go to a place of worship of a different tradition to recognize the foolishness of this. I was brought up in a fundamental Christian non-conformist sect, and early absorbed the teaching that Roman Catholicism, with its saints and its cult of the Virgin was an idolatrous, even downright wicked presence within the Christian family. Although I later parted company with my fundamentalist sect, my feelings of suspicion towards Catholicism remained, and were much compounded when I came upon the ruthless way in which, in its name, gnosticism had been exterminated (see Chapter 5).

Thus, on my first visit to St Peter's in Rome, I entered with little in the way of fellow-feeling. The visit proved to be moving because of the physical presence of that majestic building, but consciously did nothing to change my views about Catholicism. However, on waking the following morning, I found to my astonishment that my outlook had undergone a profound transformation. I now 'knew', at a deep inner level, why the Catholics revered their saints and adored the Virgin. And this 'knowing' has never left me. It hasn't prompted me to join the Catholic Church; it isn't a 'conversion' in that sense. But it is an awareness of being initiated into the devotion of all those pious souls who have found their path in Catholicism, and of having received from them the gift of kinship.

## NO PLACE FOR FANATICISM

Ramakrishna put it that the Reality which we struggle to express is linguistically like water. People call water by many different names, but water still remains water, and still quenches the thirst when we actually drink it. Chidbhavanananda summarizes Ramakrishna's teaching on the need to avoid narrowness as follows:

> The fanatic sincerely believes that his path alone is true and the others are no paths at all. He feels it his duty to attack other religions. But this attitude is born of ignorance. The fanatic helps neither himself nor others. He deals out nothing but evil. Contrary to this, same-sightedness and acceptance of all religions are born of enlightenment. This enlightenment comes as a result of one's comparing notes with paths that have not been one's own till now. It is all right for a baby to commence its life exclusively in the domain of its mother. But subsequently as the child grows it must contact others so that its outlook may expand. Acquaintance with others does not come into conflict with attachment to mother. A religious person has, in like manner, to create in him an attitude of devotional inquiry into faiths other than his own. If he does not piously seek to study the other paths, he brings on himself the misfortune of shrinking into the shell of his own religion.
>
> *Ramakrishna lives Vedanta*, p. 267

Vivekananda made the same point with great simplicity when he said, 'You should be born in church, but you should not die there'.

Even atheism, Ramakrishna taught, can be a stage towards enlightenment for some people, and may be part of their spiritual evolution. Provided atheists create 'a melting earnestness' for elevating themselves through self-effort, and keep in their minds that they are seekers after truth, then 'as fresh air passes in through an open window, truth reveals itself to a mind kept open by earnest enquiry'. The only bar to progress is closure of the gate of understanding 'with the shutters of egotism'. Such closure, as I understand it, is in fact the sin against the Holy Spirit, for which there can be no forgiveness because *until* one opens the mind there is no possibility of redemption.

But Ramakrishna was careful to point out that religious

harmony must not lead one to follow *no* particular path. This is as unhelpful as fanaticism. Unlike Ramakrishna, the rest of us have neither the time nor the capacity to practise all paths with the application they require. We must each choose the path to which we feel most suited, and pursue it with zeal. But – and this is my own interpretation – unless we are able to grasp at least intellectually the genuineness of the other great paths, then it is certain we will not have fully understood even our own.

# 10

## Objective Meditation II:
## Form and Formlessness

### MEDITATION IN VEDANTA

In view of the emphasis laid by Ramakrishna upon bhakti and jnana, the meditation practices taught by Vedanta are best looked at under these two separate headings. Both of them can be classed as objective meditation, though as we shall see the jnana quickly transcends any distinction between objective and subjective. Before discussing them however, there are some preliminary points in Vedanta which are of great benefit to the meditator.

The Vedas teach that there are three states of spiritual meditation: *sthula-dyana, tejo-dyana* and *sukshma-dyana*. The first, in which visions of saints or deities are seen and voices may be heard, is the flowing meditation dealt with in Chapter 5. The second, which in Vedanta represents a higher stage on the path and in which forms and visions disappear, is stilling meditation (Chapter 4). The third is a merging into Reality itself, an experience surpassing any other human experience. The first two of these meditative experiences allow one to enter savikalpa samadhi, while the third allows one to enter nirvikalpa.

These three states represent respectively the realization of God with form and attributes, the realization of God without form but with attributes, and the realization of God without form or attributes, and to the Vedantist they are the stages through which the meditator passes while following any of the practices dealt with in this book. (It is interesting to map them onto the Tree of Life, with the four lower sefirot corresponding to the first stage, the next three corresponding to the second, and the highest three and absorption into Ain Soph corresponding to the third.)

## THE EIGHT STEPS OF MEDITATION

In the Vedanta tradition, the meditator is counselled to follow eight important guidelines, often referred to as the eight steps of Rajah Yoga and first set out by Patanjali in his *Yoga Sutras* (Chapter 4). These largely cover points already made in this book, but they provide a valuable summary and I quote them in abbreviated form.

1. *Yama* – right conduct in everyday life; that is, truthfulness, chastity, avoidance of injury, of stealing, and of the acceptance of gifts (since gifts put us under obligation and destroy freedom of action).

2. *Niyama* – cleanliness of mind and body, equanimity, devotion to God, and the absence of greed and over-indulgence.

3. *Asana* – correct posture; in particular, a posture that allows one to sit for forty-five minutes or more in meditation.

4. *Pranayama* – correct breathing.

5. *Pratyahara* – gathering in of the forces of the mind from their habitual wanderings.

6. *Dharana* – fixing the mind upon a single idea.

7. *Dhyana* – centring the mind upon this idea for twenty minutes without a break in concentration.

8. *Samadhi* – superconsciousness, initially at the level of savikalpa and ultimately at the level of nirvikalpa.

I mentioned earlier that, although emphasizing only one or two of the yogas, the meditator need take some account of all of them, and these eight steps are an indication of how this need is met. The first two steps are karma yoga, and ensure that life is free from the desires and stresses of daily life that make it harder to concentrate in meditation. They go further and help rid us of the selfishness that would misuse any siddhis which may come through meditation. The result is the cleansing of mind and body necessary if they are to serve as a fit temple for the third aspect, the spirit. Without such cleansing, the spirit, although always present, is veiled from us.

We are fallible human beings and Steps 1 and 2 may look like impossible counsels of perfection, but they are guidelines towards which at the very least we can aspire. Steps 3 and 4 are somewhat easier and constitute an elementary though essential hatha yoga which keeps us sitting comfortably for the required period of time and (in the terms used in yoga philosophy) opens the subtle channels within the body up which energy travels during its transformation from gross to subtle, from physical to spiritual.

Step 5 involves collecting the mind, ideally through an introductory prayer, dedication or invocation – a ritual that turns the mind towards the inner world (bhakti yoga). The sixth step, *dharana*, is meditation itself (rajah yoga), with the mind centring upon the object of focus, while Step 7 is the difficult task of keeping the mind there. If and when this can be achieved for some twenty-five minutes, then Step 8 (jnana yoga) arises naturally of itself, and the meditator enters samadhi.

## MEDITATION AS BHAKTI

Whatever the meditation in which we engage, the first five of these eight stages are invariable. It is at Step 5, *pratyahara*, that differences arise, since now the meditator chooses the object of concentration. Vedanta teaches that initially this should be God with form and attributes, whether personified by an avatar, a saint, a bodhisattva, a revered teacher, or a symbol or mantra. A few – very few – people can, from the beginning, fix the mind upon formlessness, but for most of us this is very difficult. So Vedanta advises us to start at a more concrete level, and only later to 'proceed higher and attain to formlessness'. It tells us to place the focus of meditation – whether visualized, held as a thought or repeated as a mantra – in the heart centre, which in Vedanta is not the physical heart but a place just below the navel and in the interior of the body. 'There one seats the object of concentration', says Ghanananda in *Meditation*, 'The heart centre is the starting point for spiritual thought' (p. 50).

Ramakrishna laid particular emphasis upon *japa*, the repetition of the name of God (or of the object of devotion) as the focus of concentration in bhakti, and taught that it is the most accessible form of meditation. Japa is of course a version of *mantra* meditation, a widely used practice in all the great traditions. Mantra involves the repetition of a sound or series of sounds or words (silently or out loud), as for example the 'Hail Mary' of the Roman Catholics or the 'Jesus Prayer' ('Lord Jesus, son of God, have mercy upon me a sinner') of the Greek and Russian Orthodox Churches. In these, as in all traditions, the repetition of the mantra is sometimes coordinated with the breathing, either by a repetition on the out-breath or on both in-breath and out-breath. In the case of a long mantra, part is said on the in-breath and part on the out.

While carrying out these repetitions, the meditator focuses either upon the meaning of each word in the mantra or upon the sounds themselves, sometimes visualizing appropriate symbols to accompany them. Rather like 'Om', the sounds of many mantras are said to carry power in and of themselves (which is why we are told they are valueless in translation), power which takes the mantra deep into the unconscious where it continues to work even when not being recited.

This idea of particular sounds carrying creative power goes back to the beginnings of recorded history, and occurs in the teaching that it was the 'word' of God that created (or continually creates) the visible world. 'In the beginning was the Word.' 'God said, let there be light, and there was light.' The vibrations which constitute sound are thus held to be the primal 'matter' that precedes the appearance of the physical world, the first movement in the undifferentiated unity of being. Try this out for yourself on a mundane level by striking a tuning fork near a cardboard sheet on which you've sprinkled very find sand, and notice how the grains arrange themselves into geometrical shapes in response. The shapes are the visual representation of the sound wave, its signature, its unique creation.

In Buddhist and Hindu traditions, when uttering a mantra, a *mala* containing 108 beads (a number with astrological significance in India) is frequently used, with a repetition of the mantra as each bead is fingered in turn. Catholics and Muslims make similar use of rosaries and prayer beads. The mantra can also be repeated, silently and without the mala, as one goes about daily tasks, and from personal experience I know that after some months of this constant repetition the mantra seemingly comes to rest in the heart centre, where one is aware of it continuing even when the mind is actively concerned with other things. Far from distracting the concentration, this constant repetition at the background of awareness sharpens the mind by occupying the space that would normally be taken up with mental distractions.

An alternative to this constant repetition is to repeat the mantra a set number of times last thing at night, so that again it is taken into the heart centre (into the unconscious if you prefer), where it continues during the hours of sleep. And of course the mantra is also used as the point of focus in sitting meditation, either repeated aloud or silently, whichever the meditator finds most helpful.

## THE MEANING AND USE OF MANTRA

The word *mantra* is thought to be a combination of the first syllables of the Sanskrit words *manna* (thinking) and *trana* (liberation from the bondage of appearances). A mantra is therefore liberation from thinking, but over the centuries the word has also come to mean 'that which protects', indicating that an appropriate mantra is believed to guard against the perils of the outer world as well as taking one into the inner. (There are also destructive mantras of sorcery and witchcraft, as revealed in the *Atharva Veda*.)

In the Eastern traditions, each mantra is believed to have been first conveyed to the spiritual teacher with whom it is associated while he or she was in a state of superconsciousness. The mantra is therefore the 'sound signature' of the teacher, rather as the shapes in the sand are the sound signature of the tuning fork, and the teacher reveals him or herself to inner consciousness in response to the mantra when the meditator is sufficiently practised in its use.

Usually, you are given a mantra when you are initiated into the practice of a great teacher within the tradition you follow, together with precise instructions on how to use it. It is said that this allows the mantra to carry extra power, since you are hearing it from someone who heard it from someone who heard it from someone right back to the spiritual teacher to whom it was first revealed. But if you have not received any particular initiation, this need not stop you using a mantra. First learn as much as you can about the tradition you are following, and then find which of the teachers within it raises in you the strongest emotional response. Often this response comes as a sudden awareness of great love for the teacher concerned, as if they are a friend you have always known in your heart.

The next step is to take his or her mantra, regarding it as their embodiment in sound. Don't look upon it simply as a name (though names can be powerful things). Look upon it as an actual emanation, as the sound form corresponding to the visual form of the teacher. Unlike the visual form, the sound form is materially present. You can pronounce it whenever you please, and when you do, sense (don't visualize yet) that the teacher is physically present.

When sitting in meditation, the procedure now is to merge this feeling of presence with your own heart centre. Sense (still without visualization) that the teacher is seated in this centre, his or her consciousness a living and vital reality inside yourself. Now silently start the repetitions of the mantra, placing each repetition in imagination in the same heart centre, thus stabilizing the sense of presence.

The advice not to visualize during these early stages of practice is because doing so distracts the attention from the mantra. For the moment, you are working purely with sound and the sense of presence evoked by sound. However, when the practice is well established, a visualization may form of itself. This is the revelation of the teacher at the level of inner consciousness that I referred to earlier. Unlike the visualization practices discussed in Chapter 7, this visualization does not have to be built up in your own mind. It appears spontaneously, just as the shapes in the sand appear spontaneously in response to the tuning fork. The visualization may be the form of the teacher, or it may be the Sanskrit letters of the mantra. Usually you will already be familiar with these, but they will appear as if not from the memory but from a dimension of their own. Don't debate where they come from. As with the forms built up through active visualization, treat them *as if* they are real. Allow the visualization to remain at the centre of your practice, offering each repetition of the mantra to it.

If such an image does not arise spontaneously, this is of no special importance. Continue working just with the mantra in the way I discuss in the next section, or build the visualization consciously, allowing it to appear, as it were, from the energy generated by the mantra.

But as with all visualizations, don't become attached to this image, no matter how it appears. Remember that Vedanta teaches that this is only the first of the three stages of meditation. Later there will come a stage when your meditation passes into formlessness. Become attached to forms now and you will either resist this stage (thus preventing further development) or feel a powerful sense of loss (an emotion which equally stands in your way). For a time will come when even the mantra is left behind, like a ladder that has helped you climb and is no longer needed.

---

**BOX 17**
**SOME MANTRAS**

Within the Christian religion, the Jesus Prayer, mentioned in the text, has been at the centre of the meditation tradition in the Orthodox Churches of Russia and Greece. The *Philokalia*, an inspired collection of writings some of which date back to the fourth century AD, gives an indispensable account of how this prayer is used in meditation, while R. M. French's translations of the two anonymous spiritual classics *The Way of a Pilgrim* and *The Pilgrim Continues His Way* are also excellent sources of information.

Islam uses particularly *Allah ahkba* (*A-la ak-ba*), 'God is great', and *La illa ha illa Allah ho* (*Lah ih-luh hah ih-luh A-la hoo*), 'There is nothing but God'. Both mantras can be chanted on all occasions, but Islam does not encourage the use of devotional

**BOX 17**
**SOME MANTRAS**

mantras directed at saints or prophets. Nor does it encourage visualization of God in any pictorial form. For Islam, one approaches God either through attributes (such as mercy, power and love) or at the ultimate level of formlessness ('nothing but God').

Of the numerous mantras in the Tibetan Buddhist tradition, three of the most widely used are those of the Buddha, of Tara, and of Avalokiteshvara. Buddha's mantra, *Tayata om muni muni maha munaye soha* (*Ta-ya-ta om mooni mooni ma-ha moon-aye-ye so-ha*), is used primarily to awaken the Buddha mind, the mind of full enlightenment, within oneself and others. Often practised together with a strong visualization of the Buddha, this enlightenment is imagined as streaming from him in white rays of purifying light.

Tara's mantra, *Om tare ture tuttare ture soha* (pronounced *Om taray too-ray too-ttaray too-ray so-ha*), is used to help awaken the 'skilful means' necessary to liberate oneself from ignorance and fear. Tara, sometimes referred to as the 'Mother of the Buddhas', is visualized in female form, with white light flowing from her head to symbolize the elimination of negativities of body, red light from her throat eliminating negativities of speech, and blue light from her heart eliminating negativities of mind.

Avalokiteshvara, the Buddha of compassion, is visualized as radiating white, red, blue, green and yellow light to all beings, bringing compassion and relief from suffering. His mantra, *Om mani padme hum* (pronounced *Om marni pay-me hom*), sometimes called 'the great mantra', is one of the most popular of all and Tibetans are apt to chant it, with reverence and joy, when going about any of the activities of daily life.

Hinduism contains a mantra for virtually every occasion. Some are connected with a deity (an aspect of the one god), while others are more general. Some deities have more than one mantra. Among the most widely used short mantras are those of Shiva, *Shivo-ham* (*Shi-voh-hum*) – used to awaken one's own spirituality and to obtain enlightenment, and of Vishnu, *Hari om tat sat* (*Huh-ree ohm tut sut*) – used for purification and for the benefit of departed souls. *Om shanti* (*Ohm shahn-tee*), 'the peace of God', is used universally.

All the above mantras are held to be sanctified not only by the being with whom they are associated and by the quality of sound itself, but also through their use by devout men and women down the centuries. Rather like the atmosphere of sanctity sensed on entering a church or temple or mosque, they radiate an objective power all their own.

## MANTRA MEDITATION WITHOUT VISUALIZATION

I mentioned that if no visualization arises during mantra meditation, or if you choose not to build one for yourself, this is of no particular consequence. In fact, in some traditions it is considered an advantage, since there is less chance of becoming attached to forms and the progress into the experience of formlessness may be quicker. For those who dislike the idea of deities or Buddhas or bodhisattvas, the very idea of visualization may in any case be unattractive.

Whatever the reason, if you are working just with a mantra, take it into the heart centre in the way detailed earlier. Your concentration will be keener if you feel the mantra becoming a part of you rather than remaining a set of sounds which you are simply going to repeat. Look upon it as an object of bhakti, even if you don't associate it with any particular teacher – after all, it is going to help you towards self-knowledge. See it as a symbol of the wisdom deep within you, waiting to be entered. At the very least, it deserves respect.

Keep your mantra at the centre of your awareness. Try and make each repetition as mindful as the last. Once the meditation is well established, you can drop the mantra from time to time and stay focused on the space that it occupied. This isn't the limitless space of true formlessness. It is simply the finite space left by the mantra. You still have to go through other stages before you experience this limitless space but it is nevertheless an important advance.

If thoughts intrude again after a while, return to the mantra until concentration is re-established. In time you will be able to go through the whole meditation session with only a few initial mantra repetitions.

## THE ADVANTAGES OF MANTRA MEDITATION

Of all meditation techniques, mantra is the easiest to apply effectively. A mantra is more obvious as a point of concentration than the breathing, more accessible than a visualization, more effective as a way into tranquillity than a koan, and anyone who is making little progress in stilling the mind by other techniques should explore the path it offers. One of the reasons why Transcendental Meditation (TM) is such a popular meditation technique is that it is a simple form of mantra meditation in which the meditator focuses upon a single Sanskrit word and, with or without devotion to a religion or a spiritual teacher, repeats it over and over for fifteen minute sessions twice a day.

Even if you are firmly wedded to another meditation practice, it is still of great value to have a mantra, which you can repeat silently to yourself when you feel the need to calm a restless mind during the working day, or whenever – out of self-discipline or devotion – you wish to return to it. Relatively early in my first period of intensive practice with a mantra – long before I had actually been initiated into its use – I found that my mind automatically focused upon it the moment I put my thinking into neutral. Not only did this lead to feelings of greatly increased mental energy (many people are unaware of just how much mental energy the chattering mind uses up), it also helped the emergence of creative insight. Such insight arises from the unconscious, the wellspring of intuition, and by clearing the mind of the conscious thoughts that usually dominate it we unclog the channels through which the unconscious communicates.

And above and beyond everything, the mantra increases the meditator's love and devotion towards the object of practice. It is as if it taps a spring of emotion within the heart which flows through the meditator towards Christ or the Buddha or whoever, and through them towards all beings.

## THE FORMLESS ABSORPTIONS

The meditator is now ready to pass from meditation with form into formless meditation. This transition, and the stages that precede and follow it, is mapped into fourteen progressive stages by Tibetan Buddhism (see, for example, *Meditative States in Tibetan Buddhism* by Lati Rinbochay *et al.*), which are in effect a more detailed guide to the four highest stages identified by Vedanta (p. 192). These fourteen stages can be summarized as follows:

1. *Mindfulness* The meditation position is taken up and the mind turned towards meditation.

2. *Continuous Setting* Concentration is focused upon the mantra. Thoughts arise but are disregarded. Even when they no longer arise, the thought that 'thought is resting' still remains.

3. *Re-setting* Concentration deepens, and the mind recognizes and discards distractions the moment they arise.

4. *Close Setting* The object of concentration is now never lost, and *tranquillity* arises.

5. *Disciplining* Concentration becomes deeper still and *insight* begins to arise, but laxity (overwithdrawal into a trancelike state) may occur, and has to be avoided by disciplining the mind to maintain concentration.

6. *Pacifying* Laxity is overcome but excitement at the depth of one's meditation occurs, and has to be pacified by letting go of this emotion.

7. *Thorough Pacifying* Excitement is now fully overcome.

8. *One-pointedness* The mind is now fully centred upon the object of meditation, and may have the first glimpses of savikalpa (relative) samadhi.

9. *Mental Pliancy* A tingling is now felt at the top of the head as bad mental and physical states leave the body. The glimpses of samadhi may become more frequent.

10. *Physical Pliancy* The body feels soft and light and melts into (becomes one with) the object of meditation. Bliss arises and full savikalpa samadhi is entered.

11. *The First Formless Absorption* The mind becomes one with limitless space. Forms, including the object of meditation, disappear. Even 'the sound of a cannon' would not disturb. Nirvikalpa (absolute) samadhi begins to arise.

12. *The Second Formless Absorption* Even 'limitless space' appears gross and is left behind. The mind merges with limitless consciousness.

13. *The Third Formless Absorption*    Even 'limitless consciousness' appears gross and is left behind. The mind merges
with nothingness (no-thingness).

14. *The Fourth Formless Absorption*    The peak of cyclic existence is reached. All discrimination, even that between form
and formlessness, disappears and full nirvikalpa samadhi is
entered.

In the first three formless absorptions onwards, when nirvikalpa
samadhi is progressively entered, the term 'gross' is best defined
as discrimination, since *limitless space, limitless consciousness*
and even *nothingness* imply the existence of their opposites. In
the fourth formless absorption, the meditative mind passes
beyond even this level of discrimination and, in Buddhist
terminology, can now leave cyclic existence if so desired and
enter final Nirvana.

Dropping the mantra on entry into the four formless absorptions doesn't mean that the meditator never uses it again. Not
only is it kept as part of the practice while going about daily life,
it is also still used during formal meditation sessions. Having
once entered the first three formless absorptions does not mean
they can be re-entered at will. For many weeks and months,
meditation may produce neither formful nor formless awareness. The meditator remains in an arid state where the mantra
is the only comfort. This is something of what the Christian
mystics refer to as the 'dark night of the soul', the time when,
having received the divine vision, it seems to be taken away,
leaving nothing in its place.

The only way through this experience is to note it, with as
much detached interest as possible, and carry on with the practice.
One should not be tempted to abandon the practice or to change
it for something else. One continues with the mantra, day after
day, and waits for light to dawn again, as surely it will.

## JNANA IN MEDITATION

The experience of full savikalpa samadhi is a first initiation into
jnana, true insight. The meditator has now seen into the centre,

even if only briefly, and knows without doubt its reality. But the ultimate jnana of nirvikalpa samadhi still remains to be realized, and this cannot be done without relinquishing entirely the bhakti practice of focusing upon forms and attributes, and entering into the fourth formless absorption.

In many of the great traditions it is recognized that the meditator not only experiences great difficulty in undertaking this final step but also great reluctance. Having achieved savikalpa samadhi, in which the divine is experienced and bliss enjoyed, there is a natural desire to cling to this state. Why proceed further? The universe has become clear, eternity has revealed itself, the blinkers of ignorance have fallen away and love is revealed as the truth at the centre of all things. Why surrender this in pursuit of a 'formlessness' which seems to negate the experience which, after so much practice, has just been achieved?

The answer is that nothing is negated. The reality that has been experienced is an expression of ultimate reality, just as you and I are expressions of it. But this ultimate reality has still been seen through the limits of the human mind. It is, if you like, ultimate reality presented in a form that can be comprehended by a mind still restricted, however slightly, by its own concepts, its own way of filtering truth, in the manner that a prism divides light into a rainbow of colours. There is nothing 'unreal' about the rainbow. It is there, as potential within the white light, but each of its colours is only a part of that light, a limited expression of it. In attaining to that light we do not lose the rainbow, we come to know it for what it is, a manifestation of the colourless colour that transcends and creates all colours, an aspect of the origin and the source from which all colours and diversity flow.

Ken Wilber, a Westerner who has done much to bring Eastern and Western psychology together, writes of his own attainment of formlessness as:

> not a loss of faculties but a peak-enhancement of them ... no blank trance but perfect clarity; not depersonalized but transpersonalized. No personal faculties ... were lost or impaired. Rather, they all functioned, for the first time it seemed to me, in radical openness, free of the defences thrown up by a separate sense of self ... I did not watch or experience all that, I simply *was* all that. I could not see it

because it was everything seen; I could not hear it because it was everything heard; I could not know it because it was everything known. That is why it is both the great mystery and the perfectly obvious.

*Odyssey (article)*, p. 84

Elsewhere (see also Crook and Fontana, *Space in Mind*) Wilber writes that the experience of formlessness is:

not a particular experience among other experiences, but the very nature and ground of *all* experiences, high and low ... *In itself* therefore it [is] not experiential at all; it [has] nothing to do with changes of state ... The ultimate state is what I am before I am anything else; it is what I see before I see anything else; and what I feel before I feel anything else.

Ramakrishna teaches that in the modern age this experience of formlessness, jnana, is much more difficult than bhakti. In fact, if we can follow only one path, he tells us to choose bhakti, since progress is quicker and the sentimentality into which it can lead is less of an error than the dry theoretical knowledge which can result from pursuing only jnana. But the fact remains that for a complete practice, we must combine both.

## FORMLESS REALITY

Vedanta recognizes that the reason why jnana is so difficult in the modern age, no matter how ready the meditator feels to enter formlessness, is that from birth onwards we are conditioned to the presence of forms and find it hard even to conceive such a thing as formlessness. Vedanta helps by telling us that jnana is the realization (the *real*ization) that, 'I am not the body, not my thoughts, not the intellect, not the ego' and so forth. This realization is, in fact, essentially the experiential realization of the world presented to us in theoretical models by modern nuclear physicists, a world of formless energy out of which the particles which make up the atom and thus the world of forms appear and into which they disappear.

The ancient *rishis*, the sages whose wisdom created the Vedas, knew all this 3000 years and more ago, and the Buddha restated it 500 years before Christ. The world of forms, the rishis tell us, is 'mind stuff' – *maya* in the terminology of the Vedantists, *prakriti* in that of the Samkhya philosophy, *shakti* in that of the Tantrics, *samsara* in that of the Buddhists. How similar to this is the terminology of philosophers of science such as Sir Arthur Eddington and Sir James Jeans. Eddington put it that the link between the empty world of subatomic physics and the physical world as we experience it is the human mind. 'The stuff of the world is mind stuff' (*The Nature of the Physical World*). Jeans (*The Mysterious Universe*) was even more explicit; '. . . the universe can best be pictured . . . as consisting of pure thought'.

But – and here is the distinction between dry theoretical knowledge and true jnana – it is one thing to know these facts from studying the wisdom of the rishis or the work of the modern physicist, and another to *know* them in the sense of having experienced them. It is at the point of experience that belief passes over into knowing, and intellectuality becomes wisdom. And what is this point of experience? Let me take an example. You may have an excellent physicist's knowledge of the strange world within (and beyond) the atom or you may be thoroughly aware of the teaching of the Vedas or of the Buddha, and 'know' that the world of phenomena is fundamentally empty; but have you stopped to think – and, even more, to *experience* – that your own body is empty in just this same way? The atoms that compose it are no more substantial than the atoms that compose a table or a chair. Your own body is just as much *maya* as the ground upon which you walk.

## MEDITATING ON SPACIOUSNESS

Once we acquire theoretical knowledge about formlessness, we are in a sense moving into a 'mirror' stage, in which we see this knowledge reflected in our minds. However, less explicit guidelines are possible on how to go beyond this stage than can be given on the practice of other meditation techniques, for by its nature meditation upon formlessness is beyond words and concepts. Once the meditator leaves behind the mantra and visualizations, formlessness may arise of itself, but there are times when the meditator feels stranded in what is sometimes referred to as that 'terrible space between heaven and earth' (see Herrigel *Zen in the Art of Archery*).

During this time, a practice to help the mind operate without a specific point of focus is meditation upon spaciousness. Place the awareness in the point above and between the eyebrows (the 'third eye' used in visualization practice – see Chapter 7) and be aware here of nothingness, symbolized by a blank screen if need be. Thoughts, when they arise, are not watched or noted as in zazen, but allowed to pass like a murmur of conversation in the next room. The more one is centred within spaciousness, the less obtrusive this murmur becomes until finally it ceases altogether, and spaciousness embraces all things like the infinite reach of eternity itself.

## NETTI – 'NOT THIS'

Vedanta also teaches that the true practice of jnana centres around the Hindu concept of *netti*, 'not this', and requires the meditator to pass beyond each of the physical and mental characteristics which we usually take to be 'me'. In doing so, the meditator is approaching his or her true being in the same way that Vedanta approaches ultimate reality, that is, in terms of what it is not rather than what it is – 'netti, netti'; 'not this', 'not this'. The procedure is that, having established concentration and tranquillity through one's usual practice and reached what on page 201 was referred to as *continuous setting*, one transfers the focus of attention to the body, becoming aware of it as a solid presence. Like a mantra, the theme is then allowed to emerge and run repeatedly through the awareness, 'I have a body but I am not this body'. No attempt is made to 'dissolve' the consciousness of the body. Instead, as the meditation deepens, the realization arises, through the senses as well as through the mind, that although the body is a loved and cherished possession, it is not who we really are. One day the body will die and will dissolve of itself, but our essential awareness will remain.

Once this realization is achieved (it may happen quickly or over many sessions), the meditator turns attention to the thoughts that play their shadow theatre on the surface of the mind, and the theme is allowed to emerge, 'I have thoughts but I am not the

---

**BOX 18**
*NETTI* IN CHRISTIANITY

Christianity also teaches the path of *netti*. One of the most profound revelations of my life was that Christianity contains the same insights that ennoble Eastern thought. Some of these are dealt with in the discussion of gnosticism in Chapter 5, but *netti* is yet another strand in the richness of Christianity. Most apparent in the outpourings of mystics such as the anonymous writer who borrowed the Greek name *Dionysius*, Christianity has always contained a *via negativa* as well as a *via positiva*. The *via negativa* path starts from the 'unknowability' of God. Unless God reveals Him/Herself to creation, then a cloud of unknowing must always remain like a veil between us and Him/Her. The *via negativa* takes the view that any description of God, however exalted, is necessarily a human one. As Wolters puts it in his translation and commentary upon *The Cloud of Unknowing*:

> Any description however exalted is inevitably a human one, and because of this difference in kind can never be accurate or adequate. If we say that [God] is 'great' or 'most highest', or 'a person' or 'good', we use words which can only be properly understood in a human context, words which distinguish 'you' from 'me', and each of us from the next man. Manifestly we cannot speak of Deity like that ... God cannot be great or high or personal or good in our sense of the words. He ... is so much more than these that we speak more truly when we say that He is none of them, and is more worthily described negatively than positively. When the mind faces Him ... it enters a cloud of unknowing. (*The Cloud of Unknowing and Other Works*, p. 17)

If Wolters had also made the point that God cannot also be 'he' rather than 'she', or 'she' rather than 'he', then his presentation of the *via negativa*, and our recognition of its oneness with *netti, netti*, would have been as near complete as words can make it.

---

thoughts'. As with the body, this theme is repeated over and over until a realization comes that thoughts, although important and valuable, are not who we are. These thoughts arise and dissolve, while the act of watching endures, just as the audience endures while the theatre scenes in front of them shift and change. Once this realization is stabilized, the meditator turns awareness on the ego, the sum total of the small self with all its shifting moods, feelings and attitudes, likes and dislikes, and the theme is allowed to emerge, 'I have an ego but I am not the ego' (or, if you prefer 'I have a self but I am not the self').

Gradually through this practice there dawns a sense that one's being is something much more than these attributes which belong to it but which come and go, which arise from emptiness and pass away into emptiness like the rest of the phenomenal world. Thoughts come and go, feelings and moods come and go, attitudes and opinions come and go, the awareness of the body comes and goes, the in-breath and the out-breath come and go, consciousness itself comes and goes as we wake and sleep. Everything is in a state of creation and destruction except for the constant of awareness, which in the case of advanced individuals is said to remain unbroken even during the hours of apparent sleep.

There is nothing frightening about this realization. It allows us, however briefly it lasts, to glimpse how restricted our normal world view is, how isolating and disturbing. For this world view would have it that reality 'out there' is always waiting, even when life is going well, to challenge us, trip us up, rob us of what we take to be ours, outmanoeuvre us. Even the people we most love serve as reminders that we live always under the threat of loss. Though our glimpse of formlessness, of unity, may be restricted to one timeless moment, it shows us that this fragmented world view is not the real view, that our existential anxiety is a consequence of delusion rather than of vision. And whatever arises after this glimpse, we never quite lose sight of what it has revealed to us.

There is another version of this practice, used particularly in Buddhism. In this you meditate upon (or think consciously about, if you prefer) an object – any object will do but a table is a good place to start. A table consists of a top and four legs. Visualize a table if you like. Now take one leg away. Now another. Now another and another until you are left only with the top. Do you still have a table? If not, where has the table gone? You haven't taken *it* away. All you have taken away are four legs. So why do you no longer have a table? What is a 'table'? Try the exercise again but this time take the top away first. Have you a table now or only four legs? If you have no table, where has the table gone? Ultimately, what *is* the table?

Do this with as many objects as you please over several meditations but never rush over the 'dismantling' of any of them. Allow the significance of what you are doing to sink in. Don't puzzle and rack your brains. Just observe. After a time, there will come the sudden realization that 'table', 'body' and all the rest are mental constructs. Of themselves, they have no abiding and unchanging existence. And with this realization comes an experience of the formlessness of all things.

Once this direct realization arises, you are no longer looking in a mirror. Your consciousness, metaphorically, is now outside 'things' altogether and beginning to see into reality. The glimpses, the sense of *knowing*, may not last long at first. But don't doubt the insights they provide. Stay with the practice and allow it gradually to deepen.

## WHO AM I?

Closely linked to the technique of netti is that emphasized by another great Hindu sage, Ramana Maharshi (see, for example, Mahadevan's *Ramana Maharshi*). This technique belongs in a sense to Chapter 8, for 'Who am I?' is the ultimate koan, from which all other koans are derived. But in another sense it belongs to every chapter in this book, for 'Who am I?' is at the centre of all meditations as I said at the outset.

As taught by Ramana Maharshi, the question 'Who am I?' can be taken as the focus of concentration in meditation, and worked on in the way I described in Chapter 8. But as with all koans, don't look for an intellectual answer. Hold the question in the mind as a puzzle to which you know there *is* an answer, an answer that will emerge in its own time and its own way, an answer that must not be anticipated or obscured by expectations, an answer which is there like a mountain top emerging from the mists of early morning.

You can also work with the question 'Who am I?' in a duo exercise as given in Box 14 (Chapter 8). Ramana Maharshi taught also that whenever we become conscious of ourselves as the doer of an action, we should ask, 'Who is it who is doing this?' – 'Who is it who is eating?', 'Who is it who is walking?', 'Who is it who is angry/sad/happy?'. And even when we come to puzzle over questions of ultimate truth, of life and death, we should still consider, 'Who is it who asks these questions?'. In other words, we must turn all our questions back upon ourselves.

At first, you will find yourself answering the question 'Who am I?' by giving your name, but a name is only a label assigned to you by other people at birth. That can't be who you are. You may then think of yourself in terms of your relationships, as a wife or a husband or a lover or a parent, but relationships are always evolving, growing, changing. That can't be who you are either. You may next think of yourself in terms of physical or psychological attributes — your age or your likes and dislikes or your temperament or your qualities. But these again are constantly shifting and changing. Go back a few years, even a few months or a few weeks, and you will find quite radical changes in many of these characteristics. Were you any less 'you' in the past than you are now?

Finally, if your pursue this exercise far enough, there comes a blank sense of not knowing. In spite of living with yourself all these years, and in spite of your knowledge about other things, the truth is that you don't know who you are. Stay with this 'don't know'. Don't look for any more formulas, any more words. Stay with the sense of 'don't know'. Meditate on that sense. If it should fade, go back to the answers you originally gave, and see once more how unsatisfactory they are. Then meditate again on 'don't know'. As with 'mu' (Chapter 8), the answer is not to be found in intellectual speculation but in the direct reality of experience itself.

## THE FINAL STEP IN JNANA

Realization of the truth of one's own being takes one into the realm of the formless, the goal of jnana, the nirvikalpa samadhi of the formless absorptions, of pure experience without a separate individual self who does the experiencing. Yet even this goal isn't final. The meditator now has to bring this realization back into everyday life, back into the world of forms. Not as a formula to be imparted to others — we have seen many times that it is not something that can be put into words — but as an experience to be lived. How can this be done? Only by reconciling this glimpse of ultimate reality with the relative reality in which we live on this earth. To remain in the rarefied state of nirvikalpa samadhi would mean that one has failed the final test, for that would be to deny that the world of forms is a part of reality, that Samsara and Nirvana are, as the Buddha taught, ultimately one. Such a denial would mean that one had not experienced the ultimate level of nirvikalpa samadhi because one would still be located in duality, in the world of this *or* that rather than this *and* that. The opposites would once more have arisen, and as the Buddha taught, 'When the opposites arise, the Buddha-mind is lost'.

Reconciling the formless world with the world of forms is like asking, 'Has my body a "form"?' The answer is that certainly it has, even though this form is not who I am and is subject to change and growth and eventual decay. I *have* a body, and I *have* attributes. What then are these? They must be none other than *symbols of reality*, in the way that the shapes in the sand are symbols of the sound that creates them.

In this realization lies the knowledge that since the world of forms arises from the formlessness of ultimate reality, then the worlds of forms and of formlessness must in truth be aspects of the same thing. Samsara and Nirvana are one, as the Buddha taught. The wheel comes full circle, and there stands revealed an ultimate reality which embraces not only existence but non-existence. And with this revelation, the opposites of which worldly experience seems to be composed, the 'either–or' of everyday life, disappear. Even life and death are seen to be one, and in seeing this the mind passes beyond doubt and fear, beyond mortality and immortality, beyond self and not-self, and into the vastness of being. As the *Prajnaparamita* (*The Perfection of Wisdom*), that great Buddhist jnana text, puts it,

*Gate gate paragate parasamgate bodhi svaha*

'Gone, gone, gone beyond, gone altogether beyond, oh what an awakening, all hail!'

# 11

## *Conclusion*

In studying the various forms of meditation described in the previous chapters, the one system from which, like shoots from a single root, all other systems grow and flourish becomes clear. What can be said, in summary and conclusion, about this one system? Six things at least.

1. Central to meditation are the stages respectively of *concentration, tranquillity* and *insight*. Without concentration – one-pointed attention upon the focus of awareness – we cannot gather the dispersed fragments of our mind together and allow tranquillity to appear. Without tranquillity, we cannot experience the openness and the clarity within which insight can appear. And without insight, our practice cannot go beyond the point of deep relaxation.

2. Insight takes us into the inner world of our own mind. Within this inner world we must abandon intellect if we wish to make progress. The language of this inner world is intuitive and paradoxical, and is spoken through symbols, through images, through sounds, through the irrationality of the koan. In this inner world, we must suspend logical questioning and accept what occurs there 'as if' it is real. The gods or the powers which we experience within this inner world are created jointly by the actions of our own mind and the underlying creative reality of which they are the symbols.

3. For meditation to be effective it must become a part of our lives, not only in terms of the regularity of our practice but also in terms of the importance we attach to this rajah yoga of the mind. And we must place this rajah yoga within the context of karma yoga, which makes us aware of our actions, of bhakti yoga, which develops in us the power of love and compassion, and jnana yoga, which brings us to the level of wisdom and understanding.

4. The 'self', the ego, the small learned person we think we are, is an impediment to progress. In meditation, this small self is discarded as the mind centres upon meditative awareness. In place of this small self, meditation puts us in touch with a much profounder sense of our being, a sense which transforms our humanity both in our relationship with ourselves and in our relationships with others.

5. At a deeper level, all meditation systems dissolve the boundaries between inner and outer, between our own minds and the universal mind, whether we choose to call this universal mind God or Nirvana or Ain Soph or Brahman or any of the other names by which men and women have known it.

6. At a deeper level still, there comes an expansion of our own limited mind into the infinity of this universal mind, an expansion which is not annihilation, not a loss of individuality, but a reality in which the distinction between individuality and unity, as between all opposites, not only disappears but is seen never truly to have existed.

As we recognize the system that underlies all systems, we recognize why Aldous Huxley (see, for example, Isherwood's *Vedanta for the Western World*) referred to it as 'the perennial wisdom', a wisdom that has continually to be brought home to us by the great spiritual teachers, and then rediscovered by men and women within their own hearts. Each time great teachers impart this wisdom it gradually becomes eclipsed after their death, lost under a gathering mass of dogma and ritual and personal bids for power by the followers to whom they have entrusted its safekeeping. Hence the need for each of us to turn within, and enter for ourselves the path they have mapped out for us into the inner world where this wisdom is always present.

This path is meditation. How far we travel along it depends upon a number of things such as opportunity, physical health and strength, the support and companionship of likeminded people, and — most crucial of all — the strength of our own motivation. But however weak your motivation seems to be, once you have set out on this path, there is no turning back. There will be times in life when you are meditating regularly, and times when it is a struggle to find the inclination or the mental or physical space to sit even once a week. There will be times when your mind stays calm and clear, poised in the awareness that meditation brings, and other times when it chatters away ceaselessly, and you feel that no progress has been made or ever will be made. But once embarked upon the path of meditation, you will never entirely forsake it, since even when you diverge from it for a space you will never quite forget the way back.

The path of meditation is a path in tune with the flow of life itself, a path that follows to its source the creative spirit which underlies everything we do and that sustains and renews our lives, moment by moment. The creative spirit, in short, which is what life actually *is*. The more we become aware of this fact, the stranger it seems that we should go through our days on this earth without knowing what being alive actually means. We *are* alive, day by day, hour by hour, minute by minute, yet what is it, this being alive? So distracted and confused are we by what goes on in the outer world, by the demands made upon us, the things said to us and about us, that we become separated from our real nature. The mystical wedding that meditation brings about between our material and our spiritual selves ends this separation. In the mystical wedding the alchemist in us transmutes base metal into gold, our soul hears the voice of God, the Buddha-mind realizes Nirvana, the magician experiences the soaring flight of Horus into the light of eternity, and Malkuth finally unites with Kether and merges into the vastness of Ain Soph.

# References and Further Reading

The great majority of these books are currently in print, and have been selected with availability partly in mind.

Apuleius, L. *The Golden Ass*,

Ashcroft-Nowicki, D. *The Forgotten Mage: The Magical Lectures of Colonel C. R. F. Seymour*, Aquarian Press, 1986.

Barlow, W. *The Alexander Technique*, Arrow, 1975.

Benson, H. *The Relaxation Response*, Collins, 1976.

Brunton, P. *A Search in Secret Egypt*, Rider, 1969.

Budge, Sir E. A. *Egyptian Magic*, Routledge and Kegan Paul, 1972.

Budhananda, Swami, *Teachings of Sri Ramakrishna*, Advaita Ashrama, 1975.

Campbell, J. and Moyers, B. *The Power of Myth*, Doubleday, 1988.

Castenada, C. *The Teachings of Don Juan: A Yaqui Way of Knowledge*, Penguin Books, 1970.

Cheng Man-ch'ing and Smith, R. W. *Tai Chi: The Supreme Ultimate Exercise for Health, Sport and Self-Defence* (2nd edition), Weatherhill, 1967.

Chidbhavananda, Swami, *Ramakrishna Lives Vedanta* (2nd edition), Sri Ramakrishna Tapovana, 1971.

Chögyam, Ngakpa. *Rainbow of Liberated Energy: Working with Emotions through the Colour and Element Symbolism of Tibetan Tantra*, Element Books, 1986.

Chögyam, Ngakpa. *Journey into Vastness: A Handbook of Tibetan Meditation Techniques*, Element Books, 1988.

Conze, E. *Buddhist Meditation*, Unwin, 1972.

Conze, E. (trans.), *The Short Prajnaparamita Texts*, Luzac and Co., 1973.

Cooper, J. C. *An Illustrated Encyclopaedia of Traditional Symbols*, Thames and Hudson, 1982.

Crook, J. *Catching a Feather on a Fan: A Zen Retreat with Master Sheng Yen*, Element Books, 1991.

Crook, J. and Fontana, D. (eds.), *Space in Mind: East–West Psychology and Contemporay Buddhism*, Element Books, 1990.

Cox, M. *Mysticism: The Direct Experience of God*, Aquarian Press, 1983.

Dunne, D. *Yoga Made Easy*, Panther, 1965.

Eddington, Sir A. *The Nature of the Physical World*, Cambridge University Press, 1935.

Evans, C de B. *The Works of Meister Eckhart*, vol. 1, Watkins, 1924.

Evans-Wentz, W. Y. (ed.), *The Tibetan Book of the Dead*, Oxford University Press, 1960 (commentary by C. G. Jung).

Evans-Wentz, W. Y. (ed.), *Tibetan Yoga and Secret Doctrines*, Oxford University Press, 1967.

Evans-Wentz, W. Y. (ed.), *The Tibetan Book of the Great Liberation*, Oxford University Press, 1968 (commentary by C. G. Jung).

Feild, R. *The Last Barrier*, Element Books, 1985.

Fontana, D. *Dreamlife: Understanding and Using Your Dreams*, Element Books, 1990.

Fontana, D. *The Elements of Meditation*, Element Books, 1991.

French, R. M. (trans.), *The Way of a Pilgrim*, SPCK, 1942.

French, R. M. (trans.) *The Pilgrim Continues His Way*, SPCK, 1973.

Ghanananda, Swami. *Sri Ramakrishna and His Unique Message*, Ramakrishna Vedanta Centre, 1970.

Godman, D. (ed.), *Be As You Are: The Teachings of Sri Ramana Maharshi*, Arkana, 1985.

Godwin, J. *Mystery Religions in the Ancient World*, Thames and Hudson, 1981.

Goleman, D. *The Meditative Mind*, Crucible Books, 1989.

Govinda, Lama Anagarika, *Creative Meditation and Multidimensional Consciousness*, Unwin, 1977.

Grant, P. (ed.), *A Dazzling Darkness: An Anthology of Western Mysticism*, Fount Books, 1985.

Guirdham, A. *The Great Heresy*, Neville Spearman, 1977.

Gupta, M. N. *The Condensed Gospel of Sri Ramakrishna*, Sri Ramakrishna Math, 1978.

Halifax, J. (ed.), *Shamanic Voices: A Survey of Visionary Narratives*, Dutton, 1979.

Hamilton-Merritt, J. *A Meditator's Diary*, Penguin Books, 1979.

Hanson, V. (ed.), *Approaches to Meditation*, Quest Books, 1976.

Harner, M. *The Way of the Shaman* (3rd edition), Harper and Row, 1990.
Hart, G. *A Dictionary of Egyptian Gods and Goddesses*, Routledge and Kegan Paul, 1986.
Harvey, A. *A Journey in Ladakh*, Fontana Books, 1983.
Herrigel, E. *Zen in the Art of Archery*, Routledge, 1953.
Hoffmann, J. *The Sound of the One Hand*, Paladin Books, 1977.
Hyams, J. *Zen in the Martial Arts*, Bantam Books, 1982.
Isherwood, C. (ed.), *Vedanta for the Western World*, Unwin, 1963.
Jeans, Sir J. *The Mysterious Universe*, Cambridge University Press, 1930.
Julian of Norwich, Mother. *Revelations of Divine Love*, Penguin Books, 1966.
Jung, C. G. (ed.), *Man and His Symbols*, Pan Books, 1978.
Kadloubovsky, E. and Palmer, G. E. H. *Writings from the Philokalia on Prayer of the Heart*, Faber and Faber, 1951.
Kapleau, Roshi Philip. *Three Pillars of Zen*, Rider, 1980.
Kelder, P. *Tibetan Secrets of Youth and Vitality*, Aquarian Press, 1988.
Krpälvanand, Yogacarya Swami. *Science of Meditation*, Sri Dahyabhai Patel, 1977.
Lati Rinbochay, Denma Locho Rinbochay, Zahler, L. and Hopkins, J. *Meditative States in Tibetan Buddhism*, Wisdom Books, 1983.
Loyola, St Ignatius. *The Spiritual Exercises* (trans. T. Corbishley), Anthony Clark, 1973.
Luk, C. *The Transmission of the Mind Outside the Teachings*, Grove Press, 1975.
Luk, C. *Practical Buddhism*, Rider, 1971.
Mahadevan, R. M. *Ramana Maharshi, The Sage of Arunacala*, Unwin, 1977.
Masunaga, R. (trans.), *A Primer of Soto Zen: Dögen's Shobogenzo Zuimonki*, Routledge and Kegan Paul, 1972.
McDonald, K. *How to Meditate*, Wisdom Books, 1984.
Monks of the Ramakrishna Order. *Meditation* (3rd edition), Ramakrishna Vedanta Centre, 1984.
Naranjo, C. *How to Be*, Jeremy Tarcher, 1989.
Nicol, C. W. *Moving Zen*, Bodley Head, 1975.
Osborne, A. (ed.), *The Teachings of Sri Ramana Maharshi in His Own Words*, Rider, 1971.
Pagels, E. *The Gnostic Gospels*, Penguin Books, 1982.
Payne, P. *Martial Arts: The Spiritual Dimension*, Thames and Hudson, 1981.
Poncé, C. *Kabbalah: An Introduction and Illumination for the World Today*, Quest Books, 1973.

Prabhavananda, Swami and Isherwood, C. (trans. and eds.), *How to Know God: The Yoga Aphorisms of Patanjali*, Mentor Books, 1953.

Regardie, I. *The Tree of Life*, Samuel Weiser, 1972.

Reps, P. *Zen Flesh, Zen Bones*, Penguin, 1971.

Richardson, A. *Dancers to the Gods*, Aquarian Press, 1985.

Roberts, J. *The Seth Material*, Prentice Hall, 1970.

Robinson, J. M. (ed.), *The Nag Hammadi Library* (2nd edition), E. J. Brill, 1984.

Sabom, M. D. *Recollections of Death*, Corgi Books, 1982.

Scholem, G. *Kabbalah*, Dorset Press, 1987.

Sekida, K. *Zen Training: Methods and Philosophy*, Weatherhill, 1975.

Sekida, K. (trans.) and Grimstone, A. V. (ed.), *Two Zen Classics: Mumonkan and Hekiganroku*, Weatherhill, 1977.

Simonton, O. C., Mathews-Simonton, S. and Creighton, J. L. *Getting Well Again*, Bantam Books, 1986.

Staal, F. *Exploring Mysticism*, Penguin Books, 1975.

Stace, W. T. *The Teachings of the Mystics*, Mentor Books, 1960.

Steiner, R. *Knowledge of the Higher Worlds: How is it Achieved?*, Rudolph Steiner Press, 1969.

Suzuki, D. T. *Essays in Zen Buddhism* (3 vols.), Rider, 1953.

Suzuki, D. T. *Mysticism: Christian and Buddhist*, Unwin, 1979.

Suzuki, D. T. *The Field of Zen*, The Buddhist Society, 1980.

Toyne, M. *Involved in Mankind: The Life and Message of Vivekananda*, Ramakrishna Vedanta Centre, 1983.

Tucci, G. *The Theory and Practice of the Mandala*, Rider, 1969.

Vivekananda, Swami, *Inspired Talks*, Sri Ramakrishna Math, 1963.

Waley, A. *The Way and Its Power: The Tao Te Ching and Its Place in Chinese Thought*, Mandala Books, 1977.

Ward, T. *What the Buddha Never Taught*, Element Books, 1990.

West, M. A. (ed.), *The Psychology of Meditation*, Clarendon Press, 1987.

Wilber, K. Odyssey: a personal enquiry into humanistic and transpersonal psychology, *Journal of Humanistic Psychology*, 22, 1, pp. 57–90, 1982.

Wilber, K. The pre-trans fallacy, *Journal of Humanistic Psychology*, 22, 2, pp. 5–43, 1982.

Wilhelm, R. (trans.), *The Secret of the Golden Flower*, Routledge & Kegan Paul, 1962 (commentary by C. G. Jung).

Wolters, C. (ed. and trans.), *The Cloud of Unknowing*, Penguin Books, 1978.

Wood, E. *Concentration: An Approach to Meditation*, Quest Books, 1949.

Wood, E. *Yoga*, Penguin Books, 1965.

Yokoi, Y. and Victoria, D. *Zen Master Dōgen: An Introduction with Selected Writings*, Weatherhill, 1976.

# INDEX